Still Distracted After All These Years

Help and Support for Older Adults with ADHD

KATHLEEN NADEAU, PhD

hachette
BOOKS

NEW YORK

Copyright © 2022 by Kathleen Nadeau

Cover design by Amanda Kain

Cover copyright © 2022 by Hachette Book Group, Inc.

Hachette Book Group supports the right to free expression and the value of copyright. The purpose of copyright is to encourage writers and artists to produce the creative works that enrich our culture.

The scanning, uploading, and distribution of this book without permission is a theft of the author's intellectual property. If you would like permission to use material from the book (other than for review purposes), please contact permissions@hbgusa.com. Thank you for your support of the author's rights.

Hachette Go, an imprint of Hachette Books
Hachette Book Group
1290 Avenue of the Americas
New York, NY 10104
HachetteGo.com
Facebook.com/HachetteGo
Instagram.com/HachetteGo

First Edition: October 2022

Hachette Books is a division of Hachette Book Group, Inc.

The Hachette Go and Hachette Books name and logos are trademarks of Hachette Book Group, Inc.

The publisher is not responsible for websites (or their content) that are not owned by the publisher.

Library of Congress Cataloging-in-Publication Data has been applied for.

ISBNs: 9780306828911 (hardcover); 9780306828935 (ebook)

Printed in the United States of America

LSC-C

Printing 1, 2022

CONTENTS

CONTENTS

Introduction

I come to the field of attention deficit/hyperactivity disorder (ADHD) with excellent real-life credentials, thanks to my family. My older brother was brilliant but had no tolerance for homework or boredom. He dropped out of college, never to return, because he married early and had a family to support. My younger brother struggled even more because he had the double challenge of ADHD and dyslexia. Back then, we didn't know how to help students like him, and he hated school because it made him feel stupid. After graduating from high school, he entered the workforce and eventually owned his own small business, but his undiagnosed ADHD continued to haunt him. He was great at sales but terrible at managing the details, and finally went out of business. I've often thought that if my brothers had received the help available to students today, both of them might have had much easier, more successful lives.

I was one of the lucky ones in my family. I enjoyed school, and academic achievement was central to my identity. Yes, there were signs of ADHD—I sometimes "zoned out" in class and had trouble starting assignments without the pressure of a perilously close due date—but when I earned my first B in seventh grade and my first C in eighth grade, I buckled down and tried harder. I knew some tasks seemed more difficult for me than for my peers, but didn't know enough to recognize symptoms of the disorder until I went to graduate school, where I first learned about ADHD and related disorders.

The concept of learning disorders was relatively new during my grad school years. And as for ADHD, we still believed it was a childhood disorder that affected only boys who outgrew it at puberty! Girls and women my age were simply never evaluated.

But even though I recognized my brothers' struggles in the literature about ADHD, my later career focus on ADHD had nothing to do with my family and everything to do with the passage of Public Law 94.142, the Education for All Handicapped Children Act, in 1975. Parents of hyperactive children who were struggling in school suddenly had a good reason to seek a diagnosis. Before the passage of this act, the only purpose of diagnosis was to seek a prescription for Ritalin, and many parents had huge misgivings about medicating their children with "speed." But 94.142 required schools to "provide a free and appropriate education" for all children with a "handicap" (as we called it back then). Although I had started my career with a general psychotherapy practice, suddenly, in the mid-'70s, my phone was ringing off the hook with calls from pediatricians asking whether I knew how to diagnose what was then called attention deficit disorder (ADD). Parents were now eager for a diagnosis that might help their children get the support and accommodations to help them in school.

Testing and treating children with ADHD soon became a significant portion of my private practice. Most requests for evaluation and therapy came from mothers of hyperactive young boys. In those days, the primary symptom we looked for was hyperactivity. Most of the kids presented with behavior problems, such as being disruptive in class or "not listening" to parents or teachers. These kids were struggling in school and were challenging to manage at home. Nearly all of them were boys. We coached parents on behavior management techniques, pinpointed the correct dosage of Ritalin, and offered wholly misguided but well-intentioned assurances that the condition would lessen, if not disappear, after puberty.

It soon became apparent that this disorder was more complicated than it initially appeared. A surprising number of the children I tested for "gifted and talented" programs showed patterns similar to children with ADHD (distractibility, forgetfulness, and disorganization) even though they were doing well in school. Because they didn't fit the expected hyperactive and impulsive symptoms of ADHD— they were daydreaming, forgetful, and disorganized rather than bouncing out of their seat or disrupting the class—no one had asked whether their inattention might be a neurological difference rather than a personal shortcoming. But was it all connected?

I started to see another contradiction to the "hyperactive, academically disinclined young boy" image of ADD. Parent after parent of children I tested reported that they had exhibited similar behaviors as children, mothers, and fathers. And though they were well past puberty, they hadn't outgrown those challenges. These same parents continued to have difficulty arriving on time for appointments or following through on the detailed behavior charts and reward systems that we were all trained to recommend to parents in those days. Could this be the same disorder, just filtered through an adult brain?

These and other questions would end up driving the focus of my writing and clinical practice over the next four decades. My career has focused on identifying those groups within the larger ADHD population who have been underidentified and underserved. First, I developed new assessment tools and treatment protocols for adults when most doctors still thought ADHD was a childhood disorder. Later, I studied how ADHD manifested itself in girls and women. Mental health professionals all too often told them that their struggles were due to anxiety, depression, or personal failure rather than a treatable neurological difference.

Others of my patients didn't conform to the ADHD stereotype because they were professionally successful. ADHD is classified as a disability. To have a "disability," as defined in the US, one must have a physical or mental impairment that substantially limits one or more "major life activities." This description fit the kids who were performing significantly below grade level in school, but what about students with exceptional intelligence who could compensate? What about adults who had earned law or medical degrees but struggled with executive functioning deficits related to paperwork, note-taking, report writing, and general organization?

One of my patients, John, came to me after losing a wrenching fight to receive additional time on his law school entrance exam. He was one among many who sought accommodations for ADHD under the Americans with Disabilities Act (ADA), which considers ADHD and learning disorders as qualified disabilities when taking these "high-stakes" exams. At the time, there was a standard view that students who achieved the level of academic success required to be eligible for law school or medical school couldn't possibly have ADHD. Denial of accommodations for these very bright students with ADHD has driven numerous lawsuits against the National Board of Medical Examiners and others against the LSAT, GRE, and GMAT examiners, claiming disability discrimination. (Those suits are likely to continue: In 2011, the federal government published a thorough assessment of ADA compliance by the companies that produce and administer high-stakes testing to gain entrance into postgraduate education. It found that the Department of Justice had failed to develop a comprehensive approach for dealing with complaints about noncompliance. Instead, they dealt with the lawsuits on a case-by-case basis.)

To John's credit, even without accommodations on his LSAT exam, he was admitted to law school and excelled there. However, he remarked to me later that he probably would have been accepted by a better-ranked school if he'd been able to take the LSAT with the accommodations now more common for applicants with diagnosed ADHD. His story is like that of any number of physicians, attorneys, business executives, and graduate students I've worked with, all of whom benefited from an ADHD diagnosis and treatment. Just as someone with poor vision may still succeed on an exam even if they are denied access to their glasses, someone with ADHD may be able to find workarounds for their brain that functions differently. But how much more might they achieve with the appropriate support? Although the situation has improved for bright students with ADHD, we still have far to go.

Adults who mentioned their ADHD issues during appointments for their children in the 1980s are now in their retirement years. All these years later, the mental health field recognizes ADHD in adults—our best estimates are that ADHD affects some 4.4 percent of older American adults. One retrospective study, which involved having older adults complete the Wender Utah Rating Scale (WURS), which was designed to identify adults with ADHD by their recalling events from their childhood, found that approximately 5 percent of adults qualified for the diagnosis. Conventional wisdom once held that ADHD was a childhood disease, only later accepting that it might continue to manifest in our twenties, thirties, and forties. However, even today, most psychiatrists and neurologists continue to ignore *older* adults with ADHD. Research about older adults consistently reports that ADHD declines with age—but I was observing no such decline in my clients who had been diagnosed earlier in life. That contrast piqued my interest. Does ADHD wane in later years? If so, why? What is it like to have ADHD in your sixties, seventies, and older?

And so, I turned my attention to older adults with ADHD.

A huge demographic change is on the horizon. Population demographics reported by AARP indicate that by 2035 (only fifteen years into the future as I write this chapter), there will be more people over age sixty-five than under age eighteen. Think about it. More older adults than children. In other words, in only a few years, the great majority of people struggling with ADHD will be adults, including older adults. Those of us in the field of ADHD and related disorders need to stop dismissing ADHD in older adults as infrequent and less impairing.

Surprisingly, almost nothing targeting the general public has been written for or about older adults with ADHD. I saw a huge unmet need and decided to explore and write a book about my impressions, hoping to spur others to understand the tremendous and growing demand of older adults with ADHD.

The ADHD diagnosis alone, at any age, can be a very healing experience. But those who finally decide to seek a diagnosis in their sixties or seventies face barriers to finding a professional willing and able to diagnose and treat them.[1]

Despite these challenges, the stories you will read in this book are a testament to the persistence of adults who somehow got past those barriers to receive an ADHD diagnosis.

I have written about the older adults I had treated in my clinical practice. But, in addition, I decided to cast a wider net by placing an ad in a nationally distributed magazine focused on ADHD, seeking older adults with ADHD to interview in preparation for this book. Between 2017 and 2020, I interviewed 150 men and women over the age of sixty, all of whom had been officially diagnosed with ADHD by a mental health professional. The youngest interviewees were aged sixty; the oldest was eighty-four.

ADHD has the same fundamental symptoms in older adults as in younger adults, but adults may express those symptoms differently in later years. For example, someone who routinely forgot to turn in schoolwork on time as a child may grow into a retiree who misses a bill payment, even though they had enough money, for reasons they can't quite explain. Worse, problems with daily life management, disorganization, and forgetfulness can too easily be dismissed as signs of age-related cognitive decline, or worse, incorrectly attributed to the onset of dementia. If you are an older adult (or the friend or family member of one) who is reading this book and wondering whether you may be dealing with ADHD, here are some things to consider.

Do you or did you have any of the following problems?

School-related problems

- Underperforming in school
- Doing well on tests but not doing homework
- Difficulty completing papers
- Behavior problems during school years
- Being told, "You're so smart; you just need to try harder."
- Difficulties in graduate or professional school, such as not completing a thesis or dissertation
- Difficulty passing medical boards or law boards

Work-related problems

- Losing or quitting jobs due to poor performance or dissatisfaction
- Missing deadlines at work
- Never being promoted to the level that you feel you deserve
- Difficulty with paperwork

Life management problems

- Forgetting to pay bills
- Living in a messy, disorganized environment
- Smoking cigarettes and/or drinking to excess
- Getting speeding tickets
- Struggling with depression and anxiety
- Procrastinating and having difficulty accomplishing projects, even projects that initially excite you

Relationship/interpersonal problems

- Losing your temper often or being easily frustrated
- Having high levels of conflict with those close to you

- Having marital conflicts leading to separation and divorce
- Inconsistent and emotionally reactive parenting patterns

Family history

- Having children diagnosed with ADHD
- Family history of anxiety, depression, substance use disorders
- Family history of learning disorders

If some of these patterns sound familiar to you, you (or the friend or family member whose habits you're thinking of right now) may have undiagnosed ADHD. The good news is that you've come to the right place to learn more about how older adults with ADHD can lead calmer, happier, more productive lives.

Here's the other good news: People with this disorder are not alone. ADHD in adults is one of the *most* common psychiatric disorders. We have learned a lot about it, and there are better options for treatment today than ever before. If you are an older adult, you grew up during years when we knew almost nothing about ADHD, let alone ADHD in older adults. And if you are reading this book, you are in the vanguard of those seeking understanding, diagnosis, and treatment for lifelong ADHD. As you read, you will learn that it's never "too late" to be diagnosed and that diagnosis and treatment have been life-altering for many older adults.

You'll notice I'm writing most directly to those older adults who suspect they have ADHD and to the family members who want to understand better, help, and support them. I hope to increase awareness of ADHD in older adults more broadly and thus lead to better training for mental health professionals to recognize and treat ADHD in older adults, especially in cases where it hasn't been diagnosed earlier in life. I am proud to be in the vanguard of professionals studying older adults with ADHD, but I would be prouder still if this book inspired my colleagues to join me in a stronger, more informed focus on the needs of older adults with ADHD.

You also may notice something else about this book: It uses a lot of visual structure on the page. You'll find clear subheadings that signpost content and bullet-point lists that efficiently convey information. After writing several books for adults and children with ADHD, I've learned that the *visual presentation of information* is nearly as important as *the information itself.* Many of my clients struggle to finish other full-length books about topics that interest them—but they have no trouble with mine!

One more thing to keep in mind: So many adults have told me that they have a pile of books on ADHD beside their bed and haven't managed to finish any of them. To prevent this book from being added to the pile of unread ones, it should be read one chapter at a time to allow the information to sink in. Give yourself time to think about each chapter before reading another. And feel free to read chapters out of order, depending upon the issues you most want to focus on.

Living with ADHD in our later years is hugely influenced by multiple factors. Comorbid disorders, such as anxiety, depression, low self-esteem, learning disorders, and other psychiatric disorders, can complicate and intensify the effects of ADHD. And then, there are considerable differences in external factors—the level of stress older adults with ADHD encounter each day due to their life circumstances; for example, the presence or lack of support and acceptance from others in their lives; also, the number of people they are responsible for, such as aging parents or adult children who haven't successfully "launched" into independence. Another factor is how well older adults cope with their ADHD.

Despite these differences, however, I bring good news. Most of the adults I interviewed told me that life has become less stressful in their later years. In part, that's because the demands upon them have lessened as they retire from active working life and are no longer raising children; but it is also because they have developed coping skills and built stronger supports. It's those skills and supports I hope to offer here, shoring up your sense of control over your own life and offering actionable steps to improve your golden years.

I dedicate this book to today's older adults with ADHD. The more we listen to what you have to say, the easier it will be for you and those who follow.

ADHD in Older Adults: Why It Matters

What leads older adults to seek a diagnosis and treatment for ADHD?

Unfortunately, many people underestimate the ongoing impact of ADHD among older adults, including many mental health professionals. In conversation about this book with a highly educated man, he asked me why it mattered whether you have ADHD once you are retired since there are, he assumes, so many fewer demands to meet. This man, among many others, misunderstands and underestimates the human cost of living with ADHD as an older adult. We think of hyperactive children who don't do well in school, but we are less familiar with the entire arc of the life of an individual with ADHD. The fact is that ADHD impacts *all* aspects of life—how we sleep, how and what we eat, how we go through each day—forgetting and losing personal items, running late, rarely feeling prepared, underperforming, feeling judged, being misunderstood and sometimes outright rejected by others. It's not just a matter of managing academic or work life; it's about struggling to manage all aspects of daily life. And, as you'll read in this chapter, it's a matter of how little self-esteem many adults with ADHD have and how little social acceptance they feel as they go through their lives. These issues don't stop when our working years end.

Across industrialized nations, such as the United States, productivity and organization are akin to moral virtues. People with ADHD may have many strengths related to curiosity, spontaneity, and creativity. However, they typically struggle with skills referred to as "executive functioning skills," which include the abilities to plan, organize, be efficient, be aware of the passage of time, and initiate and complete tasks. These struggles result from a neurological issue: an inadequate supply of dopamine in the prefrontal lobes of the brain. Living with ADHD, especially in industrialized nations, is to live with scorn and criticism. To those who don't understand the neuroscience of ADHD, being slow, late, or inefficient is viewed as a choice rather than the result of well-documented brain differences.

An illustration of just how high the cost of growing up with ADHD can be, no matter where you're from, and how early it starts, comes from a research project I described in my book *Understanding Women with ADHD*.[1] Immigrant women from challenging backgrounds told the researcher that the most significant trauma they had experienced was at the hands of strict and intolerant teachers whose mode of discipline was public shaming in the front of the classroom. Such shaming regularly occurred when students talked in class, forgot their homework, or hadn't remembered the teacher's instructions. Although some women had escaped abject poverty, abuse, or even war, these women reported that the intolerance of and humiliation for ADHD behaviors during their school years had been among their most emotionally traumatic experiences growing up.

All the adults I interviewed had lived with undiagnosed ADHD until middle age or later. They had grown up without the understanding or support that could have reduced or prevented the pattern of family conflicts, underperformance in school, problematic relationships, divorces, unemployment, and employment in jobs for which they were poorly matched. They grew up with parents frustrated that they "didn't just sit down and do their work," that they didn't "just try harder," that they didn't listen or seem to care.

The idea that people with ADHD are squandering their potential—that they could be more successful, more organized, more prompt, more productive, but are *choosing not to*, is at the root of many adults' struggles with their ADHD. Instead, they *need different systems and sometimes medication to support their success*. Even after a diagnosis, feelings of shame, regret, and anger can linger. I call this cluster of emotions "the if-only's." A participant, Diana, put a common experience succinctly:

> *"One of my struggles is a feeling of sadness over what I would like to have accomplished (in my life) but couldn't; I think about what my ADHD has cost me."*

It's vital to recognize the effects of these emotions and their causes. Psychiatry has not yet held a reckoning for the group of Americans who are most likely to have undiagnosed and untreated ADHD: Americans over age fifty-five.

As the baby boomers retire and age, a profound demographic change is on the horizon. By 2035, the AARP reports, there will be more people over sixty-five years old than under age eighteen.[2] This demographic shift is striking given that ADHD has always been categorized as a childhood disorder. Due to the ongoing demographic changes in the population, if the field continues to focus on children and ignore older adults, we will miss caring for the *majority* of patients.

> Because of increased longevity combined with a declining birth rate, by 2035 there may be more older adults than kids and teens with ADHD.

STILL DISTRACTED AFTER ALL THESE YEARS

The number of Americans who might benefit from better understanding their brain as they enter a new phase of life is staggering.

> Because we are living longer and working longer, getting a proper diagnosis and treatment in our later years is more important than ever.

Boomers in their midfifties and beyond are different from previous generations. Rather than heading for their rocking chairs, many are still working or are diving into new projects or passions that they have time to pursue postretirement. The share of people aged sixty-five to seventy-four who are still working is projected to be 30.2 percent by 2026,[3] nearly double the rate during the boomers' prime working years. And this number is only going to rise as longevity increases. That's a statistic that would make sense to Marie.

Marie had gone to college years earlier and earned C's. "I just couldn't learn the boring stuff; I don't know why," she told me. Marie dropped out, married, and raised two children. Her path was highly challenging. Her husband fell ill, and they lost all their assets, paying for the cost of his care. In her early fifties, she lost her husband and focused entirely on the needs of her children until they grew up and left home. Then, she told me, "I wanted to go back to college." Marie had been diagnosed with ADHD as an adult, but had focused entirely on the needs of her children with ADHD until they graduated from college. Finally, she was alone and decided to complete her long-abandoned college degree. "I took Ritalin and graduated summa cum laude," she reported. Marie went on to earn a master's degree, graduating at the top of her class. Now, in retirement, she says that she is happier than she's ever been. Marie is very active in her community and works on a local newsletter for seniors. Her latest project is to learn how to build a website for the nonprofit organization where she volunteers. Now that she's learned how to learn, nothing is stopping her.

Marie is a real success story, but not everyone is so lucky. Reports from the National Council on Aging[4] tell us that at least one-third of boomers over age sixty-five (a group that's growing by more than ten thousand Americans per day) live near or below the poverty line. There are frustratingly little data on the well-being of adults with ADHD, but because impulsivity and money-management struggles are a hallmark of adult ADHD, those with ADHD are often less financially prepared for retirement. As one older man with ADHD said to me, "I'm going to have to work until I drop."

Even after they are no longer working, retired adults still have a great deal to manage—bills, taxes, endless health insurance claims, numerous doctor appointments, physical therapy appointments. One of our primary tasks is just to keep ourselves going as we age. The countless tasks of daily life, sometimes including the care of a spouse or partner who is chronically ill, demand constant management. A heartbreaking number of older adults are weighed down not only by the stress of keeping everything up to date, but by the guilt and shame they feel in struggling with basic tasks. Unaware that their struggle stems from a neurological difference, many have internalized the belief that there is no excuse for their long-standing struggles to manage their daily lives. There's some evidence that this guilt and shame leads older adults with ADHD to suffer from greater social isolation than their peers. And we now know that loneliness can kill us. Research shows that isolated adults have a lower life expectancy.[5]

But there is good news. Older adults with ADHD reported that diagnosis and treatment had a significant positive impact on their lives. The next chapter will share stories of men and women diagnosed late in life, highlighting what prompted them to seek an

ADHD diagnosis and how they have benefited from diagnosis and treatment.

KEY TAKEAWAYS FROM THIS CHAPTER

✔ ADHD is real.

✔ It affects people of all ages.

✔ No matter your age, you can take steps to improve your health and the quality of your life.

✔ Don't give up on yourself!

The Challenges of Getting Older

With or without ADHD, we all face new concerns as we age

W hen I first began to talk to my staff about my observations of older adults with ADHD, several of them laughed, asking me, "Aren't you just talking about what it's like to get old?" That question, unintentionally dismissive of the challenges of growing older with ADHD, made me realize that I also needed to consider the challenges that aging presents to all of us in order to clarify the difficulties particular to those with ADHD. What's different? What's the same?

This chapter will address the importance to all older adults

- of finding purpose in old age,
- of working to maintain engagement with family, friends, and community,
- of making our money last as long as we do,
- of deciding where and how to live as our needs change,

- of maintaining our health as we age, and
- of dealing with cognitive decline.

We're Living Longer

Our life spans in the United States have increased so rapidly that the issues we face during retirement years are relatively new concerns. When the Social Security system was put into place in 1937, providing regular payments to those aged sixty-five or older, the average life span in the US was 61.7 years.[1] In other words, most wouldn't live to collect Social Security at all, and many would only collect those benefits for a brief time. There were no "retirement years" in a general sense. Indeed, some individuals, more women than men, lived into their seventies and eighties. Many of these women lived alone or with adult children and grandchildren. There was no "retirement lifestyle" because few retirees were able to enjoy what we now have come to expect, our "retirement years."

As our "retirement years" continue to extend, we need to combat outdated stereotypes. Robert Butler, MD, was one of the earliest gerontologists to talk about the importance of having a productive, meaningful old age. Butler coined the term *ageism* to refer to society's negative associations with old age.[2] Before he wrote about the need for "meaning" in old age, society simply thought of these years as ones to spend in inactivity or, if fortunate enough, on a golf course. Today, many of us live twenty or more years past retirement, so leisure activities may not provide lasting satisfaction.

Finding Purpose

I spoke at length with a highly educated woman, Ellen, only a few months into her retirement. Her work had come to a somewhat premature end when the organization where she worked moved its headquarters. Ellen realized she needed to turn the page to a new phase of life, but what to do? She felt a bit lost and told me that she didn't want to "just volunteer" in some random sense. She had felt a strong sense of purpose in her life as a medical researcher and wanted to become involved in something meaningful and stimulating in retirement. Her career had fully engaged her brain. Ellen needed something similar in retirement to provide intellectual stimulation, a feeling of self-worth, and involvement in her community. Easier said than done! She felt unfocused and unmoored without the decades-long routine of the workweek. Ellen did not have ADHD—she was focused, organized, and efficient, yet she felt a bit lost.

In my exploration of the concerns of older adults with ADHD, I also queried a small cohort of retired adults who did not have ADHD as a point of comparison. Several among them talked of still wanting to "feel relevant." Not an easy task when many employers consider people in their fifties to be "older." We have all experienced the tidal wave of technology over the past quarter-century. Today's older adults who were middle-aged when the internet exploded in the mid-1990s often sound apologetic and self-denigrating about their level of computer literacy. Societal change, spurred by technology, has occurred perhaps more rapidly over the most recent generation than at any time in history,[3] making it challenging for older adults to keep pace with change. In a world that has rushed ahead without us, making technological changes at warp speed, it has become more and more difficult to feel relevant and competent.

> Change—extremely rapid social change—is the most important fact of life today.[4]

Maintaining Social Engagement

Our social lives often diminish as we enter retirement, primarily if most of our social connections are related to our work. But even if our social network is broad, it inevitably diminishes as friends move away, fall ill, or die. Loneliness has been connected to a greater susceptibility for physical and mental health problems[5] and is perhaps one of the most critical issues to resolve as we age. Hanna, for example, had an active social life for many years. She and her husband belonged to a wine group, a dinner group, and an active discussion group associated with their church. After her husband's death, however, she struggled with the daily isolation of living alone. "The thing I miss the most," she told me, "is having someone at home to talk to about the details of everyday life." She felt less comfortable attending the wine group and dinner group as a widow, surrounded by married couples, and eventually dropped out of both groups. Her former social life as part of a couple had been satisfying. As a widow, Hanna felt more alone as she socialized with couples. She needed to build a new social life to meet her changing needs.

Social life in retirement requires planning and initiation if it's going to happen. Building and maintaining a social network and support system is critical for leading a satisfying postretirement life. Easier said than done, however. Studies show that approximately one-third of people are affected by loneliness in industrialized countries where life does not center on family and village.[6] Everyone is susceptible regardless of income, education, gender, or ethnicity. Loneliness is defined not simply by physical and social isolation, but just as importantly by the distressing feeling that our social needs, whatever they may be, are not being met. Hanna still belonged to a wine group and dinner group that she had enjoyed with her husband, but now that she was alone, those groups no longer met her needs. Although the frequency of social interactions certainly impacts loneliness, the quality of social relationships is more important.[7] For example, Marge, an older woman without ADHD, lives in a highly socially active adult community that offers numerous activities. Despite this, she ruefully commented that she stays busy with activities to distract herself from her loneliness. Marge has many social interactions, but the quality of these interactions doesn't provide her with the intimacy that would make her feel genuinely connected, understood, and cared for.

The effects of loneliness can have a harmful health impact equivalent to smoking cigarettes and obesity.[8] The risk of loneliness increases significantly after age seventy. Furthermore, because loneliness often makes a person irritable, depressed, and self-centered, there is a snowball effect in which loneliness begets even greater loneliness. Lonely older adults may alienate those around them, resulting in growing isolation. Increasing amounts of research identify loneliness as a significant public health problem linked to a 26 percent increase in the risk of premature death.[9]

Financial Challenges

It is a big challenge for most Americans to provide themselves with a comfortable retirement. There are always many needs and desires competing for priority in our monthly budget during our working years. Current financial statistics indicate that few American households are saving even close to what they may need for retirement. The National Institute on Retirement Security (NIRS) reports that for 40 percent of all US households, their primary retirement income will be Social Security—which in 2022 paid an average of only $1,658 per month.[10] Fewer and fewer employers offer a retirement plan. With all the competing demands on an individual's monthly income, most people cannot prioritize retirement savings.

Changes in Living Circumstances in Response to Differing Needs as We Age

Daily living challenges increase for all older adults in retirement years as health issues increase and life maintenance tasks become increasingly challenging. Many are less able to comfortably drive a car, shop for and prepare healthy meals, and generally keep up household management tasks. Most adults profess a desire to remain in their home as they age.[11] Still, the costs and difficulties of aging in place often begin to fall onto adult children when limited money is available for upkeep and housekeeping, and as transportation becomes increasingly tricky.

Other choices include "over fifty-five" condo communities and increasingly popular active adult communities, such as The Villages in central Florida. According to an August 2021 article in *Business Insider*,[12] it is the most rapidly growing community in the United States. But not everyone can afford to move to a retirement community. As life spans increase and the required savings to support twenty or more years in retirement are challenging to achieve, we may see an increase in multigenerational living. One man proudly reported to me that he was about to retire, leaving his home improvement business to his son and business partner and moving into a "tiny house" that he had designed and built on a remote corner of his son's wooded property. Although this man found a creative retirement housing solution, for most families, intergenerational living is more and more challenging. Family life is less stable, given the patterns of adult children moving far away, higher rates of single parenthood, and patterns of partnering without marriage or multiple marriages that have increased over the past generation or two.[13]

Self-Care to Support Health and Extend Life

We all know that we need to eat well and exercise to stay healthy. Yet we also understand that the temptation to sit on the couch, watch TV, and eat comfort food is often more compelling. Statistics indicate that over one-third of adults between the ages of sixty-four and seventy-five are obese.[14]

Many adults over sixty-five years of age need assistance with at least one activity of daily living (e.g., eating, bathing, dressing). One comprehensive study of the needs of older adults with multiple health problems concluded that there is a tremendous need for better communication and coordination of care of older adults.[15] Health-care providers are often undertrained; primary care physicians have little time to develop a personal relationship with an older adult who has multiple health conditions. Family members find that they play the role of exhausted, untrained, and unpaid health-care coordinators.

Cognitive Decline

Cognitive decline as we age is not inevitable. Genetic factors make some of us more likely to develop Alzheimer's or other dementias. But recent research strongly suggests that general cognitive decline is strongly related to lifestyle factors. What we are learning is good news. We have much more control over our physical and mental decline than we previously believed, but what we need to do to maintain our physical and cognitive health is challenging. Maintaining a healthy lifestyle requires commitment, determination, and support from others. Dale Bredesen has been a pioneer in studying the impact of lifestyle changes in not only slowing but reversing (!) cognitive decline in older adults. He outlined his approach in his best-selling book *The End of Alzheimer's*.[16] Subsequent research has supported his findings, emphasizing the primary importance of dietary changes to protect against or reduce cognitive decline.[17] (I write about this in more detail in Chapter 9.) A big issue here is also the problem of confusing cognitive decline with undiagnosed ADHD.

Challenges Reported by Non-ADHD Older Adults

The concerns of older adults discussed in this chapter were identified by the professional community. Let's look at how well those issues align with self-reported problems. While certainly nonscientific, I queried a small group of twenty-five older adults by simply asking them to list the "top five challenges" they experienced in their daily lives.

The concerns they listed were wide-ranging as I gave them no parameters for their responses. Once I received them, I organized them into general categories to better understand the predominant concerns. The primary concerns of this group fell into the following categories:

- **Fatigue/sleep problems**—This was, by far, the most common concern expressed.

- **Difficulty maintaining healthy habits**—This concern was a close second to fatigue and sleep issues. As one woman wrote, "Since I'm going to die soon anyway, is it worth it to deny myself the food that I love and force myself to exercise, which I hate doing?"

- **Difficulty maintaining social connections with friends and family**—Family concerns were primarily related to time and distance: not seeing adult children often enough and not knowing how to build and maintain relationships with grandchildren who live at a distance.

- **A struggle to remain organized in daily life**—Many of the adults I spoke to mentioned difficulty in decluttering and maintaining order in their home amid a lifetime of accumulated belongings. Their organizational concerns also included struggling to keep up with financial and medical records, maintaining a calendar, and a general feeling of inefficiency.

- **No longer feeling "relevant" in postretirement years**—They mentioned not feeling engaged, not contributing to society, and lacking a sense of purpose.

In other words, these adults didn't sleep well, tried to but often didn't take good care of their health, felt distressed about the physical distance and limited interactions with adult children and grandchildren, and weren't happy with the state of disorganization in which they lived. As we become older and more easily tired, we become prisoners of our belongings. The last thing we feel motivated to do when we have low energy is to organize, downsize, and off-load a lifetime's worth of belongings. All that I have written about aging in this chapter applies, of course, to older adults with and without ADHD. However, those with ADHD face additional burdens that I will focus on in the next chapter.

KEY TAKEAWAYS FROM THIS CHAPTER

✔ We need to **rethink retirement** and ways to remain active and engaged for twenty or more years after the "typical" retirement age.

✔ It's important to **find a sense of purpose** during our later years—whether this involves volunteer work, family engagement, or pursuing a long-delayed interest.

✔ **Maintaining a feeling of "relevance" in the digital age** is increasingly difficult for older adults who haven't grown up using computers and smartphones.

✔ **Maintaining active social engagement** is critical to supporting our physical and emotional health. We need to add new social connections to counteract the inevitable loss of earlier social relationships due to moving away, ill health, or death.

✔ **Thinking ahead regarding a possible need for a change in housing** is essential rather than leaving these decisions until a crisis arises.

✔ **Navigating the financial environment in retirement** is increasingly difficult for most because substantial retirement benefits for most of us are a thing of the past.

✔ **Self-care is increasingly essential** to stave off health problems and maintain our mobility, yet daily healthy habits are challenging to maintain.

✔ **Cognitive decline is a worry for most of us.** Recent research suggests that a healthy lifestyle is the most effective way to maintain our cognitive abilities.

It's Hard to Understand It If You Haven't Lived It

The human cost of living a lifetime with undiagnosed ADHD

G rowing up with ADHD, most kids are showered with criticism or rejection many times a day—from parents, teachers, and coaches. "Why do I have to remind you so many times?" "Why are you always late for the bus?" "Why do you lose everything?" "Why do you always do things at the last minute?" "Why can't you just sit down and do your homework?" "You just need to try harder." In school alone, not considering criticism from parents and coaches, it is estimated that a child with ADHD could receive twenty thousand corrective or negative comments by the time they are ten years old.[1] And the feedback from peers can be even more brutal. Stephen Hinshaw's ground-breaking research[2] on girls with ADHD found that these girls tend to be either "socially rejected" or "socially neglected" by peers. Research shows that ADHD is often associated with social difficulties for children with ADHD[3] that continue in adolescence[4] and into adulthood.[5]

If you haven't lived it, you can only try to understand what it's like to feel criticized and outcast from a young age, no matter how hard you try.

Having ADHD is more difficult in some cultures than in others. I recall many years ago talking to a group of European physicists, colleagues of my husband, who politely inquired about my career focus. When I began to describe the challenges of ADHD, several of them laughed, saying, "But you are describing most of our students!" Here in the US, we value being on time, on task, and on target, all of which require good executive functioning skills, skills that are often in short supply when you have ADHD. Our culture values persistence, competition, and achievement. School, in particular, can be a very ADHD-unfriendly environment. Criticism of children with ADHD regularly occurs when students talk in class, don't complete their work, forget their homework, or can't remember the teacher's instructions.

In other ways, however, the US is very ADHD-friendly. We are a nation that accepts and celebrates second chances; we celebrate risk-taking, creative problem-solving, and entrepreneurship.

In this book, the older adults I write about lived with undiagnosed ADHD until middle age or later. They had grown up without the understanding or support that could have reduced or prevented the pattern of family conflicts, underperformance in school, conflictual relationships, divorces, unemployment, and employment in jobs for which they were poorly matched. They grew up with parents frustrated that they "didn't just sit down and do their work," that they didn't "just try harder," that they didn't listen or seem to care. Research suggests that children growing up under a barrage of parental criticism tend to demonstrate *more ADHD symptoms as they grow older compared to children with ADHD whose parents were more supportive and encouraging.* Today's adults, aged fifty-five and older, for the most part, were raised by parents who didn't understand ADHD and believed that their children could change if only they tried hard enough. They grew up feeling "different" but didn't know why they didn't fit in.

Again, Diane's words echoes many common experiences:

"One of my struggles is a feeling of sadness over what I would like to have accomplished (in my life) but couldn't; I think a lot about what my ADHD has cost me."

And even people who appear highly accomplished report life-long, painful struggles.

For example,

Richard did well in school, but struggled terribly to complete his dissertation to earn his PhD in psychology. Later, he looked back with great regret on his lifetime of angry outbursts and irritability toward his family and colleagues. Ultimately, his colleagues asked him to leave their private-practice group because his poor planning, disorganization, and irritability had become intolerable. He now works alone, a default decision that many adults with ADHD resort to because of interpersonal difficulties.

Lauren's story reflects the struggles of many women with lifelong untreated ADHD.

The youngest child in her somewhat chaotic family, Lauren grew up with an alcoholic father who was verbally abusive toward her mother. She feels sure, looking back, that her dad had undiagnosed ADHD. At age seventeen, Lauren married to escape her unhappy home life and started having children right away. In retrospect, she wishes she had stayed in school but, at the time, didn't feel that she could be a successful student: "I just couldn't focus." Lauren followed her husband's successful career while working part-time at a random assortment of jobs as her children grew up. She described her husband as "a wonderful man" and was overcome with shock when he came home one day, after more than twenty-five years of marriage, to tell her he was leaving. He said that he hadn't been happy for years because she was "too emotional" and disorganized, always doing things at the last minute. Lauren had focused on her children, trying to give them the stable, loving childhood that she had never experienced. She admitted that her abilities as a homemaker were somewhat lacking and that she may have taken her husband's support for granted. After his devastating departure, she fell into a prolonged depression.

Eventually, Lauren pulled herself together. Her alimony, combined with what part-time work she could cobble together, allows her to support herself modestly—a far cry from her comfortable lifestyle as a married woman. Her children, who had been the center of her life, are grown. Today, Lauren is "just getting along." In her early sixties, she shares an apartment with a roommate, lives near one of her adult children, and said that she would need to work part-time as long as she is able. It was not until her sixties that she was diagnosed with ADHD by a doctor who was astute enough to recognize there was more going on than her long-standing depression. Taking medication for her ADHD, Lauren feels calmer and more focused and wonders how different her life might have been if she had been diagnosed and treated when she was younger.

Lauren's story about late-diagnosed ADHD has several elements common to many with undiagnosed, untreated ADHD: dropping out of school because she felt she couldn't succeed academically; inability to earn a comfortable salary; struggling with emotional dysregulation, and difficulty maintaining order in her daily life; and little awareness of how she was impacting her partner. Her focus was on her children, and she depended upon her husband to "take care of everything else," never realizing that he had unmet needs. Looking back with regret over lost opportunities, Lauren wonders whether, had she been diagnosed and treated earlier, perhaps she would have been able to function more as an equal partner in her marriage rather than as a dependent wife. Maybe she could have decided to return to school, developing skills and building self-esteem along the way. Lauren's is an all-too-common story of loss and lost opportunity.

The impact of ADHD upon our lives can vary tremendously as our ADHD is impacted by the circumstances in which we live. Rita's story is a tragic one due to the circumstances in which she grew up. I received the following email from Rita in response to an online seminar I offered on ADHD in older adults:

> *"I was diagnosed with ADHD at age five. I came from a single-parent home. My mom had undiagnosed ADHD, and I am pretty sure my dad suffered from this affliction (ADHD) too. Unfortunately, my mother, who was diagnosed with cancer, and was a single parent with four children, could not deal with me, her child with ADHD. In the end, she put me in a foster home. I have suffered my whole life from ADHD and was fired from every job I ever held. I eventually found a way to work for myself, but it has been a struggle, to say the least. I still barely make enough to support myself and have gradually become antisocial due to being shunned by others. I have been single for nearly twenty-five years and have totally given up on finding a relationship. I live alone and work out of my house. Loneliness takes on a new meaning when you have no contact with anyone socially. I drink excessively and don't care. A lowered life expectancy would be a relief.*
>
> *"There is no cure for this affliction, and many of us just give up. I worked so hard to connect socially but to no avail. I am tired of trying to fit in and be liked. I will never fit in and be liked. And my family no longer wants anything to do with me. I am thinking of trying Ritalin again. Maybe this time."*

Rita was traumatized by being placed in foster care. Her mother was understandably overwhelmed as a single parent of four kids with a cancer diagnosis, not to mention the challenges of trying to raise a child with ADHD and behavioral difficulties. Remarkably, despite her traumatizing childhood, Rita graduated from college. We don't have the details of what she studied and what sort of work she tried to engage in following her graduation. We know that she has been chronically depressed and socially isolated. She struggles with chronic sleep problems and has never "fit in" with any social group. Her cry of despair is a striking example of "rejection sensitive dysphoria," a new term that has become part of the ADHD lexicon in recent times—a term to describe the terrible pain that results from feeling rejected by others. The depression, sleep problems, alcohol problems, social isolation, and feelings of being an outcast described by Rita are shared by many adults with untreated ADHD.

And then there is the man I call "Good-Time Charlie." He started working in the restaurant business in his early twenties and loved it.

> *"It's kind of a bohemian life, especially when you work the late shift. I would work from early evening to three a.m. and then party with my coworkers after that." Charlie described some restaurants where he worked, those with live music and an upbeat atmosphere, as "kind of an island for misfit boys." Charlie married once, very briefly, but doesn't like to feel tied down. Social relationships have always been difficult for him.. "People are attracted to me because I am fun and outgoing, but I have angry knee-jerk responses, and after a while, I lose friends and business partners." Now, he works alone. "Life is far from perfect. I'm still trying to multitask and never seem to finish anything. My 'thought tornadoes' wear me out. It's like I'm on a treadmill and can't get off. Having ADHD is exhausting."*

You may read such figures as "sixty percent of individuals with ADHD symptoms in childhood continue to have difficulties in adult life."[6] Those figures were calculated in the late 1980s when an ADHD diagnosis was an "all or nothing" affair. If you met diagnostic criteria (six or more symptoms), you "had it" and if you only had five symptoms or fewer, you didn't. Our thinking has evolved in the years following. We are slowly coming around to a consensus that ADHD is a dimensional disorder[7] in which you can have a range of symptoms from mild to severe. The more we recognize ADHD as a dimensional disorder, the clearer it becomes that ADHD persists across the life span.

If you are an adult with ADHD, you are more likely to be fired from jobs, to have held many short-term positions, and if you are among the fortunate few, to finally find work to which you are well suited despite your ADHD challenges. Many adults with ADHD resort to self-employment, a pattern described by both Richard and Rita, because they have had chronic interpersonal difficulties with employers and colleagues. Typical workplace difficulties for adults with ADHD include absenteeism, lateness, excessive errors, missing deadlines, and a general inability to keep up with the expected workload.

At home, conflictual relationships and marital breakups are more common. And the risk of drug and substance abuse is significantly increased in adults with persisting ADHD symptoms who have not been receiving medication. Most adults have "complex ADHD," meaning that they have ADHD in combination with other issues. These may include anxiety, mood disorders, eating disorders, substance use disorders, bipolar disorder, learning disorders, post-traumatic stress disorder (PTSD)—the list is long.[8] If you are an adult with ADHD, you are more likely to have children with ADHD because it is so highly heritable, which, in turn, causes further challenges. It is significantly more difficult to parent children with ADHD, especially if you are a parent who also has ADHD. Generational cycles of dysfunction often develop under these circumstances.[9]

Difficulty Creating the Structure Needed to Accomplish Your Goals

One of the common challenges of living with ADHD is difficulty creating structure in an unstructured situation—and few things are as unstructured as retirement. One day, you are working—with a daily schedule and daily tasks. The next day, your time is your "own." Even though you still have many things to take care of—all of the responsibilities of life are still there except for work—there's no schedule. You can stay up until the middle of the night; you can sleep until noon. You can stop preparing meals and simply forage in the kitchen, living on a probably much less healthy diet.

> *George had enjoyed a very busy and successful career as an architect. His days were structured, and tasks were clearly defined. Now, in retirement, he reported to me, "I find it so much harder to get things done now that I have almost nothing to do."*

And George is not alone.

Robert told me that he had looked forward to pursuing many interests in retirement that he hadn't had time for during his career. *"Now that I'm retired and have plenty of time, I don't really do any of the things I'd planned. I spend money on materials or equipment for a new hobby and then soon drop it. There's just no focus in my life."*

We'll come back to this critical topic in Chapters 6 and 7.

Maintaining Social Engagement as an Adult with ADHD

For older adults with ADHD, the challenges of maintaining a solid social network, or building a new one in retirement, are even more significant because being your own "social secretary" requires planning, organization, and follow-through. So many older adults with

ADHD have told me that they have lost friends due to the challenges of keeping in touch. "I've finally given up on sending holiday cards," one woman told me. "Many years, I purchased cards but never got around to sending them." She envies people she knows who are still in touch with friends from high school or college. "Out of sight is out of mind, for me," she told me ruefully. As an older adult with ADHD, you may have experienced social difficulties throughout your life due to problems reading social cues, forgetting, interrupting others, talking too much, or being irritable and short-tempered—all hallmarks of ADHD.

Maintaining or building a social network requires social skills, planning, and effort—things that may be in short supply for many older adults with ADHD. When I asked one older woman with ADHD whether she entertained people in her home, she responded humorously, "Not if I can help it!"

The following comments by Karen, a woman with ADHD, describe with painful clarity these social challenges:

> "I have never been able to understand the rules of conversation. I tend to either space out or blurt out something unrelated to the topic of the conversation. I try hard, but the 'rules' just don't come naturally. My interrupting makes me seem uncaring when that's the last thing I feel. I have a few friends who have ADHD, so they understand me and accept my quirks."

Karen said something vital as she lamented her social difficulties—that most of her friends have ADHD and therefore understand her. Finding or creating a group of other adults with ADHD can be a very heartwarming and healing experience. (I write about this again in Chapter 10.)

You may not recognize yourself in Karen's painful account of social rejection. It's important to remember that ADHD is a "coat of many colors." There are so many different presentations of ADHD and many adults with ADHD have excellent social skills. For example, Robert, a retired business consultant, had greatly enjoyed his career, which involved advising the owners of small to medium-size businesses. Robert loved meeting with the owners and their employees to understand their successes and challenges. He could relate easily to all sorts of people, a gift that served him well as a consultant. After retiring, Robert told me that one of his favorite pastimes was to chat with everyone he encountered as he ran errands or sat in a café with a cup of coffee. His wife would wait impatiently while he talked with one person and then another. She was very organized and kept their social calendar, whereas his gift was to engage in spontaneous encounters as he went about his day.

Financial Challenges in Retirement for Those with ADHD

Saving enough for retirement is difficult for most adults but even more challenging when adults have ADHD. Poor planning ability and patterns of impulsive spending combine to make the picture bleak for many with ADHD. Some of the older adults I spoke to commented with chagrin that they would have to work "until the day I die." Those who told me that they were financially secure in retirement in most cases attributed that security to their non-ADHD spouse's income and investment planning. High divorce rates also create a significant barrier to financial security in old age. Some of the older adults I spoke to told me of working part-time after retirement to bring in a bit of extra income.

Senior-Friendly Living Circumstances

Finding affordable housing in later years can be very difficult. If you own your own home, you may need to sell it to access your equity in the house to use for retirement income. Some fortunate few sell their home and move to a less expensive area of the US where they can purchase a much smaller home and still retain some money for retirement income. Multilevel care facilities are often too costly for the typical retiree. With little savings and only a very modest monthly income (half of seniors receive 50 percent of their income from Social Security, while for 25 percent of seniors, 90 percent of their income comes from Social Security[10]), the choices can be limited.

Some adults with ADHD who own their homes resort to renting rooms to afford to remain in their homes as long as possible. One woman I spoke to in her sixties told me that she had moved into the basement of someone else's house and, rather than paying rent, exchanged her services caring for the old and infirm husband a few hours each day to allow his wife to have time to go out.

In some families, grandparents live with the family of an adult child—an arrangement that was very common generations ago, but less and less so because today it's likely that adult children have moved far away, pursuing their careers.

If you are an older parent with ADHD, you are likely to have adult children with ADHD. They may not have the financial and emotional bandwidth to come to your support because of their own life challenges. In many, if not most, families impacted by ADHD, there is sparse "intergenerational financial cushion." The older adults with ADHD may have little retirement savings while their adult children with ADHD have little discretionary income, making it more difficult for them to help with their parents' housing needs. And, of course, having children is no guarantee of a haven in our later years. Kate told me that she had hoped to live with her daughter and son-in-law in her old age. In her late seventies, no invitation has been forthcoming from her daughter, and she has no plan B. And many older adults with ADHD are not parents, which requires them to be self-reliant at a vulnerable time in their life.

Self-Care to Support Health and Extend Life

Healthy living patterns are challenging to maintain as we get older. As an adult *with* ADHD, the challenges are only magnified. Healthy living takes planning, commitment, and follow-through. (I write more in Chapter 9 about ways that you can make it easier to develop healthy daily living habits as an adult with ADHD.) Adults with ADHD are more likely to be overweight or obese and, as a result, to suffer from the many health problems related to unhealthy eating patterns, including type 2 diabetes and heart disease.[11] Recently, the ADHD professional community is starting to pay more attention to the health needs of older adults with ADHD. I have begun to offer healthy eating coaching groups for ADHD at my clinic, focused on educating adults with ADHD about how to counteract patterns of impulsive eating, overreliance on carry-out and convenience foods, eating out of boredom, and eating to self-soothe. While many without ADHD engage in these unhealthy eating patterns, having ADHD increases your vulnerability to disordered eating patterns.

Cognitive Decline

As I wrote in Chapter 2 about Dale Bredesen's research, we have learned that unhealthy lifestyle choices are closely tied to cognitive decline. It only makes sense, then, that those with unhealthy eating patterns, poor sleep habits, and little regular exercise will be more susceptible to cognitive decline. As you will read more about in Chapter 4, it is critically important to distinguish between never-diagnosed ADHD in older adults and the onset of dementia. Sadly, when older adults seek an assessment of memory problems, very few memory clinics routinely screen for ADHD. This lack of screening creates the likelihood that never-diagnosed adults with ADHD may be incorrectly diagnosed with early signs of dementia rather than receiving adequate treatment for a highly treatable condition.

What Older Adults with ADHD Report about Their Top ADHD-Related Struggles

I explored the main concerns of older adults in two ways. First, I simply asked them to list the top five ADHD-related challenges that they experience. This approach gave them free rein to list anything and everything with no preconceived notions on my part. We organized their responses into the following categories:

1. **Organization**—They reported that they had difficulty prioritizing, planning, and following through to completion; problems with household maintenance, paperwork, and general indecisiveness.

2. **Focus and attention**—They reported distractibility, difficulty sustaining their attention, making careless errors, frequently losing personal items, and tending to hyperfocus on something of interest so that they forgot many essential tasks.

3. **Motivation and productivity**—They reported struggling with boredom, losing interest in projects they had started, difficulty with getting going in the morning, low energy, and generally feeling unproductive.

4. **Emotions**—Emotional issues ran the gamut, including depression, anxiety, irritability, self-doubt, self-pity, guilt, feelings of overwhelm, and general difficulty with emotional reactivity.

5. **Memory**—They described general forgetfulness, difficulty remembering what they had been doing after a distraction ("Where was I?"), and general difficulty with "working memory" (i.e., keeping several things in mind at the same time).

Self-Report Questionnaire

In my structured interview with older adults, I asked them to recall how they functioned on a broad range of issues in midlife, compared to current functioning in later life. Not surprisingly, many reported some problems to be less challenging in older age simply because the demands they face in retirement are significantly less than those they had faced in midlife. ADHD exists in relationship to the demands placed upon us. Using an analogy from the world of physical disability, you might report significantly less difficulty getting from place to place as a mobility-impaired person if you live in an accessible community with no stairs. The elimination of stairs doesn't mean that your disability has improved. It means that the environment better accommodates your disability. Likewise, if you are not a caretaker for others and you are no longer employed, you may find that your ADHD is less challenging. However, you continue to struggle with the many tasks of daily living. Some reported ADHD challenges have decreased, not because they have gone away, but because their post-retirement lifestyle places fewer cognitive demands on them.

I developed a symptom list in a highly informal manner by creating a long list of ADHD-related challenges that I have observed in the many adults and older adults who have come to my clinic. I then asked the 150 already diagnosed adults I interviewed to respond to the list to identify the items they viewed as most problematic. The ten most commonly endorsed items were the following:

1. Difficulty completing tasks
2. Impulse to "do one more thing" when I don't have enough time
3. Difficulty sticking to my plan for the day
4. Losing track of time
5. Difficulty handling paperwork
6. Feeling overwhelmed

7. Messiness
8. Getting regular exercise
9. Absentmindedness
10. Keeping in touch with friends

You may be interested in completing the self-report questionnaire yourself. It should be thought of as a "structured interview" that you might want to review with a mental health professional to explore the possibility that you have ADHD. The questionnaire is not a diagnostic instrument; there are no cutoff scores. Nevertheless, it may be beneficial for your mental health professional to structure a broad interview as part of your assessment process. You can find this questionnaire in Appendix A, pages 305–307.

We all face a range of challenges as we age, with or without ADHD. However, these same challenges are typically more significant for those with ADHD due to the executive functioning issues fundamental to ADHD. In addition, there are issues more specific to ADHD that further contribute to the difficulties faced by older adults with ADHD. These are the ADHD-related problems experienced throughout their lifetimes that continue to cause problems in later years with daily life management, getting things done, emotional regulation and sensitivity, memory challenges, and social relationships.

KEY TAKEAWAYS FROM THIS CHAPTER

✔ Frequently, growing up with ADHD means growing up under a shower of criticism from teachers, parents, and peers.

✔ Many older adults diagnosed with ADHD look back in regret at what might have been different if they had gotten help earlier.

✔ Adults with ADHD share the usual changes and challenges of growing older but may experience them more intensely:

  ○ More family conflicts and concerns due to intergenerational ADHD

  ○ More significant financial difficulties in late life

  ○ More difficulty finding meaning and purpose in retirement because, while intentions are good, planning and follow-through are often lacking

  ○ More difficulty maintaining healthy daily habits that require discipline and focus

✔ Older adults with ADHD continue to struggle with difficulties related to the following:

  ○ Disorganization

  ○ Lack of focus

  ○ Low motivation

  ○ Negative emotions

  ○ Forgetfulness

✔ ADHD is a "coat of many colors," and not all older adults with ADHD experience all these struggles to the same degree.

How Do You Know You Have ADHD?

Understanding and diagnosing ADHD in older adults

W hen older adults with undiagnosed ADHD experience memory issues in later years, understandably, their first worry is about dementia. And even those with diagnosed ADHD might be concerned that ADHD could make them more likely to develop dementia. Because dementia impacts so many older adults, ADHD forgetfulness can seem more frightening as older adults enter their sixties and seventies, when the likelihood of dementia looms on the horizon. *"I forgot my doctor's appointment. I can't ever find my glasses. My wife swears she told me three times that we have plans this weekend, but I have no memory of that. Is she losing it? Or am I?"*

If you are experiencing similar worries, take a look at the list of experiences common to many adults with ADHD. If you find yourself answering yes to many of the questions, then it's important to ask a professional (psychiatrist, psychologist, neurologist) to assess you for adult ADHD.

Do or did you experience:

School-related problems

- Underperforming in school
- Doing well on tests but not doing homework
- Difficulty completing papers
- Behavior problems during school years
- Being told, "You're so smart, you just need to try harder."
- Difficulties in graduate or professional school, such as not completing a thesis or dissertation
- Difficulty passing medical boards or law boards

Work-related problems

- Losing or quitting jobs due to poor performance or dissatisfaction
- Missing deadlines at work
- Never being promoted to the level that you feel you deserve
- Difficulty with paperwork

Life management problems

- Forgetting to pay bills
- Living in a messy, disorganized environment
- Smoking cigarettes and/or drinking to excess
- Getting speeding tickets
- Struggling with depression and anxiety
- Procrastinating and having difficulty accomplishing projects, even projects that initially excite you

Relationship/interpersonal problems

- Losing your temper often or being easily frustrated

- Having high levels of conflict with those close to you
- Having marital conflicts leading to separation and divorce
- Inconsistent and emotionally reactive parenting patterns

Family history

- Having children diagnosed with ADHD
- Family history of anxiety, depression, substance use disorders
- Family history of learning disorders

If some of these patterns sound familiar to you, you (or the friend or family member whose habits you're thinking of right now) may have undiagnosed ADHD.

Marty was in his seventies and was experiencing forgetfulness every day. Some of the things he forgot were relatively minor, such as "Where did I put my cell phone?" But other items were more problematic. His desk at home was piled high with mail, and he regularly received notices about bills that had gone unpaid. He and his wife, Nancy, a woman who had always had an excellent memory, were becoming increasingly worried. Fearing that his forgetfulness might be the first sign of dementia, they made an appointment with an adult psychiatrist. Together, they met with him to express their concerns. Fortunately, the psychiatrist was one of the relatively few who are familiar with ADHD in adults. He carefully interviewed the couple about examples of forgetfulness in Marty's daily life, both currently and in the past. It became clear to the psychiatrist that Marty had always struggled with planning, organization, and remembering the details of daily life. Marty had always relied on Nancy to "keep the trains running on time" at home. Because many of the patterns they described were long-standing, the psychiatrist began to consider that Marty might have ADHD rather than dementia.

Importantly, the psychiatrist asked questions about the family history. ADHD is a condition that strongly runs in families. If one family member has ADHD, other family members are likely to have it as well. He asked whether any children and grandchildren had been diagnosed with ADHD. "Yes, two of our grandchildren have been diagnosed and are taking medication," Nancy related. To their great relief, the psychiatrist told them that he believed Marty's problem was lifelong undiagnosed ADHD. He prescribed stimulant medication, to which Marty had a very positive response. The psychiatrist also told them that many other changes were needed in Marty's daily routines to help him be less forgetful and keep track of essential tasks. Marty and Nancy felt great relief and set about working together to build habits and routines at home to help Marty function more easily in his daily life.

Not everyone is as fortunate as Marty and Nancy were. Older adults concerned about forgetfulness often go to memory clinics where they are screened for dementia by neurologists for whom ADHD in older adults is not on their radar. One survey of memory clinics across the US showed that only a small percentage of these clinics even consider the possibility of ADHD when assessing memory problems in an older adult.[1]

Because so few neurologists or adult psychiatrists have received substantial training in diagnosing ADHD in adults, much less in older adults, there is a risk of overlooking ADHD and misdiagnosing mild cognitive decline or early Alzheimer's. This type of misdiagnosis is precisely what happened to Adele.

Adele had retired with her husband to Florida. She had always been a bit forgetful and disorganized. Despite this history, her husband became convinced that she was developing dementia in her seventies and took her to a neurologist for an assessment. The neurologist diagnosed her with early-stage Alzheimer's and prescribed medication typically used to slow its progression. During their periodic visits to the neurologist, her husband painted an increasingly negative picture of his wife's daily functioning. Fast-forward several years, and Adele became a widow. In conversation with her son, she told him that she had never felt comfortable with her neurologist or believed in her Alzheimer's diagnosis. Her son arranged for a consultation with a younger neurologist and accompanied his mother to the appointment. He later shared that this younger neurologist confirmed his mother's suspicion that she did not have Alzheimer's but instead had ADHD.

Link Between ADHD and Dementia

There is evidence of an association between ADHD and dementia. Research published in 2021 reported on a very large multigenerational population study in Sweden[2] that showed parents of children with ADHD are more likely to develop dementia. In addition, there is some evidence of a link between ADHD and Lewy body dementia (LBD)[3] (a form of dementia similar to Alzheimer's, but with a more rapid progression; symptoms include confusion, memory loss, disorientation, and loss of balance).

It's important to understand that studies are not suggesting that ADHD "causes" dementia, but that there is an association between the two conditions. It is not clear whether this is a genetic link or the indirect result of unhealthy lifestyle choices associated with ADHD that can lead to cognitive decline and dementia. Dale Bredesen's work on reversing cognitive decline[4] shows very hopeful and promising results indicating that, for a large percentage of people, early signs of dementia or cognitive decline are the result of poor diet, lack of sleep or exercise, and so on, and that cognitive decline can be reversed through significant improvements in daily healthy habits. (This is discussed in much greater detail in Chapter 9.)

Why Does It Matter at This Late Date If I Have ADHD?

Most people with ADHD live with it, without a diagnosis or treatment, throughout their lives. But their lives are typically more frustrating and stressful due to their ADHD. If you are in your sixties, seventies, or beyond, you may think, "If I've lived with it this long, why bother with it now?" The many older adults with ADHD I've spoken to and treated over the years tell a very different story about their late diagnosis. There is often a feeling of relief ("Now I finally know what the problem is!") and positive change among older adults after being diagnosed. Let me share a few of their comments with you.

> "I have felt reenergized in a very positive manner. I can manage not to ruminate too much on the problems I had as a child, and I am still glad that I am here, now, and learning for the rest of my life."

> "I kind of enjoy and embrace my ADHD, now that I understand it. Others may have a problem with my forgetfulness and lateness, but that's their problem! I like all its aspects, from intuitiveness to creativity to empathy. Now, I accept who I am."

> "Now that I know I have ADHD, I read about it and learned how to reduce the challenges. For example, I have learned that exercise is my best ADHD treatment. I also understand now that my struggles with time management, organization, procrastination, and motivation are not character flaws. I am much less self-critical, and I'm enjoying retirement a lot. My husband and I have a lot of interests, and we enjoy going out and doing things together. I focus more now on the positive and don't dwell so much on my ADHD challenges."

> "I'm able to set basic routines for myself now. Most important, I have much better self-esteem. I feel like I'm becoming a different

person. I still shut down at times when there are upsets with my husband, but my new awareness is very helpful, and I recover from upsets more quickly."

"I used to make lists and then feel despondent seeing the list and tell myself, 'I can't do this,' and nothing would get done. Now, I tell myself, 'Bless you—I'll do the best I can.' I try not to schedule too much in a day."

If you are like many older adults with ADHD (diagnosed or undiagnosed), you have probably grown up with criticism from the adults around you: "Why are you always late?" "You could do so much better if you tried harder!" "Why is your room such a mess?" "Why do we always have to struggle with you over getting your homework done?" "Why do you have to argue with me all the time?" Many older adults who have struggled with undiagnosed ADHD throughout their lives often feel battered by failures, failures that they and most everyone around them have attributed to laziness, poor self-discipline, low motivation, or incompetence, beginning in their youth. It's hard to grow up feeling good about yourself when you have difficulty doing the things that many of your classmates can do with relative ease. Not being able to keep up with your peers at school or with your siblings at home can lead to feeling bad about yourself. Low self-esteem is common among adults with ADHD who didn't receive a proper diagnosis and treatment when they were younger.

Why Does ADHD Seem to Vary So Much in Different People?

ADHD can be very confusing because its presentation can vary widely. Some with inattentive-type ADHD are slow, quiet, and often shy. They are unsure how to fit in with their peers and may have only one or two close friends during childhood. Others with ADHD are noisy, argumentative, rebellious, and always in motion. Some are bossy and alienate everyone around them because they want things to go their way all the time. Others are quiet and insecure, not speaking up at all. And still others can be charming and engaging, not struggling with the social challenges that so many with ADHD experience.

Many Professionals Still Don't Realize That You Can Be a High Achiever with ADHD

Although, in the minds of many people, ADHD is associated with being a poor student, you may be surprised to know that it's entirely possible to be a good student, even going to college or to professional school after college, yet still struggle with ADHD. These high-IQ adults with ADHD typically need to work twice as hard as their classmates or colleagues. No one sees the effort required; they just see the results and assume that they can't possibly have ADHD. Many middle-aged adults who have come to me for treatment have told similar stories. Psychiatrists to whom they have gone for an ADHD assessment have said, "I can tell you right now, without going any further, that you can't possibly have ADHD because you have ... [a law degree, a medical degree, a doctoral degree, etc.]." Sadly, the mistaken belief that you can't have ADHD if you succeed in your chosen profession is still quite common in the medical and mental health community.[5]

Diagnosis Can Be Missed by Adhering to the Strict Rule of "6 or More" Symptoms Being Required

According to the American Psychiatric Association's *Diagnostic and Statistical Manual*, 5th edition (DSM-5),[6] if you have five symptoms or fewer, you do not have ADHD, but if you have six or more, you *do* have ADHD. Despite this rigid diagnostic protocol, most of us in the field of ADHD are reaching a still unofficial agreement that ADHD exists along a continuum.[7] In reality, you can have mild ADHD, significant

ADHD, or anything in between. The DSM-5 diagnostic criteria were developed through observation of young boys and often don't capture the presentation of ADHD in older adults.

Diagnosis Complicated by Co-occurring Conditions

Another reason for the confusion around ADHD in adults is that it occurs in combination with many other disorders. These coexisting conditions may include anxiety, mood disorders, bipolar disorder, substance use disorders, eating disorders, personality disorders, learning disorders, autism…the list is long.[8] So, you can see why it may look very different from one person to the next. Many individuals who are reading this book may have been diagnosed with anxiety or depression without their treating professional ever considering the possibility of ADHD. In fact, ADHD is among the most common adult psychiatric conditions, but is overlooked because it is typically accompanied by other psychiatric conditions that are more familiar to mental health professionals.

Diagnosis Complicated by Waxing and Waning Symptoms

Another reason that a diagnosis can be missed is that ADHD symptoms can wax and wane throughout your day, your week, your month, even throughout your life. That's because stress levels, sleep deprivation, and demands that are placed on you all impact the level of your ADHD symptoms.[9]

The Evolution of Our Understanding of ADHD

We are also learning more and more about ADHD as time goes by. For example, fifty years ago, the emphasis was on hyperactivity, primarily seen in boys. Then, we began to focus on distractibility and difficulty paying attention, or on negative behaviors, such as being oppositional. In the mid-1990s, the ADHD professional community began to recognize that many adults had ADHD. At that same time, we began to conceptualize ADHD as a disorder of "executive functioning"—a catchall term that encompasses our abilities to plan, organize, follow through on, and complete tasks; as well as how we manage our time and our belongings—or, as one professional put it, "our ability to get our act together." But more was to come. Only recently, professionals in the field are talking about difficulties with emotional regulation—meaning that many with ADHD react with emotional intensity to many things—be it with anger, frustration, hurt feelings, excitement, or joy. Keeping track of time, tasks, and belongings plus managing our motivation level and emotional reactions are all in the mix. We are now starting to think of ADHD as a very complex disorder that impacts all aspects of self-management.[10]

ADHD Is a Misnomer

Think about this name—it implies we have a "deficit" of attention—in other words, an inability to maintain our attention or focus on an activity. And yet it is well known that people of every age with ADHD have, if anything, a surplus of attention when they are engaged in an activity that interests them. Many in the ADHD community refer to this as "hyperfocus"—becoming so intensely focused on an activity that you don't know what time it is and don't realize that someone is speaking to you or trying to get your attention.[11] It seems more accurate to think of a dysregulated attentional system, one in which you can be highly distractible under certain circumstances and able to focus intently at other times.

I once worked with Jim, a computer scientist whose hyperfocus was so intense that electronic reminders never worked for him. He would absentmindedly turn off the offending alarm and continue

*to work on whatever he was doing. At his office, the secretary
finally realized that she needed to go to his office door, knock
loudly, and call his name to get his attention to remind him that it
was time to leave for a scheduled meeting. His company benefited
enormously from Jim's "attention deficit," which if anything, was
an attention surplus.*

ADHD Can Be Considered a "Type of Brain" Rather Than a "Disorder"

Generally, ADHD is classified as a disability under the Americans with Disabilities Act.[12] You won't hear from physicians trained to diagnose and treat diseases, maladies, and disorders that there are positive aspects of having this condition that we call ADHD. The focus in medicine is to look at what's wrong and try to "fix" it. And the reason for classifying ADHD as a disability is to qualify for accommodations in school or the workplace. But there is much more to having an ADHD brain than its challenges.

We need more research on the positive aspects of ADHD that can contribute to success.[13] Most ADHD research is focused on treating the negative aspects. I am certainly not in the camp that celebrates ADHD as a "gift" and discounts its challenges, but I firmly believe that there are advantages to having an ADHD brain that deserve much more attention. A small but growing body of research is focusing on the positive aspects of ADHD.[14]

ADHD is often found among improv artists, comedians, and actors. I once facilitated a group of teenagers diagnosed with ADHD who recognized their creative gifts. They told me they took their medication when they wanted to focus on schoolwork, but chose to be off their medication to engage in creative activities. In other words, they recognized that their ADHD was the basis of their creativity, and they didn't want medication to dampen it. Of course, no matter your age, you shouldn't make unilateral decisions about medication changes without consulting with your prescriber.

Many people with ADHD thrive upon risk and crisis. People with ADHD can make excellent entrepreneurs because challenges energize them; they are risk-takers, and often see opportunities that others don't. Many people with ADHD thrive in careers that call for intense focus in emergencies. One study shows, for example, that the rate of ADHD among wildfire fighters is four times that in the general population.[15] Their brain thrives on intensity, allowing them to focus better than most in critical situations. For example, political operatives often have ADHD, thriving on the immediacy of a political campaign.

I recall consulting with a man in his late twenties who was struggling to complete his doctoral dissertation. He had taken several months off to travel and had, at one point, found himself in a Cambodian refugee camp. He described suddenly feeling energized and alive as he focused on organizing and coordinating the distribution of desperately needed food, blankets, and other supplies. By great contrast, as he returned to his doctoral thesis, he felt lethargic and unmotivated. His brain thrived in intense and urgent situations but struggled to focus when there was little or no external stimulation.

Thom Hartmann, a man with self-diagnosed ADHD, wrote a book titled *ADHD: A Hunter in a Farmer's World*,[16] in which he described those with ADHD as the "hunters" of the world, craving movement and variety. The "hunters" were able to intensely focus on "the hunt," in contrast to "farmers," those without ADHD, who preferred predictability and regularity in their lives. Thom was a gifted entrepreneur in addition to being a writer and educator. He described himself as a start-up specialist. He loved coming up with ideas and bringing them to fruition, but he knew himself well enough to know that he needed to turn over the day-to-day management of his enterprises to someone who was more of a "farmer" who could keep things organized, manage paperwork, pay the bills, and generally keep things running.

Do you recognize any of these positive traits in yourself? It is important to understand that there is much to celebrate about having an ADHD brain as you go through your journey of exploring the possibility that you may have ADHD.

Why Would Someone Seek an ADHD Diagnosis When They Are in Their Midfifties or Beyond?

I have asked many adults who were aged sixty or older when they were first diagnosed what led them to seek a diagnosis at such a relatively late date. Here's a sampling of their responses:

"I was having a lot of problems with clutter. I went to a class about getting rid of clutter and the trainer mentioned ADHD. I started attending a self-help group and finally got diagnosed."

"I was in therapy for depression. My sister gave me a book on ADHD and I recognized many of the ADHD traits in myself. I was having a lot of problems functioning at work and finally decided to retire early. Now, I'm in a support group and do a lot of reading about ADHD."

"I am a mental health therapist and I had suspected that I had ADHD for about twenty years. Finally, at age sixty, I left a job and was trying to develop a private practice. I had a lot of difficulty because of the lack of structure in a solo practice and decided it was time to seek a formal diagnosis."

"I was a nurse and did well for many years working in an ER. Then, I was reassigned to a desk job which was torturous for me. I got fired because I couldn't keep up with the required calls per hour. My supervisor told me I was disorganized and didn't always remember what I'd been told. That was when I sought diagnosis and treatment for ADHD."

"My wife attended an ADHD workshop and said that sounded like me."

"I was in a relationship with a woman whose child was 'classic ADD.' I recognized a lot of the same symptoms in myself. I wanted to get help because I was simply tired of never being able to see anything through to completion."

"My daughter, already diagnosed with ADHD, encouraged me to get tested."

"I saw a TV show on ADHD and thought, 'My God! That's me!'"

"I read an article, '10 Signs That You Might Have ADHD.' I had them all. I've always known that I was different, that something wasn't right."

"I'd been having anger problems. I would get annoyed at some little thing and I would throw something, break a dish. I went into counseling at my church and got a high score on an ADHD checklist given to me by the counselor."

"I was becoming more aware of how my lack of filters, impulsivity, and many other ADHD issues were connected to my loss of jobs and friendships. Now, in my sixties, I want to try to have a happier, more focused, and better-organized life."

As you can see, some were prompted by ongoing difficulties that they experienced; others, by reading an article or seeing a television program describing patterns that seemed very familiar; still others were prompted by family members.

Are You Experiencing Regrets over a Late Diagnosis?

Regrets and "if-only's" are natural when you realize late in life that you have a condition that may have gotten in the way of some of your dreams. But there is also often a sense of relief that comes from knowing what the issue is that has caused such challenges, followed by a feeling of possibilities opening up again. I find that it is an especially positive and healing experience to participate in a support group for older adults with ADHD. My experience in facilitating such a group was that there was a powerful sense of camaraderie and close emotional bonding that took place among the group members. For the first time, they were among a group of people who accepted them, who understood their struggles, and who appreciated them without judgment. Interestingly, there was an amazing degree of artistic talent among group members—sculptors, painters, and photographers.

Why Has It Taken So Long to Get Diagnosed?

You may be wondering why it's taken you so long to get a diagnosis—why no one connected the dots. You may be blaming yourself—but you did nothing wrong. Here are some of the many reasons why late diagnosis of ADHD happens.

A General Pattern of Underdiagnosis of Adults with ADHD

Research suggests that ADHD is significantly underdiagnosed in adults.[17] In fact, when adults with undiagnosed ADHD seek mental health treatment, they typically seek treatment for other conditions, such as anxiety and depression, which so often accompany ADHD.[18] Typically, neither the undiagnosed adult nor the mental health practitioner considers ADHD as a possible diagnosis when assessing the causes of their emotional distress,[19] which reflects their lack of training regarding ADHD in adults.

Different ADHD "Presentations"

While three official "presentations" of ADHD are still listed in the DSM-5,[20] research now suggests that these are not truly distinct types because individuals can manifest hyperactive/impulsive symptoms earlier in life, but only show inattentive symptoms as adults.[21]

Symptoms of inattentive ADHD include the following:

- Displays poor listening skills
- Loses and/or misplaces personal items (glasses, keys, smartphone)
- Is easily sidetracked by external or unimportant stimuli
- Forgets daily activities
- Has a short attention span
- Has difficulty completing tasks
- Has difficulty following instructions
- Avoids activities that require concentration
- Misses details and makes careless errors

Symptoms of hyperactive/impulsive ADHD include the following:

- Feels restless when required to sit for extended periods
- Fidgets often with feet/hands or some handheld object
- Is always on the go (this tendency diminishes with age in most people)
- Has difficulty with quiet leisure activities; wants to do something active
- Is overly talkative
- Has difficulty waiting
- Tends to interrupt others
- Blurts out answers before a question is completed
- Experiences other impulsive patterns not mentioned in the DSM-5, such as impulsive eating, impulsive spending, and impulsive decision-making

The DSM-5 describes three presentations of ADHD:

1. Predominantly inattentive (most symptoms are in the inattentive category)

2. Predominantly hyperactive/impulsive (most symptoms are in the hyperactive/impulsive category)

3. Combined type (symptoms fall into both inattentive and hyperactive/impulsive categories)

Hyperactive symptoms tend to decrease with age. Older adults with ADHD may describe feeling restless and impatient when required to wait, but typically they are no longer hyperactive.

A Long History of Limited Understanding

In the 1950s, when today's older adults were children, we knew very little about what we now call ADHD. Children were diagnosed with "minimal brain dysfunction," "hyperactive child syndrome," or "hyperkinesis," with 5 to 10 percent of the child population estimated to have these issues.[22] Due to our limited understanding of ADHD years ago, it's no wonder that few older adults today were diagnosed with ADHD as children.

Misdiagnosis

Adult ADHD rarely occurs alone. Depression, anxiety disorders, bipolar disorder, and autism commonly co-occur with adult ADHD, often leading to a focus on these disorders while overlooking co-occurring ADHD. ADHD patterns in adults, such as procrastination, lack of motivation, mood lability, anxiety, and low self-esteem, are common to other conditions that are better understood in adults and therefore more likely to be diagnosed. Furthermore, adults with ADHD often go undiagnosed because they have worked hard to mask their ADHD and to develop compensatory strategies.[23]

Chronic Underdiagnosis of ADHD in Girls

Girls are more likely to try hard in school and are less likely to present behavior problems at school. As a result, they are less likely to be referred for an ADHD diagnosis. ADHD in females often becomes more apparent and problematic when they reach puberty and fluctuating hormonal levels intensify ADHD symptoms. In the past, girls and young women were not diagnosed at the same rates as boys and, even today, girls continue to be underdiagnosed to some extent.[24]

Lack of Understanding That Stress Amplifies ADHD

Another complication is that ADHD is more troublesome when life circumstances are more demanding and stressful—for example, after a promotion to management when you are required to keep track of others' work and not just your own; while trying to complete a long, complex task, such as writing a dissertation; or after becoming a parent or following the birth of a second child. Entering situations in which the demands for strong executive functioning suddenly ramp up and stress levels increase causes ADHD to be more challenging.[25] Under lower-stress conditions, a diagnosis may not be made in the same individual who demonstrates significant ADHD symptoms under high stress.

Many Continue to Go Undiagnosed

We are now twenty-five years past the mid-'90s when recognition of adult ADHD became widespread, creating much interest and publicity. Adults who were diagnosed in 1995 in their forties or fifties are now in their sixties and seventies. As a result, we have a large and growing cohort of older adults already diagnosed with ADHD—but many more remain undiagnosed.

One research project in the Netherlands found that adults between the ages of sixty and seventy reported more ADHD symptoms than did those aged seventy-one and older.[26] Do ADHD symptoms lessen in later years? It's possible that fewer symptoms were reported by older adults simply because they faced fewer challenges in later years.

Another reason that a smaller percentage of older adults are identified with ADHD may be strongly related to Russell Barkley's research suggesting a significantly shorter life span for many adults with ADHD due to unhealthy lifestyle choices that lead to chronic diseases, such as diabetes and heart disease.[27] In other words, those over age seventy are the ADHD "survivors" as many in their age cohort are no longer alive.

What Prevents Mental Health Professionals from Considering ADHD When Assessing an Older Adult?

Given all this information, you may be scratching your head and wondering why it's so difficult for health-care providers to look at ADHD. Here are some reasons.

Lack of Training

One critical factor is lack of training. The training of adult psychiatrists barely touches on adult ADHD. And the training of child psychiatrists, of course, focuses on the needs of children. Because ADHD runs strongly in families, child psychiatrists and pediatricians are certainly familiar with the parents of their child patients reporting similar symptoms. Often, they have more experience with adults with ADHD than do most adult psychiatrists. As an example, in the Maryland town where I live, the physician treating most adults with ADHD was a pediatrician. Similarly, there is a dearth of training about adult ADHD in clinical psychology programs, with pediatric psychologists typically more informed about ADHD than are adult psychologists.

David Goodman, MD, one of the few psychiatrists to specialize in treating adult ADHD, led a study in 2012[28] to explore the comfort level of both primary care physicians and psychiatrists in diagnosing and treating adult ADHD. Only 8 percent of nearly two thousand primary care doctors were "extremely confident" in their ability to diagnose adult ADHD, and only 28 percent of psychiatrists felt "extremely confident" in making the diagnosis. Dr. Goodman and his team recommend that all psychiatrists routinely screen for adult ADHD when they are doing an initial assessment of an adult because it is so common and is so often found in combination with anxiety, depression, and substance use disorders, to name a few. Although Dr. Goodman's study did not focus on older adults, it's likely that far fewer psychiatrists would feel comfortable making the diagnosis in those over the age of sixty.

Ageism

The rare consideration of possible ADHD in older adults is also partially fueled by ageism—younger physicians can be dismissive of the needs of older adults, imagining that their lives consist only of watching TV, taking naps, walking their lapdog, and maybe volunteering a few hours a week. In the media, older adults have often been portrayed as bumbling, slow, cranky, or incompetent. My hope is that as the baby boomer generation continues to move past age sixty-five, these images will change. Consider humanitarian and theologian Desmond Tutu, who was active until his death at age ninety; Supreme Court Justice Ruth Bader Ginsburg, active until her death at age eighty-seven; Anthony Fauci, the national voice of reason during the US COVID-19 pandemic, still working full-time in his eighties.

ADHD Is Not on the Radar at Memory Clinics

When older adults complain of forgetfulness, regularly misplacing belongings, and being unable to manage the tasks of daily living, few family members first think of ADHD. Instead, the immediate concern is possible early-stage dementia. As I mentioned earlier, only one in five memory clinics regularly screens for ADHD.[29] And among these more ADHD-aware clinics, very few of them seek crucial information from family members who could provide details that these issues have been lifelong and are more likely to reflect undiagnosed ADHD rather than the onset of cognitive decline in later years.

Distinguishing ADHD from Dementia

Because dementia impacts so many older adults, the forgetfulness of ADHD feels more frightening as people enter their sixties and seventies when the likelihood of dementia looms on the horizon.

Characteristics of Different Types of Dementias

The following is a brief list of characteristic patterns found in the most common dementias,[30] to provide a basis of comparison if you are concerned about possible dementia. Of course, the most important distinction between dementia and late-diagnosed ADHD is that the dementia symptoms are recent and are a marked departure from earlier functioning, whereas in ADHD, such patterns have been there to some degree throughout life.

Alzheimer's Disease

- Difficulty recalling recent conversations and events
- Apathy and depression

Cerebrovascular Disease (Vascular Dementia)

- Poor judgment
- Difficulty making decisions
- Decrease in ability to plan or organize tasks
- Motor impairment, including a slower gate and poor balance

Lewy Body Dementia (LDB)

- Sleep disturbance
- Hallucinations
- Visuospatial impairment, such as poor depth perception, bumping into things, falling easily, getting lost in familiar environments
- No evident memory loss
- Often presents in combination with Alzheimer's disease

"Normal" Age-Related Changes in Cognition

"Normal" age-related cognitive decline can occur unrelated to dementia. These cognitive changes include the following:

- Slower speed of processing (how efficiently you can perform mundane tasks)
- Reduced working memory (the amount of information you can keep in mind at one time in order to use it—for example, the number of turns in driving directions you can keep in mind as you are following them)
- Reduced executive functioning ability (your ability to organize, plan, and follow through on multi-step undertakings)

Might even more older adults be diagnosed with ADHD if we developed a diagnostic tool that specifically addresses the challenges of later life?

As I mentioned earlier, there is growing evidence that a healthy lifestyle may decrease and delay age-related cognitive decline, and in some cases, even reverse cognitive decline.[31]

Could It Be mNCD?

Usually, individuals seek memory assessments when symptoms become worrisome to them or to another family member. The critical question is whether the memory issues are a symptom of ADHD or of mild neurocognitive disease (mNCD), formerly known as mild cognitive impairment (MCI).

Mild neurocognitive disease is generally described in this way:

- Developing difficulties with the activities of daily living—needs assistance to perform

- Confusion with simple cognitive tasks, such as adding and subtracting, orientation to time and place, difficulty naming words in a specific category, etc.

- Notable increase in mood, anxiety, and emotional overreaction

- Cognitive performance has worsened over time (known as a neurodegenerative process)

Distinguishing Between ADHD and mNCD

Are Symptoms Recent and Worsening?

The crucial difference between mNCD and ADHD symptoms that can sound quite similar is that the ADHD symptoms have been present over a long period of time. While research suggests that symptoms of ADHD decrease as one ages, the opposite is true for symptoms of mNCD. This distinction—whether memory issues are the same, improving, or worsening over time—is critical to accurate diagnosis.

ADHD is a life span disorder, whereas mNCD is a disorder of old age. Of course, it's possible that an individual has both ADHD and mNCD, which is why an accurate history is important. ADHD symptoms may have been present throughout adult life, but may have worsened due to mNCD or other health factors in older age. Too often, neurologists and neuropsychologists focus mostly on current functioning and don't get a careful and detailed history.

Can You Readily and Clearly Report Your History of Memory Issues?

While patients with mNCD typically report significant and recent worsening in their symptoms, they are often not able to give a detailed history of their decline, due to memory problems. Those with ADHD are typically able to give a much more detailed account of their challenges and do not report a recent worsening of their symptoms.

Do Close Family Members Corroborate Your Long-Term History of Forgetfulness?

Ideally, this distinction needs to be documented not only by the self-report of the older adult, but also by a spouse, an adult child, or another adult who has known the individual well over the course of many years. It can be very helpful to have a close family member complete a questionnaire describing both current and past daily functioning. One such questionnaire that can be helpful is the BRIEF-A (Behavior Rating Inventory of Executive Function-Adult Version).

(The BRIEF-A is only available for use by a qualified mental health professional, most commonly a psychologist; go to https://www .parinc.com/Products/Pkey/25 for more information.)

Do Your Symptoms Improve with Medication?

Another important distinction is that currently no drug has proven effective in the treatment of mNCD. In contrast, most older adults with ADHD report significant positive benefits when prescribed psychostimulant medications—the same medications that benefit children and younger adults with ADHD. These differing responses to medication further suggest that even though symptoms may appear similar, the underlying disorders are distinct from each other.

Do You Have Adult Children, Nieces, Nephews, or Grandchildren Who Have Been Diagnosed with ADHD?

ADHD is highly heritable. An older adult with ADHD is highly likely to have family members in younger generations who have been diagnosed with ADHD because the awareness of ADHD has grown so significantly over the past fifty years. So, although the older adult and their peers are unlikely to have been formally diagnosed with ADHD, it is probable that younger family members have been diagnosed, lending further evidence pointing toward an ADHD diagnosis in the older adult.

Questionnaires to Assist in Diagnosis

There are no questionnaires created and validated specifically designed to diagnose ADHD in older adults. Some mental health professionals have suggested using questionnaires designed for younger adults, while requiring fewer symptoms to make a diagnosis.

Common rating scales currently used in the diagnosis of adults include the following:

- Conners' Adult ADHD Rating Scales
- Brown Attention-Deficit Disorder Scale for Adults
- Wender Utah Rating Scale (WURS)
- ADHD Rating Scale
- ADHD Rating Scale-IV
- Adult ADHD Self-Report Scale-v1.1 Symptom Checklist (ASRS)

Among these, only the ASRS is available to the general public and can be used as a self-screening device; however, for an accurate ADHD diagnosis, adults should consult with a trained mental health professional, as many symptoms of ADHD may overlap with those of other disorders.[32]

Beware of mental health professionals who use the WURS as the primary measure of ADHD. It relies entirely upon an older adult's memory of their behavior as a young child and asks no questions about adult functioning. The accuracy of memories from fifty or sixty years ago is questionable, as demonstrated by recent research.[33]

It's critically important that your assessment focuses on your daily functioning over the course of your adult years. The importance of such an inquiry is to establish that your problems with forgetfulness, disorganization, poor time awareness, and frequent misplacing of personal items are long-standing and are not issues that have only recently developed.

The ASRS (ADHD Self-Rating Scale)

The ASRS is a widely used ADHD screening questionnaire for adults.[34]

It asks eighteen questions, but the first six questions—Part A—are considered the items most likely to identify adult ADHD:

1. How often do you have trouble wrapping up the final details of a project once the challenging parts have been done?

2. How often do you have difficulty getting things in order when you have to do a task that requires organization?

3. How often do you have problems remembering appointments or obligations?

4. When you have a task that requires a lot of thought, how often do you avoid or delay getting started?

5. How often do you fidget or squirm with your hands or feet when you have to sit down for a long time?

6. How often do you feel overly active and compelled to do things, like you were driven by a motor?

If you respond "sometimes," "often," or "very often" to at least five of these, you are considered "very likely to have ADHD" and to be eligible for a more in-depth diagnostic process.

The "Gold Standard" of ADHD Diagnosis Is a Careful, Informed Clinical Interview

A clinical interview to make an accurate differential diagnosis between ADHD and mNCD should be thorough and cover the following:

• Current daily functioning and whether there is a marked and recent change

• Current daily functioning contrasted with reports of prior functioning

- Whether there is a family history of ADHD in younger generations
- Academic history:
  - Were they told that they could be a good student if only they tried harder?
  - Did they turn in papers and assignments at the last minute?
  - Did they attend college, but not complete their degree?
- Marital history—age of first marriage; number of divorces; children with ADHD
- Employment history—history of multiple short-term jobs, history of being fired
- Corroboration by a spouse or close family member of what the older adult reports

A spouse can answer such questions as: Is your spouse's desk at home piled with unsorted paperwork? Does your spouse have difficulty keeping up with paperwork for taxes, for health insurance claims, and so on? Does your spouse tend to lose track of time regularly, so that they are often running late? Does your spouse often forget to put things back where they belong after they have used them? Does your spouse often forget information you have told them repeatedly, and has this been true for many years?

The bottom line is that we don't yet have a good diagnostic tool to make a definitive ADHD diagnosis in older adults. As a result, the best person to make such a diagnosis is someone who has specialized in ADHD across the life span—someone who will do a careful clinical interview of both the adult in question and their spouse. If there is no spouse, it's important to speak to other family members, such as adult children or siblings.

It is of paramount importance that the professional making the diagnosis will not leap to an easy yet possibly incorrect conclusion that your cognitive difficulties are due to age-related cognitive decline.

Neuropsychological Testing to Diagnose ADHD

Neuropsychological testing can be helpful in the process of diagnosis, but it can also be prohibitively expensive. A diagnosis can be made, without such testing, by an experienced clinician (a psychologist, psychiatrist, or psychotherapist who has expertise in ADHD) through a careful clinical interview of the individual as well as close family members. If you go to a memory clinic due to concerns about declining memory, the neurologist you see may recommend testing. Testing can provide a "baseline" of cognitive functioning that can be repeated a year or more later to explore whether there is significant decline over time. Insurance typically covers testing ordered by a neurologist to assess cognitive decline. On the other hand, if you seek neuropsychological testing on your own to assess possible adult ADHD, it may not be covered by your health insurance. It's important to contact your health insurance company to determine the coverage offered by your insurance plan before proceeding with a costly neuropsychological assessment.

Steps to take if you are an older adult and suspect that you may have undiagnosed ADHD:

- Visit CHADD's website, https://chadd.org, and look at its list of ADHD experts in its resource directory to see whether there is one in your area. CHADD is the largest and oldest advocacy organization for those with ADHD.

- Go to CHADD's website and see where the nearest CHADD support group meets. If there is one in your area, these support groups are often a great way to find recommendations for the best professionals in your area.

- Do a Google search of ADHD experts in your area (not all of them are listed in the CHADD resource directory).

- Do a Google search for ADHD coaches in your area. Typically, they would know of local treating professionals who can diagnose ADHD.

- Ask your primary care physician whether they can refer you to someone with expertise in adult ADHD.

- Call the student disability service office at a local college or university. There are so many college students diagnosed with ADHD that these offices typically know of the best treating professionals in your area.

- Medicare Part B covers the care of psychiatrists and psychologists who participate in Medicare and accept assignment of payment from Medicare.

- If you are not able to find a professional with expertise in ADHD in older adults who participates in Medicare (an all-too-common possibility), you may want to pay out-of-pocket for a definitive ADHD diagnosis that you can then take to your primary care provider, asking them whether they will prescribe stimulant medication once a formal diagnosis has been made.

KEY TAKEAWAYS FROM THIS CHAPTER

✔ A belated ADHD diagnosis can be life-changing.

✔ ADHD is a very common adult psychiatric disorder.

✔ Few adult psychiatrists have received adequate training about ADHD in older adults.

✔ Unconscious assumptions about the needs of older adults may interfere with diagnosis.

✔ More targeted assessment tools for older adults with ADHD are needed.

✔ ADHD can be differentiated from age-related cognitive decline based on personal history corroborated by family members.

✔ ADHD should be strongly considered when there is a history of ADHD diagnoses in younger family members.

✔ ADHD should not be ruled out due to anxiety, depression, or bipolar disorder, as these disorders commonly co-occur with ADHD.

✔ ADHD should not be ruled out due to academic or professional achievement, as it is quite possible to have both high achievement and ADHD.

✔ Neuropsychological testing can be helpful to assess a broad range of cognitive functions, assisting in the diagnosis and establishing a "baseline" when cognitive decline is suspected in addition to ADHD.

How Do You Know You Have ADHD?

Stimulant Medication for Older Adults with ADHD

Is it safe? How can you find an experienced prescriber?

We met Adele in the last chapter, a widow living in Florida who had been misdiagnosed with Alzheimer's and was later correctly diagnosed with ADHD. I bring her case up again to highlight the difficulties that she, among many other older adults, experienced in receiving effective treatment for her ADHD. Although you might think that her correct ADHD diagnosis was a happy ending, it was not. The neurologist who knew enough to make the diagnosis didn't know enough about ADHD treatment for seniors, in particular, about the safety and efficacy of stimulant medication for most seniors. Mistakenly, the neurologist told her, "You have ADHD, but there's nothing you can do about it."

There are many things that can be done to reduce ADHD symptoms at any age. In this chapter, I will talk about how stimulant medication can be highly effective. But medication is far from the only thing that is useful to reduce ADHD symptoms. In later chapters, I will discuss other effective approaches, including psychotherapy, stress management, ADHD coaching, and lifestyle changes. It's never too late to benefit from an ADHD diagnosis and treatment.

Why Prescribe Stimulant Medication to Older Adults?

The life led by a US adult has changed significantly over the past generation. Many older adults are still working in their first career or diving into a new project or passion that they now have time to pursue. While some over age sixty-five continue to work, there are many cognitive demands placed upon those seniors who are fully retired; for example, a complex health-care maze to navigate, finances to manage, and technology to master. We need our brain to function well at every stage of life. Stimulant medication remains the most immediately effective way to reduce ADHD symptoms and enhance cognitive functioning. Four in five adults report a positive response to stimulant medication.[1] The ADHD medications currently available truly can help.

In later chapters, I write about many things that are therapeutic when you have ADHD. But these supports are not available in all areas, and when they are available, they pose a significantly higher financial burden than medication alone. Therefore, I have chosen to discuss medication first.

On and Off Medication: A Tale of Persistence and Struggle

Kristen, now in her sixties, has been on a journey of many years to recognize and find treatment for her ADHD.

Kristen was bright and had done well academically, albeit with lots of last-minute papers and cramming for exams. It was "real life" that was challenging for her.

Fortunately, she married a focused and organized fellow who made sure that bills were paid and all of the critical things happened on time. Kristen attributed her constantly messy house, with unwashed dishes in the sink, as a reflection of her focus on the more important things in life, such as hanging out with her three kids. She commented, "I'm much better at 'being' than 'doing.'"

Like many people diagnosed in adulthood, Kristen began to suspect her own ADHD following her eldest child's diagnosis, when she was in her late thirties. Soon after her son's diagnosis, she was in a bookstore and came across a book on women with ADHD. She remembers having a very emotional epiphany as she recognized herself in most of the descriptions of other women in the book.

Too embarrassed to contact a psychiatrist, she tried one of her son's short-acting stimulants. Thirty minutes later, "I had a strong urge to stand up and do something. I wanted to load the dishwasher and wipe the countertops. . . . I felt alive, engaged, not, as I had feared, strung-out. . . . For once, there was no barrier between me and what I needed to do." A short time later, she called a psychiatrist who, after a brief and fairly casual discussion, gave her a prescription for stimulants.

Fast-forward fifteen years and Kristen, now in her fifties, is told by her GP, after ordering an echocardiogram (ECG), that she will no longer prescribe stimulants to her because of the potential cardiac risks. Even after a second ECG gave her a clean bill of health, her GP refused to prescribe more than a very small (20 mg) dose of Vyvanse. "I know that my psychiatrist would continue to prescribe my regular dose of Vyvanse," she remarked, "but I don't trust him." The psychiatrist was too casual about prescribing stimulants, whereas her GP was overly cautious. Clearly, neither had expertise in adult ADHD.

CHAPTER 5

Meanwhile, she found a doctor who spent time and listened to her but who was opposed to prescribing stimulant medication. As a physician trained in integrative medicine, he wanted to use a more natural, holistic approach. He suggested that she go on a very-low carb diet and prescribed a variety of nutritional supplements.

The end result was that after years of benefiting from Vyvanse, and after consulting with three very different physicians who did not communicate with one another, Kristen was left to make her own treatment decisions. She felt most comfortable with the integrative medicine doctor and decided to follow his approach. She made this decision even though she told me that stimulants had been much more effective in helping her to stay on track and accomplish her daily tasks. Like many other adults who didn't feel that their prescriber truly listened to them, Kristen chose to stop taking stimulant medications.

Each physician viewed her need for medication through their own lens—her GP from an overabundance of caution, her psychiatrist from a too-casual position, and a functional medicine doctor from his strong bias against stimulants, and all without any in-depth knowledge of ADHD.

Furthermore, Kristen's son with ADHD, now an adult, is also experiencing difficulty in finding an informed professional to prescribe medication. His most recent effort led him to a skeptical primary care provider who assumed he was "drug seeking" and refused to write a prescription.

Today, Kristen manages her ADHD through a strenuously followed low-carb diet, nutritional supplements, and yoga. She has resigned herself to living a disorganized life, telling herself that this is "who she is." Her son continues his search for a prescriber.

Stimulant Medication for Older Adults with ADHD

77

Kristen's and her son's experiences in seeking medication to treat their ADHD paint a disturbing picture. Sadly, adults with ADHD in many parts of the US don't have access to professionals with real knowledge and experience in treating adult ADHD.

> The number one reason that adults with ADHD report for their decision to stop taking stimulants is their feeling that their physician isn't listening to them.[2]

ADHD Medications 101

Medications that are most effective in treating ADHD affect dopamine and norepinephrine, neurotransmitters that play a role in improving attentional and behavioral issues associated with ADHD. Both psychostimulants and nonstimulant medications are used to treat ADHD.

Psychostimulants

Psychostimulants are the most widely used medications for treating ADHD symptoms in adults, the same medications used to treat children and adolescents, although the FDA has not yet studied and approved *all* stimulants used for children and teens for the treatment of adults. ADHD medications currently approved for adults include methylphenidate (brand names Focalin, Focalin XR; Concerta; Daytrana; Metadate CD) and amphetamines (brand names Adderall XR and Vyvanse). Most people with ADHD respond well to medications in either "family" of stimulants (methylphenidates and amphetamines), while some respond better to one than the other. The physician makes a choice to initially prescribe a medication in one of these two "families" of stimulants, starting with a low dose and gradually titrating up to a "therapeutic" dose, monitoring your response along the way.

If you don't find that the medication that your physician first prescribes is effective, then it's important to experiment with other medications to determine which works best. If you have any family members already diagnosed with ADHD who are benefiting from stimulant medication, it would make sense to let your prescriber know and discuss the choice of trying the same medication that has been effective for your family member.

Short-acting preparations generally last approximately three to four hours; long-acting stimulants vary in their duration of efficacy, with some lasting six to eight hours and others as long as ten to twelve hours. Individual responses may vary widely, as some people metabolize medications more rapidly than others do. Most people prefer longer-acting medications because they avoid the ups and downs of short-acting stimulants wearing off and needing to be taken again during the course of the day. Some adults find that they need a "booster" short-acting stimulant as their longer-acting stimulant wears off late in the day. This is something you should discuss with your prescribing physician. A "booster" can reduce what is called the "rebound effect," a feeling of significant fatigue as a long-acting stimulant is wearing off, and can also help adults have better coverage to help them focus during evening activities.

In a recent survey by Dr. Thomas Brown,[3] not being on a stimulant during the evening was the most common unmet need of adults with ADHD. ADHD impairments occur 24/7 and people benefit from taking medications throughout the day. Adults must be at their best throughout the day but must also continue to perform at a high level in the evening, when they might be doing paperwork or managing finances. Many patients and their doctors have concerns about a second dose of the ADHD stimulant medications disrupting sleep. If this is a concern of yours, try taking a nap after lunch one day while on a full dose of your stimulant medication. Due to the paradoxical effect that the stimulants calm and soothe the hyperactive component of people with ADHD, most people find that they sleep better when they take an additional evening dose of stimulant medication. This no-risk trial nap proves in advance that additional doses of stimulants will not disrupt sleep.

Hundreds of studies have been conducted on children, teens, and adults to examine the effects of stimulant medication—probably more research than on any other category of medication—but older adults' response to medication has yet to be studied. A recent large meta-analysis of multiple studies of the effectiveness of stimulant medication[4] found that a broad range of both stimulant and nonstimulant medications used to treat ADHD were effective in adults as well as in children and adolescents. Recent studies show that many patients over age fifty experience beneficial effects of medications used to treat ADHD.[5] And, although long-term studies on adults have not yet been done, many adults have taken stimulant medication for years and continue to benefit from them while experiencing no ill effect.

Is Methylphenidate (MPH) or Amphetamine (AMP) Preferable?

Both MPH and AMP increase the levels of dopamine and norepinephrine in the synapse where brain cells connect and communicate, but each does it differently. We have no test to indicate which will work best for you. Most people respond well to both AMP and MPH. You can begin by discussing with your physician, who will decide which one to prescribe. They will then carefully increase the dose to see how you respond. If you do not have an optimal response to the first one you try, then your physician can prescribe another and observe your response to that. If you are one of those relatively rare people who don't respond well to either MPH or AMP, there is the option of taking a combination of the two.

Do Stimulant Medications Work for Everyone?

Positive response to MPH or AMP is about 70 percent.[6] This means that 30 percent of people either do not respond to or do not tolerate the first stimulant medication they try. It is important for you to understand that finding the optimal medication and dose is a process that takes time and close coordination with your clinician. When both MPH and AMP are tried in combination, about 85 percent of people get a robust, life-changing level of benefits with very good tolerance of minor side effects. But again, that means that 15 percent of people who try the standard stimulants (i.e., about one in seven people) either do not get benefits or cannot tolerate the side effects, or both. It's ideal to seek a specialty consultation from a clinician who has many years of experience with the medication treatment of ADHD. It's important that neither you nor your physician conclude that stimulants aren't for you after a negative or nonresponse to the first stimulant that you try.

Although most adult psychiatrists will state that they treat ADHD in adults (it's a very common condition, so all psychiatrists have seen it), this doesn't mean that they have expertise in ADHD. Look for psychiatrists who are associated with a specialty clinic that treats ADHD, either a private clinic or one that is associated with a teaching hospital. Other ways to find psychiatrists experienced in treating adult ADHD is to contact the student health center of a nearby college or university. ADHD is so common among college students that many student health centers typically have a full-time or part-time psychiatrist available to treat their students. Another way to search for ADHD specialists is through CHADD, the largest national ADHD advocacy group in the US. Its website, https://chadd.org, contains a list of ADHD specialists across the country.

How to Find a Prescriber Who Is a Good Match for You

- If you can find an adult ADHD support group, members can be a great source of information about the most qualified people in your area.
- Inquire at the health centers of nearby colleges and universities. Most have prescribers who treat students on campus and know a lot about adult ADHD.

- Look for prescribers associated with local practices that advertise themselves as specialty clinics for ADHD.
- Look on the websites of national ADHD advocacy organizations, such as CHADD (https://chadd.org) and ADDA (https://add.org), which list experts in many parts of the US.
- Look for child psychiatrists in your area who specialize in ADHD. Many of them treat adults as well.
- Don't settle for a prescriber who casually offers a standard stimulant to "see if it works."

Will I Become Dependent Upon Stimulant Medication?

Many adults who are new to ADHD fear that if they start taking stimulants, they will become dependent upon them and will have to take them "forever." There is a real misunderstanding on the part of some people who equate stimulant medication with highly addictive drugs, such as cocaine. Yes, they are both stimulants, but psychostimulant medications taken as prescribed are not addictive. Furthermore, longer-acting stimulant medication has very little possibility for addiction or abuse because it is designed to enter the bloodstream in a moderate, prolonged pace to maintain a consistent level of focus and alertness throughout the day.

Possible Side Effects of Stimulants

For adults, side effects are typically not severe and can include insomnia, loss of appetite and weight loss, anxiety, and some cardiovascular effects.

- **Insomnia** can be managed by carefully monitoring how late in the day you take stimulant medication. Because there are both short-acting and long-acting stimulants, if you find that your long-acting stimulant leads to insomnia, speak to your prescriber about shifting to a shorter-acting medication.

- **Loss of appetite and weight loss** are typically temporary side effects. If you are one of those rare individuals who continues to experience loss of appetite, talk to your prescriber about taking short-acting stimulants so you can schedule your meals for times before you take your medication in the morning, then after the effects wear off midday.

- **Anxiety**—If you experience anxiety or jitteriness when taking stimulants, you have several options. First, consider taking a stimulant from the other "family" of stimulants. Quite a few people report that this solves the problem. You may also be extra sensitive to stimulants and require a smaller than normal dose to manage the jittery feelings you may experience. If you have an anxiety condition in addition to ADHD, you may need to take both stimulants and an anti-anxiety medication together.

- **Cardiovascular side effects**—If you have normal blood pressure, cardiovascular side effects include mild increases in blood pressure and heart rate. A few long-term large-scale controlled studies of cardiovascular effects[7] found that stimulant use was not associated with increased risk of heart attacks, cardiac death, or stroke. Regular monitoring of blood pressure is recommended in adults taking stimulant medications.

Other Stimulant Treatment Considerations

As I mentioned earlier, it is important to seek a prescriber who is highly experienced in the treatment of ADHD. As you will read later in this chapter, older adults with positive responses to stimulant medication typically work closely with a physician to find the best medication and dose. Of note, some adults have a need for greater focus at specific times of day and may need to change the timing or dosage, perhaps adding an immediate-release stimulant to boost focus during a high-demand period of the day. Even when older adults are no longer working, there remain many tasks, such as paperwork, insurance claims, and financial management, which require increased focus and concentration. But beyond activities that require a focus on details, stimulants are also helpful to help you to manage all of the many tasks required to lead a functional daily life.

Nonstimulant Medications

When an older adult with ADHD doesn't respond well to stimulants or cannot tolerate side effects of stimulants, nonstimulants can be tried. I should note that, in general, nonstimulant medications are found to be less effective.[8] Here is a rundown of the current non-stimulant medications in use.

Atomoxetine (Strattera)

Atomoxetine (Strattera) was the first nonstimulant approved by the FDA for the treatment of ADHD in adults (it is also approved for children and adolescents). Unlike stimulant medication, Strattera takes longer to produce beneficial effects and can have mild, nonmedically significant cardiovascular side effects of a slight increase in heart rate and blood pressure. If you are already taking medications for anxiety or depression, be sure to talk to your physician about potential negative interactions with Strattera.

Antidepressants

Antidepressants classified as SNRIs (norepinephrine reuptake inhibitors, which have a direct effect of increasing the neurotransmitter norepinephrine) have been seen to have a positive effect on the core symptoms of ADHD. Treatment of ADHD with an SNRI is considered an off-label use, but it is used very commonly with adults, especially by physicians who are hesitant to prescribe stimulants to older adults.

Clonidine and Guanfacine

Clonidine (brand names Catapres; Kapvay) and guanfacine (brand name Intuniv) have been approved for ADHD in children and may also be helpful in adults. Clonidine and guanfacine are usually used in combination with a stimulant medication and rarely by themselves. They primarily impact the impulsive-hyperactive components of ADHD, while the stimulants mainly impact distractibility. Clonidine and guanfacine can be expected to decrease the "revving inside" and the need to be constantly doing something, a phenomenon reported by many people with ADHD. Fortunately, they calm feelings of restlessness without causing sedation or grogginess. They also tend to reduce the "hyperactive brain" pattern reported by many adults, of having many thoughts going on in their mind simultaneously. About 40 percent of children and adults do not respond to either guanfacine or clonidine.

The following chart contains basic information about the most commonly prescribed medications. Many newer formulations of stimulant medication, as well as some nonstimulant medications that your physician may choose to prescribe, are not included in this list.

Medication	Duration	Type & Notes
STIMULANTS		
Methylphenidate		
Concerta	Extended release 12 hours	Tablet
Daytrana	9 hours	Transdermal patch; applied to skin

Medication	Duration	Type & Notes
Jornay PM	Extended release 12–14 hours	Capsule; taken before going to sleep
Metadate CD	Extended release 8–10 hours	Capsule
Methylphenidate HCl	Extended release 6–8 hours	Tablet
Ritalin	Immediate release 3–4 hours	Tablet
Ritalin LA	Extended release 8 hours	Capsule
Ritalin SR	Sustained release 8 hours	Tablet
Dexmethylphenidate		
Focalin	Immediate release 4–6 hours	Tablet
Focalin XR	Extended release 8–12 hours	Capsule
Dextroamphetamine		
Dexedrine	Immediate release 3–4 hours	Tablet
Dexedrine ER	Extended release 5–10 hours	"Spansule"
Methamphetamine		
Desoxyn	Immediate release 4–6 hours	Tablet
Mixed Amphetamine Salts		
Adderall	Immediate release 4–6 hours	Tablet
Adderall XR	Extended release 10–12 hours	Capsule
Mydayis	Extended release 14–16 hours	Capsule

Medication	Duration	Type & Notes
Amphetamine Sulfate		
Evekeo	Immediate release 4–6 hours	Tablet
Lisdexamfetamine		
Vyvanse	Extended release 10–13 hours	Capsule
NONSTIMULANTS		
Atomoxetine		
Strattera	All day 24 hours	Capsule; starts working in a few days, but may take longer to see full effects
Guanfacine		
Intuniv	Extended release 24 hours	Tablet
Bupropion		
Wellbutrin XL	Extended release 24 hours	Tablet; takes 8 weeks to fully experience benefits

What to Expect from Medication Used to Treat ADHD

Medication doesn't "cure" ADHD, but it helps temporarily reduce some of the challenges of ADHD. It's a bit like putting on a pair of eyeglasses. If you take off your glasses, you still have vision problems, but when you wear them, you can see more clearly.

Medication doesn't suddenly make you better organized or more on time, but it does reduce impulsivity, giving you a bit more time to think about what you are doing. It improves focus and therefore can help you complete tedious, detailed tasks with fewer errors, and, to some extent, it increases self-awareness. Some medications reduce emotional overreactions so common among those with ADHD.

In my experience, many prescribing physicians do not provide detailed information about what to expect or any structured way for their patient to measure and monitor the benefits of medication. In fact, many adults have reported to me that their physician simply asks very general questions, such as "Is it helping?"

Keep in mind that adults with ADHD are impacted to different degrees and in different ways by the disorder. Some of the challenges experienced by an adult with ADHD may be the result of conditions associated with ADHD, such as anxiety, mood disorders, bipolar disorder, eating disorders, substance use disorder, and so on. Due to the complexity of ADHD, which is often accompanied by more than one additional condition, it's very important for you to understand the interactions of your various disorders so that you can participate actively in assessing the effectiveness of stimulant medications as well as the impact of other medications you may be prescribed for related conditions.

In the various accounts of responses to medication that I share in this chapter, it's clear that response to medication is highly variable. Some describe it as life-changing; others, as helpful in some respects; and still others report little benefit or intolerable side effects. Each case is different, and the more other psychiatric conditions come into play, the more complicated it may be to find an effective course of treatment that addresses all of your conditions.

> Pills don't build skills.

There's one key thing to remember. While medication can put your brain in a more functional state that allows you to make better decisions, build better daily habits, and develop organizational skills, the medication won't do this *for* you. But medication can make it easier to make these critical life changes with support from coaches, psychotherapists who specialize in ADHD, and adult ADHD support groups.

Finding the Right Medication(s) for You

It is critical to work with your physician to carefully monitor both positive responses to medications as well as negative side effects, to carefully balance benefits and risks over a period of time. I have provided a form in Appendix B (page 309) to use on a weekly basis to help you closely monitor your reactions to medication, including improvements and unwanted side effects. You are welcome to make copies of this form for your personal use. I strongly suggest that you start each week monitoring your reactions while avoiding comparing your current ratings with previous ones. This will provide you with more accurate tracking of medication response. Then, collect these weekly charts and take them to your prescriber each time you see them.

You should also ask for feedback from your psychotherapist, if you are working with one. Typically, your psychotherapist has significantly more time to spend with you and can provide their observations of your responses to medication perhaps more accurately than your physician, who will likely have less time to go through such an analysis. Through this sort of careful monitoring, other medications or the addition of other types of ADHD treatment (including psychotherapy; changing daily habits involving sleep, nutrition, and exercise; stress management techniques; and coaching or tutoring to improve daily life management) can also be considered. All will be discussed in detail in later chapters.

Your practitioner has no way to know in advance which of the two most common families of stimulant medications (methylphenidate and amphetamine) and which dose will be most effective for you. Typically, your practitioner will prescribe a stimulant medication, starting at a low dose and gradually increasing the dose every few days until you improve. There are individual differences in how rapidly we metabolize medications (and therefore how long they will be effective), in how sensitive we are to a medication (and therefore how much is needed for effective treatment), and which stimulant medications will prove most effective. It's important to work with an experienced prescriber and to develop a collaborative relationship with them to work together to find the most effective medication and dose. Don't conclude too quickly that the medication "doesn't work" or "doesn't feel good." It's important to be patient, to keep a daily record of how you feel and function on each medication that you may try, and to work together with your physician to find the right medication or combination of medications.

Improving Functioning and Quality of Life

Many physicians judge the effectiveness of medication by measuring the reduction of the "core symptoms" of ADHD while overlooking what may be the most significant challenges experienced by older adults. The official symptoms of ADHD were developed through studying the behavior patterns of children and often don't include the many ADHD-related challenges affecting adults. A better measure of the effects of medication is how it improves your general quality of life—your ability to cope more effectively with the demands of daily life management, your interpersonal relationships, and your general sense of well-being. These quality-of-life measures are contained in your weekly tracking of medication benefits and side effects.

What If My Stimulant Medication Stops Working as Well as Before?

It is rare for an adult who has had a good response to stimulant medications to lose that response over time.[9] Tolerance to any side effects often occurs in just a matter of a few days but reduction in the benefits of stimulant medications almost never occurs with adolescents, adults, and older adults. Once a person determines their best medication and dose, it typically remains unchanged for the rest of that person's life. If you think that your medication is not working as well as it once did, contact your clinician for advice. It is probably not due to tolerance and loss of effectiveness; rather, it may be caused by hormonal changes (especially in women in their fifties as they go through menopause), by an increase in certain lifestyle habits (such as a high-sugar diet, poor sleep, or lack of exercise), by increased stress, or by increased daily demands. In other words, it's important not to rely solely or mostly on medication to address increasing ADHD symptoms. Increasing the dose of your stimulant in an attempt to regain efficacy is rarely advisable;[10] in fact, it is never a good idea to adjust your medication on your own without consultation with your clinician. Always take your medication(s) as prescribed and consult with your doctor before making any changes.

Treating "Complex ADHD"—ADHD Combined with Other Conditions

It's important to understand that in adults, ADHD rarely occurs alone.[11] Most ADHD in adults is "complex" because most adults with ADHD, 80 percent or so, have been diagnosed with other conditions, including depression, anxiety, and bipolar disorder. Treating ADHD is not just a matter of taking a stimulant, any stimulant. In addition, you may need to take other medications to treat anxiety or mood issues. All of these need to be coordinated. Women whom I interviewed often reported coexisting anxiety and/or depression and many of them were taking both an antidepressant and a stimulant.

Collaborate with Your Physician and Be Patient

Individuals vary tremendously in their sensitivity to particular medications as well as how rapidly they metabolize them—all of which means that you need to develop a collaborative working relationship with your prescribing physician in which you are problem-solving, tweaking doses, experimenting with long-acting vs short-acting medications, and considering nonstimulant medications if there is significant interference with sleep or other side effects. The process requires patience—not an easy thing, but very beneficial to you in the long run.

Too many people who are ambivalent about taking medication have an initial response that they don't like and impulsively decide not to take medication, instead of working with their physician to solve the problem. The solution to which balance of medications should be exactly tailored to you.

Perhaps you need a lower dose. Perhaps you need a different medication. The majority of adults with ADHD with whom I have worked over the years find significant benefit once they find a treatment regimen that has been specialized for their needs.

The following stories illustrate the importance of working collaboratively and patiently with your prescriber to find the medication(s) that will work best for you.

> "I developed tachycardia (fast heart rate) on stimulants. Fortunately, my doctor was very experienced in prescribing stimulants to older adults. He put me on a very low dose and then very gradually increased it to the point that the stimulant was really helping with only very slight tachycardia. He assured me it was safe and that's a trade-off I was willing to make."

> "I started on one stimulant but it made my heart beat fast and it was scaring me; then I went to a different stimulant and now I'm on a nonstimulant, which doesn't raise my pulse rate."

> "At first, I took medication and it wasn't right; I'm very sensitive to medication; a year later I told my PCP and he prescribed a lower dose twice a day and that worked very well."

> "I started on stimulants that didn't really seem to work—I still lost my job. Then, I went to someone who 'didn't believe in ADHD,' who wouldn't prescribe another stimulant. Finally, I heard of an ADHD

specialist and waited many weeks to see him—now I'm taking a
higher dose of a long-acting stimulant and it's really helping—I no
longer have anger outbursts."

As sometimes happens, this last individual was treated by two prescribers who were not ADHD specialists. To this man's credit, he persisted, found an ADHD specialist, and finally experienced good results.

I find that some adults who feel anxious or ambivalent about taking stimulants are more likely to impulsively stop taking medication without consulting with their doctor. Some may be looking for confirmation that stimulants are a bad idea. So, instead of consulting with their prescriber, they take matters into their own hands, believing that their hesitancy to take stimulants is justified. Sadly, these adults rob themselves of the opportunity to benefit from stimulant medication that could help them to lead a calmer, less stressful life.

You may have a very atypical reaction to medication, but it's important that you don't immediately conclude that stimulants aren't beneficial for you. Rob wrote to me:

"Stimulants weirdly act as a sedative for me; I only take it occasionally
when my brain is so busy that I can't focus at all; I take a very low
dose because I have severe rebound when it wears off."

Another example of an unusual reaction is a man I saw in therapy for ADHD. He was a tall, full-grown man, but could only tolerate one-quarter of the standard stimulant dose typically prescribed for a child. Taking this microdose helped him a great deal, but any more made him feel anxious and jittery.

Bottom line, the great majority of adults benefit significantly from taking stimulant medication. For those few who cannot tolerate side effects, other types of medication may be helpful (see the chart I provided on pages 85–87); however, these second-line medications are rarely as beneficial as stimulants. Don't accept a second-line medication simply because your prescriber is inexperienced and therefore hesitant to prescribe stimulants to older adults. Look for a prescriber with significant experience in treating adults with ADHD.

Potential Roadblocks in Seeking Medication

You may be reading this and thinking, "Great, I think medication really is for me—let's get started!" But sometimes there are barriers— and it's good to be aware of them. Here are some of the most common.

Difficulty Finding a Physician with Adequate Training and Experience

Part of the reluctance among physicians to prescribe medication for ADHD in older adults is the surprisingly inadequate training they receive, given that adult ADHD is one of the most common adult psychiatric disorders. For example, although bipolar disorder occurs at a rate about half that of adult ADHD (2.4 percent of adults experience bipolar disorder[12] compared to 4.4 percent for adult ADHD[13]), adult psychiatrists are much more familiar with the treatment of bipolar disorder. One of the complicating factors preventing psychiatrists from considering the possibility of adult ADHD in their patients is that both mood and anxiety disorders are very common among adults with ADHD. Since psychiatric training focuses much more on anxiety and mood disorders, psychiatrists are more likely to address these issues while overlooking undiagnosed ADHD. What's important to understand is that adults with ADHD are *more* likely than those without ADHD to have depression, anxiety, substance use disorders, and personality disorders.[14] As a result, consideration of possible ADHD should be standard for psychiatrists conducting a careful diagnostic assessment of a patient with these co-occurring disorders. Even when a psychiatrist recognizes ADHD in a patient, a standard treatment approach is to first focus on the co-occurring disorder.

A common but misguided treatment approach is the physician who tells you, "Let's see what your response is to medication for your (anxiety, depression, or bipolar) and then see if there are still ADHD symptoms present." What's wrong with this approach is that treating the ADHD first will often lessen the impact of co-occurring conditions, such as anxiety and depression.[15] It makes more sense to address the ADHD first, and then assess what symptoms of anxiety and/or depression remain.

Josh Geffen, MD, a psychiatrist and ADHD specialist practicing in Brisbane, Australia, writes, "Like many psychiatrists, we began our medical and psychiatric training in the last century. We were taught that patients with adult attention deficit/hyperactivity disorder (ADHD) had a dubious diagnosis and were probably seeking stimulants for nefarious purposes. Doctors working in this field were viewed with suspicion. They were regarded either as gullible, permissive clinicians or, worse, unscrupulous suppliers of stimulants to drug seekers."[16]

Dr. David Goodman, one of the few psychiatrists with a specialty in treating older adults with ADHD, reports that the typical psychiatrist receives less than a single day of instruction on the diagnosis and treatment of adult ADHD.[17] The instruction of child psychiatrists, of course, focuses on the needs of children. If you are an older adult seeking treatment for ADHD, your best bet may be to find a child psychiatrist or even a pediatrician who is willing to treat adults. (All child psychiatrists have also been trained in adult psychiatry prior to their specialization in child psychiatry.) Because ADHD runs in families, child psychiatrists and pediatricians are certainly familiar with the phenomenon of parents of child patients reporting similar symptoms.

Nationwide, there is an enormous shortage of physicians adequately trained in the diagnosis and treatment of adult ADHD. It is

Stimulant Medication for Older Adults with ADHD

certainly easier to find expertise in or near large metropolitan areas in the US. If you live within a reasonable driving distance of a specialty center, often associated with a medical school or university, it may be helpful to seek a diagnosis and to begin treatment at one of these centers and then transfer your care to a local physician who is willing to follow the treatment protocol that has already been established. If your treatment is complicated by other conditions, such as anxiety, depression, or bipolar disorder, it may be best to periodically check in with a specialist to make sure that your medication regimen is still effective, while your general or primary care physician writes your prescriptions.

Consulting with an expert is good medical practice. Although a consultation with an expert in the field can be costly, I often advise those adults seeking ADHD medication expertise that such a consultation can be a good investment in their treatment. Once the expert has established a diagnosis and found an effective medication regimen, they can then transfer their care back to a more affordable local prescriber who can continue what has been prescribed by an expert in the field.

Such consultations often alleviate a great deal of anxiety in both the patient and the doctor. Consultations also allow a clinician with less expertise to feel less anxious about prescribing stimulant medications to an older adult by sharing the responsibility with another clinician.

Too many adults are told by their prescribing physician, "The risks of taking stimulants at your age outweigh the benefits." While the "young-old" with ADHD—in their sixties and seventies—may be met with reluctance to prescribe stimulants to treat ADHD, these same stimulants are regularly prescribed to the "old-old" in their eighties and beyond in nursing homes to decrease depression and lethargy.[18] If you encounter a reluctance by your physician to prescribe stimulants due to "risk," you are simply dealing with a physician who is uninformed. Of course, it makes sense to screen for any cardiac risk as an older adult, but it doesn't make sense for a physician to express an uninformed, blanket resistance to prescribing stimulants to older adults. (More about this issue is discussed a bit later.)

Confusing Diagnoses: Mild Cognitive Decline or Lifelong ADHD?

When older adults complain of forgetfulness, of regularly misplacing belongings, and of being unable to manage the tasks of daily living, few family members or physicians first think of ADHD. Instead, the typical reaction is to fear cognitive decline related to the early stages of dementia. ADHD should especially be considered as a diagnosis in an older adult when there is ADHD diagnosed in adult and child relatives, because ADHD is so highly genetic. Refer back to Chapter 4 for more on this important topic.

Health/Safety Concerns

Too many adults hear from a physician who is inexperienced in treating adult ADHD that the risks of taking prescribed stimulants outweigh the benefits for older adults. Although the evidence to support these cardiac risks appears minimal, a thorough history should be taken before beginning a stimulant. Most physicians don't feel confident in prescribing stimulant medication to those with cardiac concerns.[19] Your physician should make appropriate referrals as indicated for assessment of cardiac risks.[20] While there is some evidence suggesting that psychostimulants can increase heart rate and systolic blood pressure, and concerns about cardiac complications need to be explored, they should not be the cause to automatically rule out the use of stimulants in older adults without specific contraindications.[21] Heart rate and blood pressure should be monitored as a matter of course during treatment. If there are cardiovascular effects, reducing or stopping psychostimulants generally reverses them.

If you are an older adult with one or more significant health problems, already taking multiple medications for diabetes, blood pressure, high cholesterol, or other common diseases associated with age, your physician may err on the side of caution and refuse to treat your ADHD with medication. Many older adults I've known have been able to safely take stimulants despite other compromising health conditions. Due to inexperience and hesitancy on the part of many physicians, it may be advisable to seek a consultation and initial treatment with a psychiatrist experienced in treating ADHD in older adults and then shift treatment to a more local, more affordable physician once your medication regimen has been established.

General Physician Reluctance

Even at my ADHD specialty clinic, some prescribers have been very reluctant about, if not outright opposed to, prescribing stimulants to adults over age sixty, whether or not there were any complicating medical issues. Such reluctance is based on assumptions about risk, with many physicians not making a truly informed decision. In a study that surveyed physicians about their confidence in managing adult ADHD and coexisting heart disease, few physicians (5 percent of primary care physicians and only 13 percent of psychiatrists) reported that they were "extremely confident" in treating ADHD when there were cardiac concerns.[22]

Among the many older adults with ADHD whom I interviewed, a few reported that stimulant medications weren't considered by their physician or weren't continued due to serious chronic preexisting gastrointestinal (GI) problems. Two of these individuals had undergone gastric bypass surgery. Others reported an increase in blood pressure that led their physician to discontinue medication.

Here are some examples of adults who were not able to get past physician resistance to prescribing stimulants to older adults:

- "My psychiatrist prescribed stimulants, then she changed her mind and won't prescribe them."

- A physician, clearly uncomfortable with treating ADHD in older adults, "discontinued a low dose of Strattera when my BP rose slightly and refuses to consider other stimulant medications."

- In a third case, a woman had taken stimulant medication for years with very good effect, starting when she was in her forties. When her prescribing physician retired, she searched far and wide without finding another physician willing to prescribe stimulants to her now that she was in her late sixties.

Is It Depression or Something Else? Complicating Conditions

Comorbidities (coexisting psychiatric or other medical conditions) complicate the issue of which medications may be appropriate for the treatment of ADHD in adults.

Denise, an older woman whom I saw in psychotherapy, reported to me that her physician would not address her ADHD until her depression was "under control." She had been in treatment for depression for many years and had taken numerous different medications with partial, but not full, remission of her symptoms. I recommended to her psychiatrist, who did not have specific expertise in ADHD, that he consider adding stimulant medication. I reported to him that many adults I had worked with found that both their anxiety and depression had significantly decreased after they began taking medication that targeted their ADHD. He agreed to add a trial of stimulant medication to her long-standing prescription to treat her depression and Denise reported an immediate improvement both in her ability to focus and accomplish tasks, as well as a reduction in her level of depression.

In my experience, in many instances, depression and anxiety in adults with ADHD are the result of untreated ADHD and can show significant improvement when the ADHD is treated directly.

A number of potential complications require both expertise and experimentation. For example, although as many as 25 percent of adults with bipolar disorder also have ADHD, those with bipolar disorder may not have a positive reaction to stimulants. In fact, in some cases, stimulant medication may trigger a manic episode. In other cases where an older adult has been diagnosed with anxiety, stimulant medication may increase anxiety levels. In these cases, antianxiety medications may need to be introduced, or, if already prescribed, may need to be increased. What's equally important to know, however, is that many adults who had been in treatment for anxiety and/or depression for years reported that the addition of stimulant medication decreased their levels of depression and anxiety.

Limited Ongoing Support on the Part of Prescribers

Even when medication is prescribed, quite a few adults reported that there was little careful monitoring or follow-through. *"My doctor just prescribed me a stimulant and told me to let him know if it helped."* This lack of thoughtful monitoring and engagement on the part of the prescriber often led to poor adherence to the prescribed medication. A study in 2012 of adults treated for ADHD reported that many felt abandoned by their health-care provider. "Medication use was often inadequately monitored with little or no follow-up by health-care professionals, leading to poor adherence and a sense of abandonment from the healthcare system."[23]

Unaffordability of Treatment for Older Adults

Cost of treatment is an important consideration for many older adults. Many adult psychiatrists, especially those with greater expertise, do not participate in Medicare, making even a single consultation unaffordable for many older adults on a limited budget.

And many health insurance companies do not cover the cost of psychostimulant medication for ADHD in adults. These two factors unfortunately preclude the use of stimulants among older adults on a limited budget. It seems that insurance companies persist in the outdated belief that ADHD is a childhood psychiatric disorder. There is an enormous need for advocacy on the part of ADHD advocacy organizations, such as CHADD (the largest ADHD advocacy organization in the US—https://chadd.org) to lobby insurance companies to revise their standards to be in line with current knowledge that ADHD is a life span disorder and that those with ADHD can benefit from medication at any age. Several people who participated in my study reported that they did not take stimulant medication because they could not afford it.

Dr. David Goodman writes in a series of blogs on his website (https://addadult.com) that his patients have complained for years about their health insurance not covering the cost of their ADHD medications. Goodman writes that in 2018 things became even worse as insurance companies shifted to a tier system that requires patients to try less expensive Tier 1 medications for ADHD before the company would consider approving a Tier 2 or Tier 3 medication. Of course, the newer and often more effective medications are ranked as Tier 3, while older, generic medications that are often less effective are Tier 1. This system has been instituted to lower the cost of coverage by health insurance companies. As Dr. Goodman reports, prescriptions are also denied claiming that the dose exceeds the FDA-approved maximum, or that the number of pills exceeds what the company has "contracted" to cover in a given month.

Obtaining ADHD medication is growing increasingly difficult for adults. Previously approved medications are likely to be denied. While you launch an appeal, with the assistance of your prescriber, be prepared with a plan B of alternative medications if your appeal is denied. While appeals to insurance companies are increasingly denied, Dr. Goodman encourages all adults caught in this conundrum to make a formal appeal to their state's insurance commissioner, who has the patient's interest in mind and will forward the appeal to the insurance company. In Dr. Goodman's experience with his own patients, these appeals from an insurance commissioner are successful at least half the time.

One older adult shared with me, *"Medicare wouldn't pay for stimulants. They just wanted me to be on an antidepressant, which never helped. I finally found a physician who was willing to treat my ADHD. I am taking generics because my insurance won't pay for name brand. I'm feeling calmer, less intense, less attached to my ideas, to things—can let go of things now."*

Multiple sites offer information about where to find prescription assistance if your prescribed medication is unaffordable for you or you do not have health insurance coverage for prescription medication. Doing research on prescription assistance may seem daunting because it is exactly the type of task that is typically difficult for those with ADHD. This is the occasion to look to a friend or family member for support in conducting this research. Don't give up because it seems too complicated! You'll be glad you asked for help and got it done.

For information about prescription assistance and other ways to make medication more affordable, go to Appendix D (page 314).

Other ways to reduce the cost of treatment:

- Consider being diagnosed by a psychiatrist and then, once you are on a stable regimen, transfer your care to your primary care physician. Many primary care physicians feel more comfortable treating adult ADHD if there is a recent history of diagnosis and treatment by a psychiatrist.

- Consider being diagnosed by a clinical psychologist who specializes in ADHD who can then write a letter to your primary care physician documenting the diagnosis and recommending a trial of medication. Many primary care physicians feel more comfortable prescribing Schedule II drugs when there is documentation in your chart that a careful, clinical diagnosis has been done by an ADHD specialist.

In Their Own Words: Older Adults and Medication

The overwhelming majority of older adults whom I interviewed reported a very positive benefit from taking medication to treat their ADHD. Here are some of their reports:

"I was afraid to take medication, then I tried it and have increased the dose. I've never slept better. Now I don't freak out and make everyone miserable. When I have a task, I get it done."

"Stimulants helped my concentration; I'm able to read now. It also addressed my apathy in a way that antidepressants hadn't."

"I went on stimulants and was able to read a book in three days. Meds stop me from blurting out, but it doesn't slow my speech. If I don't take them, I can be untactful and rude."

"With medication, I'm able to focus and stay focused—it's also helped [to regulate] my sleep and [improved] my relationships."

"I don't interrupt people and talk over people the way I did before. I don't have to interject a comment or a story into every conversation."

"It helps my productivity."

"It gives me some 'get-up-and-go.' "

"It made it more possible for me to function at work."

"It made me feel clear and calm."

"If I didn't take it, I would feel more anxious and agitated."

"The medication gave me an awareness of myself—I am having amazing realizations—I think if I had been treated earlier, my marriage wouldn't have ended; now I'm not as chaotic and have the ability to think things through."

"When I don't take stimulants, sometimes it's like I'm in a fog—then I take them again and things clear up."

"Without stimulants, I am totally unproductive and sleep twelve hours a day. Medication gives me more energy, more motivation. I have more ability to concentrate and it has really improved my self-esteem."

"I have so much more self-awareness; I'm feeling like a new person and getting rid of old clothes and other things that aren't 'me'— suddenly I can organize and actually get things done."

"Stimulants have helped me to finally conquer my eating disorder— I was mostly purging. When my anxiety increased because I felt overwhelmed, I would eat to calm down—then I started bingeing and purging. With stimulants, I feel calmer and don't binge anymore."

"Five days after starting the medication, I was a different person. Before, I was forgetting things all the time; I gained a much higher level of confidence. Before, people were always judging me all my life."

"I've been taking stimulants for over twenty years. Medication has helped with focusing, paying attention, completing daily activities, and organization. It has also helped me to get along better with my wife and with people at work."

"I am a physician. When I'm not taking my meds, it's like night and day. I'm not as nice to patients and staff; I'm disorganized and just want to get from one room to the next. I didn't enjoy my work and did the bare minimum. When I'm on meds, I'm less stressed. My wife sees such a difference when I don't take my medication."

"I sometimes characterize the effect of the meds as helping me care about a project. Not just being able to focus on the project, but actually caring about it. In my fuzziest moments, I just don't care about the task I'm doing."

"Taking stimulants was an absolute life-changing treatment. I had difficulty understanding how I had survived sixty-two years without it. My whole world changed when I was on the medication."

"Medication made a huge positive difference in me and my work productivity. If anything, at my age now I can visualize and see through far more complex problems and design far more complex mechanical devices to eliminate these problems than I ever could. Without it, accurate complex thought and design solutions are virtually impossible."

> Stimulants are like a lens for your life instead of for your vision—they clear everything up.

But Stimulants Aren't for Everyone—and They Can't Do Everything

While most adults I spoke with had good experiences, some interviewees had varying levels of success, from little to moderate:

"I'm not sure stimulants ever helped, but they didn't do any harm; now I'm on a mood stabilizer."

"No medication has really worked, and the side effects were debilitating. It wasn't worth it. Stimulants made me feel edgy—like I had drunk too much coffee."

"I have tried many medications and none of them was helpful."

"I haven't had improvement in motivation and focus that I would like. I still have the piles and messes in my house that I would like to be able to eradicate."

"It helps a great deal, but life is far from perfect. Medication doesn't cover all the bases. A lot of my issues are related to my lifestyle. But medication helps me focus when I need to."

"Stimulants calm me down, but don't really seem to help with focus."

I have deliberately removed the names of stimulant medications from the quotes I have included in this chapter because I do not want to endorse any particular medication. The older adults I spoke to were prescribed a variety of stimulants—some in the methylphenidate family, some in the dextroamphetamine family, and some nonstimulants used as second-line treatments for ADHD. Many physicians, especially those less experienced in treating older adults, automatically lean toward nonstimulant alternatives, although studies show that they are typically less effective.[24] They are an excellent alternative, however, if side effects or medical conditions preclude you from taking stimulants.

Too many psychiatrists focus on "symptom reduction" when symptom reduction is only half the battle. Treatment should target not just "symptoms," but should place more emphasis on your daily life functioning. In other words, the "symptoms" of ADHD don't really address the struggles that you face every day that result from your ADHD. It's critically important that you and your prescribing physician pay more attention to whether the medication helps you function well in your daily life. Using the ADHD Medication Benefits and Side Effects Tracking Form, found in Appendix B, will allow you to focus more on improvements in your daily life functioning.

The remarkable number of very positive reports on the effects of stimulants are direct quotes from people whom I interviewed. In no way, however, do I want to suggest that taking stimulants are the only, or most important, treatment for your ADHD. In the following chapters, I will address other very important aspects of treatment to improve your overall quality of life and improve your daily functioning.

KEY TAKEAWAYS FROM THIS CHAPTER

✔ It's not always easy to find a prescriber who has expertise in treating older adults with ADHD. (I have provided suggestions to ease your search.)

✔ If you have difficulty finding a local physician experienced in treating adult ADHD, it can be useful to initially consult an expert and then bring that expert's recommendations to your local physician for follow-up treatment.

✔ A large number of stimulant and nonstimulant medications are used to treat ADHD. Refer to the ADHD medications chart (page 85) to see the whole range of available medications.

✔ Stimulant medications are significantly more effective in reducing ADHD symptoms; however, other medications can be useful if stimulants cause negative side effects or are not advisable due to health problems.

✔ Concerns about cardiac risks when older adults take stimulants are often overblown; however, it is always important to monitor blood pressure and pulse rate when taking stimulants as an older adult and also important to consult a cardiologist prior to taking stimulants, especially if you have a history of heart disease.

✔ Many insurance companies will not cover the cost of newer, brand-name medications, but increasingly they will cover the cost of generic, and sometimes less effective, stimulant medications.

✔ Work in collaboration with your prescriber to find the right medication and the right dose; don't stop taking prescribed medication without first consulting your prescriber.

✔ It's important to carefully record your responses to stimulants and other medications prescribed for related conditions. I have included a weekly chart (Appendix B, page 308) to provide a convenient way to record your response to medication to share with your prescriber.

✔ It is common for adults to have "complex ADHD" (ADHD in combination with anxiety, depression, or other issues) and, as a result, to be prescribed other medications in addition to stimulants.

✔ Stimulants can't solve everything, and they are not for everyone, but a remarkable number of adults to whom I have talked report very positive benefits from taking stimulants.

Learn to Understand, Accept, and Thrive with ADHD

Solution-focused psychotherapy for older adults with ADHD

The experience of ADHD varies widely from one person to another, with a broad range in the severity of symptoms and the types of symptoms, many of which overlap with those of other psychiatric disorders.[1] Many mental health providers who are not ADHD specialists, unaware of the range and complexity in the presentation of ADHD, view ADHD as a relatively simple set of issues related to "paying attention" that can be addressed by stimulant medication and a bit of "psychoeducation" to help the patient understand their ADHD. Nothing could be further from the truth. ADHD is accompanied by many other disorders, the "comorbidities" I mentioned in Chapter 4, making it complicated to sort out what to treat and how to treat it. And most important, ADHD is a 24/7 disorder that impacts most aspects of life, not just your ability to "pay attention."

What Are You Seeking "Treatment" For?

If you are seeking therapy for ADHD, the first order of business is to clarify what *your* primary concerns are. You may not be sure what to focus on and you may not be aware that many of your life challenges are possibly related to your ADHD—for example, sleep problems, poor eating habits, substance use issues, anxiety, depression, family conflict, or social isolation. Often, members of the public, misled by the name "attention deficit disorder," also think that the main issue is difficulty in "paying attention." To the contrary, ADHD can also impact almost every aspect of your life.

Your therapy should begin with an assessment of what needs to be changed in your life, followed by prioritizing your most pressing issues. An experienced ADHD specialist will deftly weave back and forth during a single therapy session to allow you to talk about what's on your mind, to process feelings, and to problem-solve—all with the goal of helping you feel and function better in your daily life.

How Do You Compare to Other Older Adults Who Are Challenged by ADHD?

I asked each older adult whom I interviewed to share with me the "top five challenges related to ADHD" that they experienced at their current stage in life. While your individual circumstances may lead you to develop a different "top five" challenges list, it might be useful to consider the issues that emerged from my discussions with a large group of older adults with ADHD.

Top Five Concerns Expressed by Older Adults with ADHD

- Being disorganized
- Emotional concerns—anxiety, depression, and emotional dysregulation

- Lack of motivation/being unproductive—"I can't seem to get anything done."
- Social problems, including isolation and problematic interactions with others
- Memory problems—being absentminded and forgetful

If you would like to compare your responses to other older adults with ADHD, I have created a self-report questionnaire that you will find in Appendix A on page 305. This questionnaire was completed by the older adults I interviewed.

Share your questionnaire responses with your therapist, paying most attention to the items on which you scored yourself the highest—doing this is the first step in prioritizing what to work on with your therapist.

Finding a Therapist to Help You Address Your ADHD Challenges

ADHD is such a common condition that almost any therapist will say they have experience in treating ADHD. In fact, if you search for a therapist on the Psychology Today website (https://www.psychology today.com/us/therapists), you'll find *many* people in your area who list ADHD as a condition that they treat. But beware! A therapist who doesn't list ADHD as a primary focus of their practice is probably not going to provide the care that you need. It's true that you may need a therapist who also treats anxiety, depression, and the whole long list of conditions that often accompany ADHD. But if ADHD is just one condition on the list of conditions that the psychotherapist claims to treat, they are almost surely not a therapist with significant expertise.

One good place to start in your search for a psychotherapist who is an ADHD specialist is at CHADD's website. CHADD is a long-established advocacy organization for those with ADHD across the life span. It lists professionals who specialize in ADHD (https://chadd.org/professional-directory) as well as organizations that treat ADHD (https://chadd.org/organization-directory).

Although it's not always easy to find a psychotherapist who is truly a specialist, there is gradual, growing awareness among psychotherapists of the more specific needs of adults with ADHD. ADHD specialists are more likely to be found in urban areas. Now, in the age of increasing online psychotherapy, it is much easier for those who don't live in urban areas to connect with and receive treatment from a psychotherapist. Medical and mental health licenses restrict treatment by licensed practitioners to residents of the states in which they are licensed. However, among psychologists, changes are taking place through an organization called PSYPACT[2] that a growing number of states have joined (at the time of my writing, twenty-six states have joined and that number is rapidly growing) in an agreement to allow psychologists who join PSYPACT to practice across state lines so long as you live in one of the states that have joined PSYPACT. Visit https://psypact.site-ym.com/page/psypactmap to find out whether your state is a participant. If so, you automatically have access to a much broader field of psychotherapists to choose among.

Another possibility is to work with a highly experienced ADHD coach. Some of them have worked in the field for many years and may even have a mental health background in addition to their coaching certification. ADHD coaches are not restricted by state licenses and can work with anyone no matter their geographic location. Coaching services are not covered by health insurance, but in many cases, coaching fees are significantly less than those of psychotherapists. Chapter 8 shares more information about how to find a qualified coach.

Buyer Beware!

It is very important to understand that therapists with limited experience with ADHD can actually do harm through misinterpreting the following ADHD behavior patterns, for example:

Being late for appointments may be misinterpreted as "resisting" treatment, low motivation, or immaturity, instead of looking at this behavior through the ADHD lens of forgetfulness and poor time management.

Not following through on agreed-upon tasks or actions may be viewed as treatment resistance or low motivation, rather than as a classic symptom of ADHD that needs to be addressed by providing more structure and support.

Emotional volatility may be incorrectly diagnosed as borderline personality disorder, instead of understanding that impulsivity, rejection sensitive dysphoria, and emotional dysregulation are all related to ADHD.

What ADHD-Focused Therapy Should Entail

Standard psychotherapy that is nondirective, introspective, and focused on feelings and relationships can be helpful if you also have anxiety or depression. Many clients over the years have come to my clinic saying that they have been in therapy that helped their anxiety and depression but that never focused on ADHD issues. Effective therapy for ADHD also needs to address the core elements of ADHD that have to do with executive functions.[3] Be sure that your therapist understands the executive functioning deficits associated with ADHD and uses a clear, direct, and pragmatic approach rather than only exploring feelings and psychological blocks. ADHD-focused therapy should help you improve your ability to do the following:

- Accomplish your goals, both large and small
- Be more reliable and on time
- Organize your belongings
- Remember—what's been said and what you've promised
- Have better control over intense emotional reactions
- Stop impulsive behaviors that take you off task
- Refocus after internal or external distractions

If your therapist refers you to a coach to address your needs to improve daily life functioning, you are not working with an experienced ADHD therapist. Yes, as you will read in Chapter 8, a coach can be highly effective in helping you develop better ways to manage your tasks, your time, and your daily life in general. But your therapist should also address these issues, offering life management techniques and giving you "homework" to practice these techniques between sessions. Typically, I only refer a client to a coach if the client is generally functioning well and feeling well, but just needs specific help; for example, in structuring their day, downsizing their household belongings, or completing paperwork tasks.

A Brain-Based ADHD Therapy Session Should Provide Structure

"Talk therapy" is often unstructured. The therapist might open with a general question, such as "How are things going?" or "How are you feeling?" and then will let you lead the discussion, asking some clarifying questions and helping you better understand what relationships and life events have contributed to how you are feeling. The problem with this approach, when you have ADHD, is that there is often no continuity from session to session. You may not even clearly recall what was discussed in the preceding session and just jump in, talking about whatever happens to be uppermost on your mind that week. When you have ADHD there are typically many different things on your mind, and therapy may begin to feel directionless as you jump from topic to topic.

A brain-based ADHD-focused therapy session should provide structure and support to help you stay on track in addressing your concerns, using approaches such as the following:

- A written summary of topics, goals, and "assignments" to practice during the week
- A review of the previous session to create continuity
- Bringing you back to the topic under discussion if your mind wanders to something else
- Helping you understand how your brain functions
- Providing tools to counteract tendencies that get in the way of accomplishing your goals
- Interweaving a discussion of feelings and personal history with a focus on building self-management tools to live a more satisfying life in the present
- Educating you to understand how you can reduce your ADHD symptoms through brain-healthy daily habits (discussed in detail in Chapter 9)

There are many ways that therapy can help:

The diagnosis itself is therapeutic. Recognition that you are not "to blame" for your behavior does not mean that you are not "responsible" for changing those behaviors. ADHD doesn't serve as an excuse but rather as an explanation for your dysfunctional patterns. An ADHD psychotherapist should help you change your thought patterns to enable you to stop blaming yourself for past mistakes and begin to understand that you have a real and treatable condition.

Learn to Understand, Accept, and Thrive with ADHD

Psychoeducation is therapeutic. "Psychoeducation" is the process of a therapist providing you with an in-depth, sophisticated understanding of ADHD and how you are affected by it as an older adult. Good psychoeducation can set you on the path to developing a positive, problem-solving approach to managing your ADHD challenges.

Bringing your spouse or partner into the treatment process can be therapeutic. When your spouse or partner understands how you are impacted by ADHD, they can begin looking at frustrating behavior differently. The therapist can guide the older couple to develop a positive, problem-solving approach to ADHD. Psychoeducation of older couples impacted by ADHD can help a non-ADHD spouse or partner to develop more realistic expectations. Treatment is less likely to work if the non-ADHD spouse or partner expects their ADHD partner to "be fixed" without their participation. Couples' psychoeducation can lead partners to work together, to have reasonable expectations, to understand which tasks are best assigned to each partner, and to support each other in working toward long-term change.

Using a hands-on approach in the therapy session can be therapeutic. I have had clients bring large boxes of unopened mail to my office because they felt anxious and overwhelmed at the thought of opening it at home after avoiding it for so long. Bringing the box to my office and sitting in a separate room, opening the mail, knowing that they would have a therapy session with me at some point while they tackled their mountain of mail, gave them the courage and support to accomplish it. For others, the biggest challenge may be making a difficult phone call. There have been many times when I've told a client, "If you can't get yourself to make the call during the week, then we'll have you make the call in my office during our next session." I've helped college students to register for classes during their session, providing them with guidance about creating an ADHD-friendly schedule. In another instance, I sat with an older woman as she wrote a very difficult email to her daughter—one she'd been avoiding writing for weeks.

Recognizing your strengths is therapeutic. Too often, the focus of ADHD therapy is on the negative. What's getting in the way? What do you need to change next? It's also essential to recognize, celebrate, and emphasize the strengths you bring to the table. The grandparent who may not be the best at remembering to send birthday cards or gifts to grandchildren may also be the fun, spontaneous, creative grandparent with whom the grandchildren love to spend time. I recall with great fondness spending time with my grandfather, who surely had ADHD. One of the oft-told family stories was how he had forgotten to bring the train tickets from the hotel room as my grandparents were setting off on their honeymoon. He would take me for long, rambling walks, telling me all sorts of interesting things along the way. We might have been a little late returning for dinner, but he was the grandparent whose company I most enjoyed.

Changing self-defeating thought patterns is therapeutic. The therapist may ask you to examine long-practiced, reflexive negative thoughts, such as *"I'm a screw-up!" "I always fail." "I'll never be able to change."* Such thoughts immediately trigger negative feelings. A central, overarching issue for those living with ADHD is the self-blame and outright self-loathing that many engage in. The therapist works to help you reframe your failures and mistakes through a lens of self-understanding and self-compassion. ADHD isn't the result of characterological flaws; it is the result of neurophysiological differences in the brain that can lead to certain types of underfunctioning. This change in thinking shifts the inquiry from "Why am I such a failure?" to "How can I improve my cognitive functioning?"

Learning self-calming techniques is therapeutic. Our understanding of ADHD continues to change. It is now clear that problems with intense emotional sensitivity (rejection sensitive dysphoria) and emotional overreactivity (emotional dysregulation)[4] are important aspects of ADHD for many people. Mindfulness-based cognitive therapy (MBCT) is a good approach to use if these are issues that you struggle with. MBCT incorporates a daily mindfulness practice.

This is a new treatment approach that combines changing your self-defeating thought patterns, learning strategies to better manage your daily life, and learning mindfulness techniques to improve your focus and calm your emotional reactivity. This new combined approach using both mindfulness and cognitive behavioral therapy (CBT) shows a lot of promise.[5]

Participating in ADHD therapy groups is therapeutic. Another, frequently ignored, aspect of treatment is the healing power of working toward change in a group setting. So often, adults with ADHD, especially older adults with ADHD who were not diagnosed until late in life, have a history of countless experiences of feeling stupid, embarrassed, and ashamed because of things that they have forgotten to do, have done late, or have done incorrectly. They feel "less-than" most of those around them. A group experience can provide powerful therapy as older adults participate for the first time with others who have struggled with most of the same challenges, problem-solving together and encouraging one another when the going gets tough.

Effective Therapy Needs to Be Comprehensive and Coordinated

As I've mentioned throughout, ADHD is typically accompanied by at least one other psychiatric condition, if not several. Even when ADHD is "uncomplicated," there are often two to three mental health professionals involved in treating an adult including a psychiatrist, a psychotherapist, and often a coach.

Ideally, the mental health professional with whom you work in psychotherapy to treat your ADHD should provide you with a range of services rather than referring you to numerous different professionals each providing their own service. Working with multiple service providers is unaffordable for most people and unnecessarily complicated. For example, in my own work with clients, I work hard to provide a range of services that might include individual therapy while also including a spouse or other family members as appropriate, rather than referring my client to a "family therapist" to work on family issues. I also integrate coaching into my psychotherapy with clients, helping them to engage in practical problem-solving about how to organize their day, lead a healthier lifestyle, improve problem sleep patterns, and so on.

Your Psychotherapist as "Case Coordinator"

One of the strong recommendations in a recent article on diagnosing and treating ADHD, written by a group of well-known ADHD experts, was that your ADHD psychotherapist should function as your "case coordinator." What does this mean? A case coordinator is someone who helps you with your communication with various treatment providers. A case coordinator is your guide, coordinating your treatment between all your other providers, working closely with you to understand your particular needs and difficulties, and helping you in finding other types of support that you may need.[6]

One critical part of the role of case coordinator is to work in collaboration with your prescriber, should you be taking medication as part of your treatment. Due to time limitations, many prescribers are unable to engage in an in-depth discussion of your medication responses. Your psychotherapist has more time to spend with you and more opportunity to engage in a careful assessment of the benefits and side effects of medications.

Unfortunately, many adults with ADHD find themselves having to coordinate their own care, a task for which they are poorly suited. Because organization, planning, and prioritizing are usually in short supply for adults with ADHD, it is incumbent upon the psychotherapist to become the case manager and to not expect the adults with

ADHD themselves to keep track of sharing records and scheduling coordinated appointments.

What Can You Do If Your Therapist Doesn't Incorporate These Approaches?

As strange as it may sound, you may need to coach your therapist to better understand your needs:

- Ask whether you can record the session to review it later during the week.
- Ask for a summary email outlining what was talked about and what you agreed to work on during the week.
- Tell your therapist that your conversation tends to ramble and that you need them to bring you back on topic should you start rambling.
- Ask your therapist to provide concrete information and recommendations about how to build more effective daily habits.

Don't Work with a Therapist Who Doesn't Address Practical Changes

If you find yourself with a therapist who believes that the practical changes you need to make require working with a coach (rather than working through them in therapy), you may want to consider finding a new therapist. While it is very true that working with a coach to accomplish specific goals can be very helpful, an ADHD therapist should also help you build tools to become calmer, more organized, able to accomplish tasks, and develop brain-healthy daily habits that will improve your cognitive functioning. (See Chapter 8 for more about working with a coach and when you should choose a coach rather than a therapist.)

What Are Some of the Most Critical Issues to Focus On in Therapy?

Keep in mind, as I said earlier, we are all impacted differently by ADHD. Not all the issues I list below may be among your primary needs.

- **Developing emotional regulation skills**—Emotional intensity and ADHD often go hand in hand. As one woman described her adult daughter with ADHD, "Whatever you can say about her, you can add the word *very* to the sentence. She becomes *very* angry *very* quickly. Her feelings are hurt *very* easily. She tends to be *very* impulsive in her emotional reactions, often saying things that later she *very* much regrets." If you have difficulty controlling your emotional reactivity, a therapist with some background in dialectical behavior therapy (DBT), a type of cognitive behavioral therapy, can help you learn and practice emotional regulation skills to keep your emotional reactions from creating yet more problems in your life. Whereas cognitive behavioral therapy tries to identify and change negative thinking patterns and pushes for positive behavioral changes, DBT also entails learning many techniques for self-calming and emotional regulation.

- **Understanding how low self-esteem contributes to emotional sensitivity and overreactions**—Many people with ADHD develop a very negative self-image after years of being criticized and feeling like a failure. A CBT approach can help you quiet your inner critic that tells you such things as: *"It's hopeless, I'll never change"* or *"I'm such a loser and always have been,"* and instead gives you constructive messages that can lead to positive change, such as *"I'm making progress," "I may not be great at being organized, but I am a creative problem-solver,"* or *"I'm going to* *look for people who recognize the good in me and don't just focus on my challenges."*

CBT to treat ADHD has been considered the most useful approach, but more recently experts in the field have written that ADHD is more complex than previously thought and that a broader focus of treatment is needed to help adults with ADHD who struggle with emotional regulation problems.[7]

- **Understanding how impulsivity provides jet fuel to your feelings**—People with ADHD tend to react before they think, leading them to act on their emotions, doing and saying things that they may later regret. You may find that stimulant medication can reduce impulsivity, giving you a much-needed moment to think about consequences before you react.

There Is No Quick Fix

In my experience working with adults, change is an ongoing, lifelong process. It involves focusing on a wide array of issues—marital issues, financial issues, quality of life issues, and so on—and possibly involving major lifestyle changes in the process. There are many things that can be highly therapeutic. Your approach to ADHD, whether you work with a therapist, a coach, an online support group, or a supportive friend or family member, needs to be custom designed to address your most challenging concerns.

In the next few chapters, I will introduce other therapeutic interventions that can be woven into your treatment, including the following:

- **Ways that you can help yourself**—developing new habits and patterns by yourself or with the support of a friend or family member

- **Working with an ADHD/executive functioning coach**—often more accessible than truly ADHD-informed psychotherapy

- **Stress analysis and reduction**—recognizing the role that stress plays in increasing your ADHD challenges and problem-solving to reduce sources of stress

- **Building ADHD-friendly environments**—home environments, social environments, and more general community environments

- **ADHD psychoeducation and support groups**—the highly therapeutic experience of sharing both challenges and solutions in a group of others who understand and accept you because they face similar issues

- **Developing brain-healthy daily habits** that can improve your cognitive functioning and overall sense of well-being

- **ADHD-focused couples training** that can take place as a couple or in a group of couples

KEY TAKEAWAYS FROM THIS CHAPTER

✔ It is important that your therapist understand that ADHD is a complex disorder that affects you 24/7 in many aspects of your life and is not just a matter of "having difficulty paying attention."

✔ Many therapists claim to treat ADHD among many other conditions. To get the best treatment, look for someone who truly specializes in ADHD.

✔ An experienced ADHD specialist will interweave a focus on improving daily life functioning with more psychological issues, such as feelings of self-doubt and shame, anxiety, depression, and interpersonal issues.

Learn to Understand, Accept, and Thrive with ADHD

✔ ADHD is a "coat of many colors" and can impact people very differently. The first task of therapy is, with the help of your therapist, to clearly identify your challenges and your individual goals.

✔ Your therapist should function as your case manager, interfacing with any other treatment providers you work with, such as a prescriber of ADHD medication or an ADHD coach.

CHAPTER 7

Ways to Help Yourself

Self-management strategies to reduce your ADHD challenges

There are many things that you can do yourself to address your challenges and begin to lead a more functional and satisfying life.

First, Educate Yourself about ADHD

The more you know about ADHD, the better you can understand your challenges, make positive changes in your life, and stop blaming yourself.

Read about ADHD

Reading books can be very difficult for many with ADHD. So many adults have told me that they have a pile of books on ADHD beside their bed and haven't managed to finish any of them. I have included in Appendix C (page 313) a short list of some of the best books on adult ADHD. If you are not a reader, however, you might learn more by purchasing an audio version of some of these books and listening to them. Some of my clients tell me that they often listen to books on ADHD as they drive in their car—making good use of what could be wasted time.

If books are not the best way for you to learn, you're not alone. If a book feels overwhelming, you may be more successful reading shorter articles from *reputable* sources. I have listed some of these sources in Appendix C.

Educate Your Family about ADHD and How It Impacts You

As you learn, share your knowledge with your family and others close to you. ADHD is real. It's not "just an excuse," as many falsely believe. At the same time, we all need to take responsibility for our ADHD, especially as it impacts those around us. Most likely, you are not the only family member who is impacted by ADHD. And those family members who are not impacted need to understand how it impacts you. The goal is constructive communication and problem-solving. (Read more about this in Chapters 11 and 12 on relationships and parenting.)

Learn Through Attending (or Forming) ADHD Support Groups

You may be fortunate enough to live in a community that offers adult ADHD support groups. Some of these groups are sponsored by the national ADHD advocacy organization CHADD. If you are not so fortunate, support groups offered online by ADDA (another ADHD advocacy organization; go to https://add.org) are of excellent quality. Another place to look for adult ADHD support groups is through Meetup (https://www.meetup.com). There are many Meetup groups across the country that have been formed by an adult with ADHD who wants to meet and learn from other ADHD adults.

During the first year of the COVID-19 pandemic, my clinic offered a free online support group for older adults with ADHD. This group, attended virtually by people across the US, became a real haven for many of the group members. Sally, one of the group members, joined because she suspected that she had ADHD. Through the group, she found resources in her area and sought an ADHD diagnosis. Sally told me that her group experience had been very positive.

> *"If it wasn't for the group, I don't know what I would be doing. In learning about ADHD in the group it's like I keep finding puzzle pieces, but I don't yet have the whole puzzle put together. I feel like I've found my flock. We're all strange birds that understand each other."*

Sally is still participating in the group, which is now self-led by the group members. She tells me that she's "still on an adventure" learning about herself and ADHD.

Treatment Advertised Online—Don't Be Duped—Do Your Own Research

ADHD has become a big business. Many people are looking for ways to get help and many companies are responding to this growing need. Be aware that while there is certainly reputable information on ADHD treatment online, there is also information offered by entrepreneurs trying to sell you their services or their products, many of which are not scientifically supported. Be sure to dig deeper and look for the credentials of people offering such products and services. Many individuals and companies online take advantage of individuals who are worried about taking medication, for example, and try to sell them a nonmedical "magic cure" for ADHD.

If you come across a device, treatment approach, or dietary supplement that claims to treat or cure ADHD, one simple way to protect yourself against unscrupulous individuals or companies is to do a quick online search about the product or service by typing "Google Scholar" into the search bar before the name of the product or service. You will quickly be shown research articles that may either support the claims or, more likely, report that these products or services are only minimally helpful, if at all. If there is no research supporting the product or service, that's an indication that it's probably not effective or possibly even harmful. Any reputable company wants to provide research to support its claims.

> Be careful about products and services that you read about online. Only use trusted online ADHD resources for reliable information. (See Appendix C, pages 311–313.)

Now That I've Done My Homework, How Do I Get Started?

Identify Your Goals and Focus on Your Priorities

With the best of intentions, many adults with ADHD make a long list of goals, some of them reasonable, others less so, and then dive in trying to change too many things at once. In my book *ADD-Friendly Ways to Organize Your Life*,[1] I offer lots of slogans to help you remember key points. One of them is this:

> E.A.S.T. is least successful!
> (E.A.S.T. stands for "Everything at the Same Time")

Instead, I advise:

> Pick just one, then get it done!

In other words, don't defeat yourself with enthusiastic but unreasonable goals. In the ADHD Life Skills coaching groups offered at my clinic, we spend a lot of time teaching people techniques to help them be more successful in reaching their goals. Many books on the market claim to offer the most successful ways to build habits and accomplish goals. One of my favorites, which is based on extensive academic research, is *Tiny Habits* by BJ Fogg, PhD,[2] the founder of Stanford University's Behavior Design Lab.

We all know "what we need to do." For example, anyone with ADHD can walk into my office and tell me, "I need to be better organized." ... "I need to get up on time in the morning." ... "I need to stop yelling and losing my temper when I'm frustrated." ... "I need to get things done." Sure, you know *what* you need to do, but a therapist can help you figure out *how* to do it.

Internationally known ADHD authority Russell Barkley has popularized a phrase in the ADHD community—that for people with ADHD, "The problem isn't not knowing what to do, it's not doing what you know."[3] I think, in some ways, this phrase doesn't quite capture the problem. Everyone, with or without ADHD, "knows what to do" but often doesn't do it. "I know I should quit smoking." ... "I know I need to organize my closets." ... "I know that I should exercise more." The world is filled with smoking cessation clinics, personal organizers, personal trainers, and fitness programs because, although

> When you have ADHD, the problem isn't that you don't know *what* to do. The problem is that you don't know *how* to do it.

people know *what* to do, they don't know *how* to get themselves to do it. The same is even truer when you have ADHD.

When You Encounter Difficulties Following Through on Your Goals, It's Time for Problem-Solving

Ask yourself these questions:

What's getting in my way?

What would make the desired behavior easier to accomplish?

Is my goal realistic? Sometimes we set ourselves up for failure with unrealistic goals.

Problem-Solving

You can problem-solve with a therapist or coach, but you can also problem-solve with a family member or with a fellow ADHDer.

Here is an example of problem-solving for ADHD:

Problem: Angry Overreactions

Problem-solving (here's one example to illustrate the process):

1. **First, identify your triggers.** Your triggers might be:
   - When you're tired at the end of the day
   - When you have not had a good night's sleep
   - When you are trying to do something that is difficult for you
   - When you are repeatedly interrupted as you try to focus on a task
   - When your spouse criticizes you
   - When you feel like a failure

2. **Then, problem-solve.**

Consider each situation that may trigger anger, then start looking for ways to reduce or prevent your emotional overreaction.

- If you are irritable and angry due to fatigue:
  - Lie down and rest.
  - Sit outside and relax for a few minutes.
  - Tell your family that you need some alone time.
  - Look for ways to reduce your daily stress level.
- When irritability is due to poor sleep:
  - Do you lose track of time and stay up too late? If so, would a recurring reminder help you be more aware of bedtime?
  - Do you stay up late and fall asleep in front of the television? Try going to bed, turning out the light, and listening to a podcast or recorded book instead. You'll have a better night's sleep if you are in bed when you doze off. (The importance of sleep and techniques to improve your sleep patterns are presented in Chapter 9.)
- If your irritation is fueled by frustration:
  - Identify recurring sources of frustration—work with your therapist to consider whether some of your frustration is due to unrealistic expectations of yourself or of others.
  - Work with your therapist to develop calm-down tools.
  - Work with your therapist to change your habit of "taking your frustration out on others."
  - Explore whether your frustration is due to chronic overcommitment.

- If you dislike being interrupted when deeply focused on a task:
  - Warn your family or colleagues in advance that you don't want to be interrupted.
  - Shut your office door.
  - Calmly remind the person not to interrupt.
  - Give those around you a time frame for how long you need to not be interrupted.
- When you feel criticized by your spouse:
  - Many families affected by ADHD fall into patterns of blaming—it may be helpful for your spouse to join you in therapeutic problem-solving to break a long-standing pattern of blame and criticism. (See Chapter 11 for more about couples' issues when you have ADHD.)
- When you feel like a failure:
  - Low self-esteem is one of those "feelings issues" that is so important to focus on in therapy; living with untreated ADHD can lead to feeling defensive and negative about yourself; understanding that ADHD is not your "fault" and learning ways to reduce ADHD challenges can also help you build your self-esteem.
  - Consider whether your expectations of yourself are unrealistic.
  - Take a moment to consider whether you engage in black-and-white thinking that leads you to believe that one small mistake equals a huge failure.

Your problems may be something other than angry overreactions. Whatever your challenges, the problem-solving process is the same:

1. Identify the problematic pattern.

2. Identify the situations or triggers that lead to this problematic pattern.

3. Then, problem-solve to reduce or eliminate those situations or triggers.

Structure and Support

Many adults with ADHD have told me that they feel like a failure in therapy because they never follow through on the "homework" they were supposed to complete between sessions. "If I'm not going to do the homework," they reason, "then I might as well stop therapy. I hate coming in to tell the therapist each week that I haven't followed through on my promises." What's missing is adequate *structure* and *support* to help you follow through on your intentions. I will return to these two very important words—*structure* and *support*—repeatedly. It's easy to figure out what you "ought" to do at home to improve your daily functioning. The real work of ADHD therapy begins when your good intentions aren't enough. That's where *structure* and *support* come in.

> To make lasting changes in your life, find the structure and support you need to succeed.

The key to successful change is to figure out the right level of *structure* and *support* you need to accomplish a particular task or to make a change in your habits, behaviors, or emotional reactions.

Activities that are very difficult for you may always call for a high level of structure and support. But you don't always need to turn to a professional to help with very difficult tasks. Sometimes the solution is to reconsider how tasks are divided at home, or at work if you are still working. If you have family members who live with you, you may need to divide the responsibility for tasks differently so that yours are more within your skill set. The same goes for tasks at work. The most successful adults with ADHD have managed to find adequate structure and support in the workplace and have had work that allowed them to focus on their strengths.

Other tasks may require a very high level of structure and support initially (for more information, see Chapter 8 on ADHD coaching). Later, as you build strong new habits, your need for support may lessen. Structure and support can be provided by your therapist or an ADHD coach in combination with problem-solving. Structure and support can also be provided by family members or friends once you have determined with your therapist or coach the best way to approach a particular task.

And don't hesitate to turn to experts when a task feels too daunting. One commonly daunting task faced by many older adults with ADHD is off-loading a lifetime's accumulation of belongings prior to moving into a smaller retirement home. Working with a downsizing expert can help you decide what to keep and what to off-load when making this major life transition. Can't afford or find a professional organizer or downsizing expert? Turn to other options, such as an accountability buddy (at https://www.focusmate.com) or a friend or family member serving as a "body double" while you work, bit by bit, to off-load and downsize (more on "body doubles" in just a bit).

Make Peace with Your Need for Extra Help

The first step, and sometimes the most difficult step, is to accept that you need assistance. So many older adults are mired in self-blame. "I *should* be able to do this," they tell themselves, despite evidence to the contrary. After a lifetime of being told, "You can do this; you just need to try harder," it's likely that you often tell yourself the same thing. Instead of "trying harder" and failing, your goal is to understand how your ADHD brain works best and then look for the structure and support you need to succeed.

Use a "Body Double"

A body double is someone in the same room with you, not engaging in a task with you, but simply offering their presence to keep you accountable and on task. Sometimes, just the presence of a friend or family member is all you need to move forward to accomplish your goal. You're much less likely to keep stopping the task to attend to other things while your friend or family member has dedicated time to support you in completing your task. The "body double" can be engaged in their own activity so long as it doesn't distract you from your task. They are not actively helping; they are simply there for support. Here is an inspiring example of how much a body double can help in completing a long-term project.

Emily was a writer who contacted me for assistance after being very "stuck" on a writing project for many months. She just couldn't seem to get started, always finding something else that "needed to be done" because the writing project had come to feel like an overwhelmingly difficult task. I suggested to her that she find a "body double" to simply sit in the same room with her while she worked on her project. Emily contacted me again about six months later, excitedly telling me that she had finished her writing project. She had asked her elderly mother, who lived nearby, to come over to her house after breakfast each day and simply spend the morning sitting with her. While her mother read, spent time online, and drank coffee—parts of her normal morning routine—Emily sat at the dining room table writing. She reported to me that having a "body double" had worked almost magically for her, keeping her on task.

Focusmate

Another highly affordable way to create structure and support in your life is to sign up for a service called Focusmate (https://www.focusmate.com). For a nominal monthly fee, with a Focusmate account, you can go online with another Focusmate member at a specified time to engage in a task that has been difficult for you to accomplish on your own. The task might be an exercise routine, an organizing task, bill paying, anything that you're having difficulty accomplishing. Your Focusmate partner is someone who also needs structure and support.

To use Focusmate, sign up for a Focusmate session online at a specific time on a specific day. Your Focusmate times can be regular and recurring, if you prefer. For example, you could sign up for a Focusmate session Mondays, Wednesdays, and Fridays at seven a.m. to support your exercise routine. At the beginning of each "coworking session," you and your randomly assigned Focusmate partner declare your task to each other and agree to stay "on camera" (on your phone, tablet, or laptop) so that you are truly "accountable." You can see that your Focusmate partner is working and they can see you. Focusmate provides an easy and highly affordable way to increase the structure and support in your life. Recently, Focusmate has allowed the formation of task-specific groups where everyone in the group is focused on the same sort of task.

ADHD reWired

ADHD reWired (https://www.adhdrewired.com) is another online option offering help for ADHD. ADHD coach Eric Tivers offers online coaching groups for the ADHD community. Graduates or "alumni" of the coaching groups can then access ongoing "accountability groups" that allow members, all adults with ADHD, to log on to a Zoom call, declare their intended task, and then get to work online. This service differs from Focusmate in several ways: (1) all of the participants identify as having ADHD; (2) these are groups rather than one-on-one sessions; and (3) participants are encouraged to be supportive and interactive as they work on their intended tasks. ADHD reWired has formed a large online ADHD community in which participants can find structure and support.

ADDA

ADDA—the Attention Deficit Disorder Association—is a long-established nonprofit organization created to support adults with ADHD. For a modest monthly fee—$5.00 per individual, $7.50 per couple—you can access classes, seminars, and support groups—all online (https://add.org). Of particular interest to older adults are the following groups:

- Virtual Peer Support Group for Women 50+
- Productivity Power Hour (support group for getting things done)
- Healthy Habits and the ADHD Brain work group
- Retired persons weekly check-in work group

ADDA is a volunteer organization of adults with ADHD. If you would like to form an elder ADHD support group of people who all live near you, ADDA is happy to facilitate the formation of a group and will even offer you guidelines about how to form and maintain a successful support group. As an ADDA member, you'll meet your "tribe," other adults who really "get it" when you talk about your goals and struggles.

Improving Cognitive Functioning

This is at the core of changing problematic ADHD patterns. When I talk to a new client, I introduce my approach saying, "My job is to teach you as many ways as I know that can improve your cognitive functioning." That may include medication, but also a wide range of other approaches:

Brain-healthy daily habits

- **Sleep**—Adequate and restorative sleep can have a big positive impact on the functioning of your prefrontal lobes; and conversely, chronic poor sleep patterns negatively impact your prefrontal lobes, intensifying ADHD challenges.

- **A healthy diet**—A low-sugar, low-starch diet, with plenty of fruits, vegetables, whole grains, and low-fat protein, can provide your brain with a steady, reliable supply of blood glucose, which fuels your brain.

- **Daily *aerobic* exercise** can increase your brain's production of brain-derived neurotrophic factor (BDNF), which can enhance learning new skills.

- **Stress reduction** involves both reducing stress in your daily life as well as learning stress reduction techniques, such as mindfulness, to lower your stress reaction to the inevitable stressors in life.

- **Vitamins and other supplements**

- **Exposure to nature**—"green breaks"—getting outside into nature once or more per day

- **Positive social interactions**—daily connections to friends and/ or family

All these brain-friendly daily habits are discussed in more detail in Chapter 9.

Learn to Feel Calmer Through Developing a Daily Mindfulness Practice

Even ten to fifteen minutes a day of mindfulness can help you reach a place of calm detachment from problems that could cause you to feel hurt, furious, or defeated. Read more about mindfulness for treating

ADHD in Chapter 9. A wonderful resource for helping adults with ADHD build and maintain a daily mindfulness practice can be found in Lidia Zylowska's book *Mindfulness for Adult ADHD*.[4]

If you have difficulty following a daily mindfulness routine, look for an "accountability partner" online. As mentioned earlier, Focusmate is an easy service through which to find a partner to help you follow through on your commitments to yourself. It's entirely free if you use it three times per week or less and is available at a very modest monthly cost if you want to use it more often.

Bottom line, with or without a coach or a therapist, making significant life changes is up to you. Medication can increase your ability to focus, helping you be more aware of your behaviors throughout the day, but learning to manage the problematic aspects of your ADHD is always a work in progress. Your goal is not to try to become someone without ADHD; your ongoing goal is to make changes in those behaviors and habits that are having a negative impact upon you and those close to you.

As I discuss more in Chapter 11, on marriage, keep in mind that being the partner with ADHD doesn't mean that you need to be "fixed" while your non-ADHD partner sets the standards. Remember, many positive traits associated with ADHD may bring value to your life and to your relationships—such traits as being creative, being a risk-taker, being able to hyper-focus, being lively, being fun, and living in the moment. As several adults with ADHD have humorously remarked, "I'm a human being, not a human doing!" Your goals are to learn to change patterns that get in *your* way, not to always try to live up to the arbitrary standards of others.

KEY TAKEAWAYS FROM THIS CHAPTER

Treatment from a professional with expertise in ADHD is not the only way to manage your ADHD. Some approaches that you can work on at home or with a fellow ADHD partner include the following:

✔ Educate yourself by reading about ADHD or listening to legitimate podcasts or YouTube recordings.

✔ Look for support groups—either in person or online.

✔ Set reasonable goals for yourself.

✔ Look for structure and support from friends and family.

✔ Learn to problem-solve.

✔ Build brain-healthy habits (more about this in Chapter 9).

Working with an ADHD Coach

Learn strategies to make better decisions, build habits, and change behaviors

There is tremendous value in ADHD coaching. One coach[1] described coaching as the "missing link" between your desire for change and achieving successful change. A study in the Netherlands interviewed a group of adults who had opted for coaching over psychotherapy. These adults had to pay out of pocket for coaching, even though mental health services were available to them at no cost. They explained that they appreciated the optimistic, strength-based, solution-focused approach used in coaching. In contrast, they found that mental health care focused on deficits and symptoms. Instead of feeling like a "patient" with a "diagnosis," they felt that they were partners with their coach in gaining a better understanding of how to approach life and deal with future problems.[2]

Most coaching takes place by phone or video connections in a one-on-one format. At my center (https://chesapeakeadd.com), we also offer group coaching where group members focus on a particular set of challenges. For example, one of our coaching groups for college students focuses on study and organizational skills; another, on daily life management skills for adults; and yet another group teaches participants ADHD-friendly ways to build a healthier relationship with food. One group treatment approach that was studied focused on organization and time management skills and was found to be very helpful to the adults who participated. The group approach offers support as well as the opportunity to use other group members as models as you work to make changes in your daily life. Furthermore, in a group setting coaching is more affordable.[3]

A growing body of research documents the efficacy of coaching. The great majority of that research has focused on college students' academic performance.[4] As the field expands to coaching adults with ADHD in life skills, its extension to older adults with ADHD is growing.[5] There is some emphasis on the cross-training of therapists as coaches so that they can conduct both sorts of interventions, as appropriate, during the course of treatment.[6] While we have a staff of coaches at my center, I also strongly encourage all our therapists to learn coaching techniques and to incorporate them into the ongoing therapy. If you can find a therapist also trained in life coaching or ADHD coaching, you have most likely found someone who can attend to all your needs as an older adult with ADHD.

Cost and Affordability of Coaching and Other Services

Typically, coaching costs less per hour than psychotherapy, often 50 percent less, although coaching fees vary significantly from one geographic area to another and from one provider to another. The downside of paying for coaching is that it is not covered by health insurance and is an out-of-pocket expense.

CHADD (https://chadd.org) has published an online article about many different routes to finding low-cost or no-cost services—see Appendix D (page 314).

When You Are Ready to Take Action but Aren't Sure How

Many older adults with ADHD are living alone and have never had the benefit of learning how to manage their ADHD challenges. And while it may seem that life gets easier after kids are raised and work life is finished, many other challenges often lie ahead—including poor health and limited finances. Here are a few comments made by some of the adults I interviewed:

"Now that I'm retired, life is unstructured. It's all up to me."

"I don't get out enough during the day. Loneliness pervades my life, but I don't want the upheaval of a relationship."

"I had to retire due to my tardiness and disorganization."

"I'm sometimes up to two or three at night and then I crash, fully clothed."

"My eating is sporadic. Today, I've had nothing to eat."

"I can't get myself to do paperwork, taxes, or chores—when I wake up, I just hit the computer and try to stay in touch with friends that way."

The First Step Is Figuring Out Whom You Should Work With

Should I Work with a Coach or a Therapist?

There is overlap between how ADHD therapists and ADHD coaches approach work with their clients. Good ADHD therapists incorporate coaching techniques into therapy. And good ADHD coaches certainly incorporate psychoeducation to teach their clients about ADHD—including an assessment of what emotional issues may be getting in the way of change. In general, however, there are many aspects of ADHD that coaches are not trained to address, such as emotional regulation, family relations, self-esteem issues, and co-occurring psychiatric conditions. Some people with ADHD work with both a therapist and a coach, but for most older adults with ADHD, this team approach is cost prohibitive. The information that follows is meant to help you decide which path is best for you.

Advantages of working with a coach:

- An ADHD coach is typically much easier to find than a therapist who specializes in ADHD.
- Coaches can legally coach anyone anywhere, whereas psychologists, psychiatrists, clinical social workers, and counselors are restricted to working only with clients who live in the state(s) in which they are licensed.

Advantages of working with a therapist:

- Your therapist is trained to treat your ADHD as well as the multiple issues and psychiatric diagnoses that can accompany ADHD.
- Your therapist can combine a focus on emotional and relational issues, so common when you have ADHD, with a coaching approach to help you problem-solve and build constructive habits.
- Therapy is covered by many health insurance policies.

A therapist is going to be more helpful if any of these situations apply to you:

- Feeling socially isolated and/or having social difficulties
- Feeling depressed and demoralized
- Experiencing anxiety
- Binge eating or overeating
- Sleeping poorly
- Feeling badly about yourself

- Being unable to make decisions or making poor decisions impulsively

- Experiencing conflicted family relationships

An ADHD coach is the better choice if the following statements describe you:

- Generally feel well emotionally

- Are not hampered by significant relationship issues, such as a recent separation or divorce or a conflictual marriage

- Have a supportive social network

- Specifically want to focus on improving executive functioning skills, such as organization, time management, and creating routines and completing tasks that are challenging for you

How Does a Coach Help?

An ADHD coach can provide assistance in several areas:

- Structure
- Support
- Accountability
- Collaboration
- Solutions

Structure

Structure is provided through regular coaching sessions that help you focus on the challenges that most interfere with your goals. In some cases, more structure is needed and a coach might meet with you twice a week for a half hour each time rather than weekly for one hour. Structure is also sometimes provided by your coach through email or text reminders between coaching sessions, to help you stay on track as you work to try new approaches or build new habits.

Support

Support is provided by your coach through their understanding and encouragement. They have experience in successfully helping others who had your same struggles, and can give you a more positive outlook when you feel you are failing. They can help you measure your progress using a more reasonable yardstick.

Accountability

Whether or not you have ADHD, you are more likely to build a new habit or skill if you are accountable to someone as you practice and work toward your goal. Whether we are trying to prepare for a marathon, to learn a foreign language, or to change the way we eat so that we are healthier, we all do better if there is someone at our side—an athletic coach, a dietitian, a tutor—who we are accountable to and meet with regularly. You and your coach together can decide how often you should report on your progress.

Collaboration

A coach isn't going to *tell* you what to do. A good coach is going to talk with you about what you've tried in the past and help you understand what has gotten in the way of reaching your goal. The two of you will problem-solve together.

Solutions

While the problem-solving is collaborative, your coach has the advantage of having worked with numerous people who also have ADHD, and therefore is familiar with a broader range of possible solutions that you may not be aware of.

Working with a Coach Can Be Life Transforming

If you experience memory problems, such as forgetting what you've been told, and suffer from limitations in your ability to make good decisions and maintain order in your daily life, these challenges have a profound negative consequence for all the important aspects of a functional and satisfying life.

Cognitive and executive functioning is still often overlooked by psychiatrists,[7] but when they are not addressed, your treatment will be less effective in helping you achieve a connected and productive life. Even if you have functioned pretty well throughout your life, you can still face significant challenges in managing your daily life in your later years. This is another reason that working with a coach can be so helpful.

Finding a Coach Who Works with Older Adults

No ADHD coach training program focuses specifically on older adults. There are "retirement coaches" who help people through that transition and "elder coaches" who support adult children in caring for aging parents, but none of these coaches specialize in the challenges of ADHD in later years. When interviewing a coach with whom you may want to work, the primary questions to ask are these:

- Do you have significant experience working with adult ADHD?
- Have you ever worked with older ADHD adults?
- Can you describe to me the sorts of issues that you have focused on when coaching older adults?

Make sure that they have experience helping adults with your most challenging issues. It's also critical to ask yourself during this initial interview, "Do I feel comfortable with this person? Do they understand my challenges? Are they easy to talk to?"

Are There Times When a Coach Should Refer You to a Therapist?

For coaching to work, you need to be ready for active problem-solving and action. If you are "ready" to create routines and build habits and receive the right level of support from your coach, you should see steady progress. When you are stalled and something is clearly getting in the way of making changes, it may be time for your coach to refer you to a therapist to focus on deeper issues that may be obstructing your progress. For example, if you have recently lost your spouse, you may need to work through your grief and loss before you are ready to productively work with a coach. Other reasons to work with a counselor or therapist include if you are struggling with a decision about whether to move away from family to a more affordable retirement community and can't seem to move forward; when your low motivation may be related to depression; when your poor diet and household clutter are related to depression; or when your social anxiety keeps you socially isolated.

Here is a story that illustrates the different roles of therapists and coaches.

Louise, an older woman with ADHD, was working with a coach to support her through the major life transition of selling the home she had lived in for many years. She had lost her husband the year before and was feeling financial pressure from the costly upkeep of her family home. Her adult children had very different opinions about what she should do. Her son strongly objected to her selling the home he had grown up in. He imagined that, in a few years, he could afford to buy the house from his mother to keep it in the family and provide more room for his growing family. Her daughter, on the other hand, saw how difficult it was for her mother to take care of the house maintenance, much of which had been done by her father before his death. The daughter strongly believed that it was time to sell the house. In addition, Louise felt overwhelmed by loss and grief. Every time she started to clear things out, the memories came flooding in. She decided that a coach might help her to organize and sort through things more efficiently. However, after a few coaching sessions, it became clear that Louise was not ready for coaching. Despite her best intentions, she had made little progress in sorting out her lifetime's worth of belongings. Her coach talked to her about readiness for coaching, which emphasized taking action. It seemed clear to her coach that Louise wasn't ready to make decisions and would benefit from psychotherapy to process her grief after losing her husband, to communicate her needs more clearly to her adult children, and to make a decision that was right for her regarding the sale of her house.

Louise worked with a psychotherapist who included her adult children in some of the sessions. A few months later, she was clearer about her own needs and better prepared to advocate for herself when speaking with her son. In therapy, Louise came to realize that her son wanted to hang on to the family home because it was a way to hold on to the father he had lost.

Having made peace with her own loss, she was then able to communicate sympathetically with her son, who gradually came to realize that it was best for his mother to sell the house. Louise made the decision to put the house on the market, and contacted her coach again for support in discarding and downsizing. This time, she was ready and her coaching proved to be a great help.

Issues That Can Be Addressed with a Coach

As with many other things related to ADHD, a coach can really help with some issues specific to older adults.

Drowning in e-Communication

If you were born in the middle of the twentieth century, you didn't grow up in a digital world. Many older adults find technology to be overwhelming and don't have good systems to manage technology as an older adult. I offer a colorful illustration of that overwhelm: I emailed an older woman with ADHD and received this auto-response: *"Please phone or text me to let me know you emailed me—I am too far behind on my email and have given up checking it for the month of June."* Her citing a specific month notwithstanding, I received that message nine months after she created her auto-response! Clearly, she was still drowning in emails nine months later. Her well-intended but ineffective effort to get back on track reflects the utter overwhelm that many older ADHD adults experience.

Life keeps coming at us, fast and furious in this digital age. Today, we receive more communications in a year than our grandparents received in a lifetime. Between emails and social media, keeping up can consume a major portion of every day. When you have ADHD, it becomes so overwhelming that there is a tendency to give up and shut down, like the woman quoted here. And very important emails can become lost amid the flood of spam and irrelevant emails. Ease of communication is both a blessing and a curse. It's important to find a middle ground between spending major portions of the day trying to keep up versus simply shutting down and being out of communication.

One man with ADHD told me that he had over ten thousand unopened emails in his inbox, and so he simply gave up and closed his email account. Many women tell me that they are up late into the night, compulsively checking the Facebook postings of friends and relatives. It's critical to find a middle ground—a way for important people in your life to communicate with you while not allowing digital communications to rule your life. One woman created a new email account and told only a select few friends and relatives of its existence. A man with ADHD closed his email account with glee and great relief, creating an auto-response saying that if the emailer really wanted to get in touch, to call him, reverting to the old-fashioned way of staying in touch. A coach who is up to date with the world of technology can help you find systems to reduce your technology overwhelm.

Buried in Stuff

I'm going to share with you several stories of older ADHD adults who found themselves overwhelmed by their belongings. Recent research has demonstrated that "hoarding disorder," an official psychiatric diagnosis, and ADHD are commonly found together, with about one in five ADHD adults also struggling with hoarding disorder. We used to believe that hoarding behavior was a form of obsessive-compulsive disorder (OCD), but it is now understood as a separate disorder and one commonly associated with inattentive ADHD.[8] *Hoarding* is defined as excessively acquiring things, living in a state of clutter that interferes with daily life, and difficulty discarding belongings.

However, even if you aren't one of those adults with ADHD who also has hoarding disorder, you may still have tremendous difficulty organizing, managing, and decluttering your home environment.

Vince, an older man with ADHD, contacted me, asking for help, and told me with desperation in his voice that he wanted to sell his house and downsize, but feared that he would be stuck in his house until he died. He explained that his wife had eventually left him, in large part due to his chaotic collection of items that grew over the years and took over the house and yard. He had been living alone for a number of years, with the chaos increasing year by year. He was eventually rescued from his plight by working with a professional organizer. The organizer helped him to tag those furniture items and other belongings that could reasonably fit into a two-bedroom condo. Then, a junk hauler was called to clear out the house, donating what could be of use and taking the rest to the local landfill. Vince had to leave the premises while all this was going on, as he realized that he would be chasing the truck down the street trying to retrieve belongings that he didn't need but felt attached to.

Steve was an aging scientist who had lived alone for many years following a divorce. His only child, a middle-aged son, was called by the property manager of his father's apartment, who told him that if he didn't come to help his father dig out the apartment, the manager would be forced to call the health department and evict Steve. The apartment was filled with paper—books, journals, and loose papers—that he had accumulated over a long career. Steve had never mentally made this shift to online digital resources. He saw all his papers as an extension of himself and an archive of his professional career and could not be convinced to off-load any of them. His son arrived, feeling great frustration, to deal with the situation. Like Vince, Steve decided to move to a new apartment and start over, with the help of a very hands-on, supportive professional organizer. The chaos that Steve's son had to deal with led to a rupture in their relationship, making him feel more alone than ever.

And then there was Marcy, who had lived in the same older and no-longer-charming home, in the inner suburbs of a large city, which she had purchased when her sons, now in their thirties, were preschoolers. Her marriage had faltered and she raised her sons as a working single parent, trying as hard as she could to take care of their needs, cooking, driving them to their ball games and music practices, but never having the time or money to keep up the house. Now, in retirement, she imagined she would have plenty of time to organize her home. No matter how hard she tried, however, the mess only seemed to grow. She would haul all the items out of one upstairs bedroom, creating even greater chaos in the adjacent rooms, and then become overwhelmed, not knowing what to do. One of her sons came home for a visit and was appalled and worried by what he found. He worked for days, trying to help his mother off-load decades of belongings that she no longer used or needed, and resolved to return in a few weeks' time to help her finish the job.

In each case, Vince, Steve, and Marcy had been able to manage their professional lives, but their "bandwidth" had been taken up with work, leaving little energy or desire to manage their home environment. There was no time for planning, organizing, off-loading, and rearranging. And when they finally faced the mountain of accumulated belongings, the task was insurmountable. What's important to understand is that none of these three was a "hoarder" in the classic sense of the word. They had not engaged in compulsive acquisition; they weren't intensely attached to their belongings, unable to let go. They simply hadn't managed to make the thousands of decisions required to get rid of unused items over the years to maintain an orderly home.

Many coaches also function as professional organizers. Professional organizing is usually a hands-on process where the organizer comes to your home to help you sort through and organize your belongings. Some are specialists in working with older adults who are downsizing in preparation for a move to a smaller retirement home.

Clutter and Disorder

In the preceding section, I wrote about being "buried in stuff," as an older adult with ADHD. This pattern is typically related to being unable to let go of things as well as to avoiding the decisions required to off-load accumulated belongings.

In this section, I write about a different but related pattern—daily clutter and disorder. As an example of the difference, I'll share a story of a woman who struggled with both patterns—hanging on to countless unused items and with a pattern of creating clutter wherever she went.

> *Harriet and her husband had collected belongings, papers, you name it, for decades and had long ago run out of storage space. In her late fifties, Harriet decided to take some graduate courses and was up against a deadline to turn in a paper. She decided to move into a motel room for a few days so that she wouldn't be distracted by all of the clutter in her home. In her next therapy session with me, she reported that she had taken her computer, papers, books, and clothing to the neat and tidy motel room and, within the course of an hour, she had re-created the cluttered and chaotic environment she had tried to escape by leaving home for a few days.*

In other words, you can be "buried in stuff" stored in the basement, the attic, closets, or even an off-site storage unit, while your living environment is relatively orderly. In contrast, this section has to do with the daily creation of clutter—newspapers left on the floor beside your chair; cups and glasses strewn around the house; mail dropped unopened on the hall table; clothing tossed on chairs and railings; dirty dishes, pots, and pans left on the counter; shoes kicked off and left where they dropped; and packages brought into the house but not put away.

There are numerous studies that show we don't function well when we are living in a chaotic environment. In 2011, researchers using functional magnetic resonance imaging (fMRI)—a type of brain scan done while the person is performing a task— found that clearing away clutter resulted in better focus and greater

> Decluttering your environment can "declutter" your mind.

ease in processing information, and improved working memory (the number of things that we can keep in mind without writing them down). Problems with focus, processing speed, and working memory are all negatively impacted by ADHD. In addition, those with ADHD typically have difficulty maintaining order in their environment, which gives them a double dose of ADHD—the first dose resulting from their ADHD brain, and the second resulting from the distracting clutter of their environment.[9] Clutter can even trigger unhealthy eating patterns! One research project placed undergraduate females in either an orderly or a chaotic kitchen environment and found that those in the chaotic kitchen made more poor food choices, especially overeating sweets.[10]

A visually, physically cluttered environment negatively impacts your ability to focus, to process information, to make good decisions, and to readily recall information that you want to keep in mind. So, if one of your goals in managing your ADHD is to be more focused and productive and able to accomplish things you'd like to do in retirement, then a messy, cluttered environment may be one of the most important things to tackle to help you get down to the tasks that are meaningful to you. A coach can help with this.

> Disorder is the product of postponed actions and decisions.

When faced with the question "Should I keep this or get rid of it?" the default decision, the easiest decision, is to keep it. And when that default decision is made countless times over decades, an older adult with ADHD is left with a mountain of clutter at a time in their life when they have lower energy and when they may have strength and mobility challenges as well as health problems.

If this is your situation, a coach can help you develop new habits that can prevent you from accumulating even more clutter and can allow you to gradually create order in your home. A coach can teach you that creating order is a constant, daily process rather than a single huge project. In my book *ADD-Friendly Ways to Organize Your*

Life,[11] I advise adults with ADHD to "think like a restaurant server." Instead of allowing a big mess to accumulate and then engaging in a big cleanup project, restaurant servers are constantly in the process of making a mess and then cleaning it up, walking across the restaurant picking up items as they go to put them back where they belong.

Overwhelmed by Medical Claims and Costs

If you have ADHD as an older adult, you may also be in poor health. The typical seventy-year-old has multiple physicians, takes multiple medications, and may have undergone surgery or is anticipating surgery. The US medical system is anything but simple, and your primary care physician may not have time to take on the role of case manager as you navigate treatment by various providers and struggle with the complex insurance system that involves both Medicare and secondary insurance coverage.

Tracking appointments, medications, insurance claims, and medical bill payments can become more than many older adults with ADHD can manage. If this is your situation, be sure to ask coaches that you interview whether they can help you develop simple systems to keep up with it all.

Managing Finances

Although many of the adults that I interviewed were financially stable and prepared for retirement, in almost all instances, their financial stability was due to the earning power and money management skills of their non-ADHD partner. It's important to note that being financially comfortable is the exception, the privilege of higher-functioning older adults who married someone who took their financial stress off their shoulders.

A more common reality is the situation of one man I interviewed who told me, "I'll have to work until I drop." The majority of adults with ADHD have experienced underemployment and unemployment over the course of their working years. And many didn't have the consistent self-discipline to save for the future rather than spending in the moment.

An ADHD coach can help you become more aware of and begin to change spending patterns and financial decisions that keep you constantly feeling stressed over financial concerns.

When Our Time Is "Cluttered" with Distractions

A cluttered environment negatively impacts our brain functions. The same is true for "cluttering" our time by living in a "reactive" rather than a "proactive" way. In "reactive mode," we are distracted by whatever catches our attention. We see something, pick it up to take it where it belongs, and then, when we get to another room, we become distracted by something we see there, and never get back to our initial task. Our time is "cluttered" by distractions that we react to. We think of something we meant to order online, and in the blink of an eye, we have become distracted and a five-minute task becomes two hours or more of wandering the internet "window shopping," or worse, actually shopping. We allow our days to become "cluttered" with random tasks that distract us from a more important task.

"If I don't do it now, I'll forget it!" This is the refrain that I hear so often from adults with ADHD. The reason they meander from one task to another in no particular order is that when something occurs to them, they feel compelled to do it immediately for fear that they will forget it if they wait until later. There are numerous satirical accounts of the ADHD brain in action. The following is an actual account by an older woman with ADHD.

"I told myself that this was the day that I was going to gather all of my tax papers for the accountant. I'd been putting it off for weeks, but now was the time! I knew I'd need a cup of coffee to

*help me focus, so I went into the kitchen to make myself a cup.
When I dumped the old filter full of coffee grounds in the trash,
I realized that the kitchen trash can was full. I quickly pulled out
the bag to take it to the trash can outside, when I noticed that all
of my neighbors' trash cans were at the curb, ready for pickup. I
rushed to pull my cans out to the street just in time for the trash
truck, when I ran into a neighbor who asked me whether I would
like to have some of the ferns she was thinning out in her garden. I
love ferns and didn't want to pass up the opportunity, so I walked
to her yard to gather the ferns, bringing them back into my yard.
Well, I couldn't leave them to dry out or they wouldn't last until
I could plant them, so I went back into the garage to gather some
newspapers from the recycle bin to wrap the ferns in, planning to
moisten the newspapers to keep the ferns fresh when I suddenly
realized that I should have taken the recycle bins to the street too.
I rushed them out too late for the recycling truck and ran into a
friend walking her dog. She invited me to join her. It was such
a nice day. How could I say no? I wanted to get more exercise. I
went inside to grab my sneakers, put my dog on a leash, and joined
her. Half an hour later, I was back at my house and walked in the
kitchen door when the phone rang. I answered the call, which was
from a member of the homeowners' association reminding me that
I had not paid my homeowner dues. I profusely apologized and
went immediately to my desk to write a check, telling myself that I
would put the check in an envelope and take it to the mailbox—no
more procrastinating! However, my checkbook had no checks in
it, so I started sorting through the drawers of my desk, looking
for more checks, when I came across the charging cable for my
smartphone that I had been looking for everywhere. I grabbed
it and went to look for my phone. I began to feel hungry and
glanced at my watch. It was lunchtime. I went into the kitchen
and noticed the coffeepot, still open, with no new coffee filter. I had
been running since the moment when I had dumped the old coffee*

grounds and had never made that cup of coffee I had so badly needed three hours earlier to help me focus on organizing my tax papers. Oh well, maybe after lunch."

Do your days go like this? It's exhausting to stay in reactive mode. This woman had been rushing around all morning, didn't plant the ferns, didn't pay the overdue bill, never got her cup of coffee, certainly didn't organize her tax papers. Who knows how long it took her to find her smartphone. Her time is "cluttered," making it almost impossible for her to focus on her original, very important task— organizing her tax papers. If this is you, a coach can work with you to recognize your reactive impulsivity and get back on track after a distraction or interruption.

Mail and Paperwork

Just as digital communications can create a huge pileup for older adults, so can paper communications. A coach can help you develop the habit of dealing with your mail as it is delivered—putting junk mail directly into the recycle bin and taking important paperwork to your work area—a home office or a desk in your living area—where you deal with items that require immediate action and file papers that need to be saved.

Habit-Building to Streamline Your Daily Routines

One woman I interviewed jokingly remarked, *"If it weren't for bad habits, I wouldn't have any habits at all."* Building habits is a core element of taking charge of your daily life so that you meet your goals. Habits have everything to do with feeling calm, reducing stress, taking good care of yourself, and reaching your goals.

Here are a few common ADHD habits that may be getting in your way:

STILL DISTRACTED AFTER ALL THESE YEARS

- Impulsive spending
- Not putting things away after you use them
- Not having a place where things belong
- Not having a regular bedtime
- Not getting regular exercise
- Not keeping in touch with friends and family
- Not planning meals
- Not getting outside each day
- Taking on too many projects and not completing them
- Not planning times to accomplish important tasks

You get the idea. Bad habits lead directly to feelings of overwhelm and to poor health through unhealthy eating habits, lack of exercise, poor sleep habits, and chronic stress.

Habit Development

Habit development is one of the most important things to work on with a coach or therapist. Multiple books have been written on habit development. One of my favorites is *Atomic Habits* by James Clear.[12] His book can guide you through successful habit building, by not taking on too many things at a time and by not setting yourself up for failure with unreasonable goals. Another is *Tiny Habits* by BJ Fogg.[13]

> Your coach can guide you as you learn to:
> - Make new desirable habits easier to do
> - Make old unwanted habits harder to do

So many adults I spoke with lamented their inability to accomplish things that they want to do—planning, getting started, and following a task through to completion. This can be very difficult for adults with ADHD because it's so easy to be interrupted or be distracted by something and then forget to come back to your task to complete it.

> *"When I was raising my kids, I never had time for my art. I always thought I would get back to it when I had more time. Now, I'm retired, but I'm still not doing art. Instead, I'm just doing random tasks, going on social media or surfing the internet."*

> *"I always thought I would like to learn a foreign language and then live abroad for a while. All those years when I felt tied down to my work, I dreamed of learning Spanish, maybe going to a language immersion program and then living somewhere in Latin America where the cost of living is much lower. Instead, I just seem to stay stuck in my rut. I'm not even sure what I spend my time doing, but it's sure not spent learning Spanish. I bought a computer program to help me learn Spanish and I've only used it a few times."*

In the end, the goal of coaching is not simply to focus on "tidying up" your life. The goal of coaching is to clear the path so that you can accomplish things you've always dreamed of doing.

ADHD coaching has matured as a profession over the past twenty-five years, with extensive training and credentialing. But because it is not a profession that requires licensure, anyone can hang out a shingle and call themselves a coach. It's important to do your homework and learn about the training and certifications of any coach that you consider working with. In Appendix C (pages 311–313), I have provided the names of a few organizations that offer ADHD coach training that are well established and highly regarded. You can look on these sites to find qualified ADHD coaches.

KEY TAKEAWAYS FROM THIS CHAPTER

✔ Coaching is helpful when you are ready to take action but aren't sure how.

✔ Coaching focuses on the practical aspects of daily life—managing your time, your tasks, and your belongings.

✔ Coaching can provide accountability, structure, and support.

✔ Coaching can help you when you are struggling with

- Email

- Paperwork

- Habit development

✔ Coaching can help you get on track to accomplish the things you've dreamed of but not yet accomplished.

Brain-Healthy Daily Habits

Lifestyle changes to improve daily functioning and overall life satisfaction

ADHD is genetic; it runs in families. There is no single "ADHD gene." Multiple genes are involved in the transmission of ADHD from one generation to the next.[1] We can't do anything about the genes we inherit, but the field of epigenetics is teaching us that you can change the ways that your genes work by making changes in your behavior and your environment. This chapter focuses on lifestyle choices that, for good or for bad, play a powerful role in determining your longevity, daily functioning, and overall life satisfaction.

Is It Too Late to Make Effective Lifestyle Changes?

If you are an older adult with ADHD, you may wonder whether lifestyle changes at your age can really make a difference. You may believe that it's impossible to make those changes at your stage in life, especially because ADHD makes healthy lifestyle choices more difficult. Russell Barkley, a preeminent ADHD authority, writes that ADHD is associated with what he terms "low conscientiousness"; that is, that people with ADHD are more likely to do what appeals to them at the moment than doing what they know is good for them in the long run.

This chapter will focus on ADHD-friendly ways to begin to build a more brain-healthy lifestyle. And you don't have to be perfect for the changes you make to have a powerful positive effect upon your daily functioning and well-being.

What the Research Says about ADHD and Unhealthy Lifestyle

Several studies show that those with ADHD are at greater risk for the following:

- Become addicted to cigarettes and have greater difficulty quitting[2]
- Eat fast food and junk food[3]
- Abuse alcohol and other substances[4]
- Avoid regular exercise[5]
- Experience unhealthy sleep habits[6]
- Become socially isolated[7]
- Be overweight or obese[8]
- Develop type 2 diabetes[9]

And all these unhealthy lifestyle choices can have a cascading effect on older adults, causing struggles with depression,[10] demoralization, and high levels of chronic stress.[11]

The impact of unhealthy lifestyle choices made by adults with ADHD is huge. Russell Barkley found that the average life span of an adult with ADHD is *significantly* shorter on average—11.7 years shorter for those with hyperactive/impulsive ADHD and 8 years shorter for those with inattentive ADHD.[12] Accidental death and suicide both play a role[13] in a shorter life span of adults with ADHD, but an unhealthy lifestyle is a major factor, in terms both of life span and in quality of life as we grow older.

Now for the Good News

To offset Dr. Barkley's bleak news, Dale Bredesen, a leader in the field of geriatric medicine, offers some very encouraging findings demonstrating that older adults *can* make changes that dramatically improve their cognitive functioning and overall quality of life.[14] Currently, his research is being replicated at the National Institutes of Health (NIH) in an exciting project called the ReCODE project. (ReCODE = **Rever**sal of **CO**gnitive **DE**cline).[15] The groundbreaking news that cognitive decline in old age is reversible is only just beginning to reach the ADHD community.

Dr. Bredesen studied older adults whose cognitive functioning had significantly deteriorated. All the adults in his pilot study had reached the point where they had to retire early or were having difficulty functioning in their daily lives. Once he prescribed a range of healthy daily habits to them, over the course of the next two years almost all of them began to greatly improve in cognitive functioning, some even returning to work, while others were feeling and functioning much better.

What's important to understand is that perfection is not required. The improvement reported by Dr. Bredesen occurred even though none of the people in his study completely followed his recommendations about sleep, diet, exercise, brain training, and nutritional supplements.

Dr. Bredesen's approach involves working with a coach with whom you

> You don't have to follow healthy daily habits perfectly to achieve a real benefit.

check in regularly to help keep you on track as you change your daily habits. Remember the idea of "structure and support" that I introduced in the previous chapter? Dr. Bredesen discovered that all older adults needed the support of a coach to be more successful at making the significant lifestyle changes that he prescribed. For more information about Dr. Bredesen's approach, go to https://www.apollohealthco.com/dr-bredesen/.

Although Dr. Bredesen's program was designed to improve the cognitive functioning of older adults with cognitive decline, his recommendations apply to everyone who experiences challenges to cognitive functioning. If you are an older adult with ADHD, following brain-healthy daily habits will have a positive impact both on your ADHD and on any age-related cognitive decline.

Stimulant Medication May Help You Build Brain-Healthy Daily Habits

While having the support of a coach or psychotherapist is ideal when you are working to develop brain-healthy habits, taking stimulant medication may help as well. Stimulants can improve your focus and reduce impulsivity, so that you are more likely to succeed in building and maintaining brain-healthy daily habits. Because stimulant medication reduces impulsivity, it therefore can help control impulsive eating and binge eating. In fact, Vyvanse, a long-acting stimulant, has been FDA approved for the treatment of binge eating disorder.[16] Research indicates that stimulants can also help improve sleep patterns in adults with ADHD.[17]

Getting Started in Building Brain-Healthy Habits

Habit building can be very difficult for those with ADHD. As I wrote about at length in Chapter 8, adults with ADHD are much more likely to achieve lasting behavior changes if they have adequate structure and support as they are working to make those changes. Furthermore, working with an ADHD coach will help an adult guard against attempting to make too radical a change or too many changes at the same time. Impatience and a tendency to underestimate the challenges of achieving a new goal can be self-defeating patterns. One woman I spoke to purchased a popular health book, glanced through it, and concluded, *"It's impossible to do what he recommends."* She moved from an interest in changing unhealthy behaviors to an immediate feeling of defeat and hopelessness without ever taking the first step. Don't let this happen to you. As I introduce brain-healthy daily habits, I want to remind you of several things:

- **E.A.S.T. is least successful (E.A.S.T. = Everything at the Same Time).** I am going to suggest many lifestyle changes that can positively impact your quality of life and reduce the impact of ADHD, but it's important to prioritize and build brain-healthy habits one at a time. Don't set yourself up for failure by trying to do too much too soon.

- **Watch out for black-and-white thinking.** If you take an "all-or-nothing" approach to dietary changes or exercise, for example, you'll set yourself up for failure. Habits are built gradually, and there inevitably will be backsliding. Knowing and accepting that your efforts will be imperfect will help you move on from your inevitable slipups and keep you on the path toward improvement.

Prioritize which brain-healthy habit you want to work on first. Ask yourself what is having the most negative impact on your quality of life. Are poor sleep patterns making you feel tired every day? Is social isolation making you feel down? Pick one and work on it for a while before you try to add another brain-healthy habit to your routine.

MENDSS is an acronym I created to help you remember the brain-healthy daily habits I introduce in this chapter. **MENDSS** stands for:

M = Mindfulness/Mindfulness Meditation/Stress Reduction
E = Exercise
N = Nature
D = Diet
S = Sleep
S = Social connections

MENDSS
Brain-healthy habits to "mend" your mind and body

Each MENDSS habit has its own section in the following pages. Feel free to scan through to pick the MENDSS habit that you want to focus on first.

M MINDFULNESS/MINDFULNESS MEDITATION/ STRESS REDUCTION

Mindfulness and mindfulness meditation are different but related, and both can be very helpful in reducing stress and increasing your ability to focus.

Mindfulness is a specific way of living as you go about your day. It involves slowing down, paying careful attention to your sensations (what you feel, hear, see, smell, taste), and being mindful of what is happening and fully engaging in it, while suspending judgment about the experience—just noticing what is.

Mindfulness moments can be engaged in throughout your day. Some with ADHD have told me that although they experienced difficulty in developing a daily practice of mindfulness meditation, they found that it was very helpful to build mindful moments into their daily activities. Times when you may feel restless or impatient, such as waiting in line or stopping at a traffic signal, are perfect situations to practice mindfulness moments. Instead of tapping on your steering wheel impatiently, wondering how long the red light will last, try using every stoplight as a signal to start slow, deep breathing while paying close attention to your breath. You may surprise yourself and find that stoplights become moments to relax and feel calmer! We can engage in mindful eating, mindful conversation (allowing you to focus on what the other person is saying, rather than leaping ahead to what you want to say next), even mindful laundry folding.

Mindfulness meditation is related to mindfulness. It is a more serious and focused "practice" of mindfulness whereby you sit for a designated period of time, focused on one thing (an object in your view, your breath), and repeatedly bringing yourself back to that single focus when your attention wanders. It is a powerful tool to help you feel less stressed by your daily life challenges and also a tool to strengthen your ability to intentionally focus. Dr. Lidia Zylowska, in her book *The Mindfulness Prescription for Adult ADHD*,[18] outlines her treatment program for adults with ADHD based entirely on mindfulness meditation. Daniel Siegel, MD, an internationally recognized authority on the mind–body connection, writes this in his foreword to Dr. Zylowska's book:

> The way you focus your mind can actually change the structure of your brain. No kidding. By taking the practical steps in this book you can strengthen the connections in your brain that support a more focused way of living...When you learn a practice like being mindfully aware, you activate and then strengthen the executive circuits of the brain responsible for such things as attention, regulating emotions, being flexible in your responses, insightful, empathic, and even being wise.[19]

Many people with ADHD believe that they are unable to practice mindfulness meditation. *"I couldn't stand it,"* one of my clients said to me. *"Just sitting there, doing nothing, and trying to keep your mind from wandering? That would drive me crazy!"* The ability to sit and meditate mindfully comes with practice. But for those who find it especially difficult to sit still for a period of time, there are other approaches that may be more ADHD-friendly. One technique is to practice mindfulness meditation in motion by walking while focusing your attention on a single thing, such as your breath, or the sensation of taking each step, and repeatedly bringing your attention back to your breath as it inevitably wanders. Other people with ADHD have reported to me that it is easier for them to mindfully meditate while taking a long hot shower. They find that the warm water relaxes them and allows them to meditate longer without feeling restless. It is the very act of repeatedly refocusing your attention after it wanders that helps you build your capacity for calm, extended focus.

The ADHD brain is often highly reactive, responding immediately and with little thought when we experience hurt, anger, or frustration. This reactivity makes us difficult to live with and can lead to the loss of friendships and the erosion of family relationships. Mindfulness meditation is a powerful antidote to emotional reactivity.

> Between stimulus and response there is a space.
> In that space is our power to choose our response.
> In our response lies our growth and our freedom.
> —*Attributed to Viktor Frankl*

Practicing mindfulness helps you create that space between stimulus (the events that upset you) and response (your reaction to upsetting events). Before you react, take a deep breath and relax! Mindfulness moments (focusing on slow, deep breathing at a traffic light, for example) can have very positive benefits; the same is true when you are annoyed or in conflict with a family member at home. Intentionally slowing down, focusing on your breath, and sending yourself compassionate messages can calm your brain so that you can respond to conflict in a calmer and more thoughtful manner. Mindfulness meditation has been shown in many studies to reduce stress levels and to increase your ability to focus.[20] If you find that you are not able to practice mindful meditation alone, you may benefit from the structure and support of an online or in-person mindfulness group.

Here are a few ADHD-friendly ways to build mindfulness into your day:

- Start your day with a few minutes of mindfulness. Stand up, stretch, look outside, and practice slow, deep mindful breathing to a count of fifty.

- Practice mindfulness whenever you are forced to wait during the day—whether standing in line or waiting at a traffic signal. Again, focus your eyes on something and take slow, intentional deep breaths until the line moves or the light changes.

- A few moments of mindfulness just before bed can set you up for a better night's sleep—just sit or stand, focus on an object, and take fifty slow, deliberate, mindful breaths.

E EXERCISE

Exercise is not only good for the body, especially the heart, but is also powerfully good for the brain. So good that some adults have "treated" their ADHD exclusively through vigorous exercise every day. More recent research has begun to study the cognitive benefits of exercise for older adults in a more nuanced way, comparing different categories of exercise: aerobic exercise, strength/resistance training, and motor training (exercise involving complex movement that requires motor learning, such as tai chi, pickleball, Ping-Pong, and so on).

Aerobic Exercise

For older adults, vigorous exercise may not be appropriate, but, as John Ratey, MD, writes in his book *Spark*,[21] as little as twenty minutes per day of aerobic exercise can prompt the brain to produce brain-derived neurotrophic factor (BDNF), which promotes the creation of new neurons, improves memory, and also promotes the growth of dendrites, those tiny filaments that connect neurons, connections that are created as we learn new things. What's more, very recent research suggests that the hormone irisin, produced by the body through aerobic exercise, improves cognitive functioning in the brain.[22] Bottom line: one of the best ways to preserve or even improve cognitive functioning is through aerobic exercise.

Dance

Dance has also been shown to be very good for the aging brain.[23] Recent research[24] has demonstrated that music and dancing are very health promoting on a number of levels simultaneously. Dance benefits our brain because it is aerobic in nature, improving overall cognitive functioning and increasing oxygen to the brain, while involving complex, coordinated movement, which has been shown to enhance more specific cognitive functions related to executive functioning. Square dancing, in particular, is good for our brain because it involves attention, memory, flexibility, balance, and aerobic movement. In addition, dance enhances our mental and emotional well-being because it involves social interaction.

Tai Chi

Like square dancing, tai chi requires learning complex movements. Sometimes it is described as "meditation in motion." Although I know of no research supporting tai chi as particularly suited to those with ADHD, my experience is that it is a much more ADHD-friendly form of meditation because tai chi doesn't require you to sit still and concentrate. Tai chi promotes improved global cognitive functions and memory, especially verbal working memory.[25] Just as important, research shows that the practice of tai chi lowers stress levels, reduces anxiety, and even has positive effects on depression.[26]

Strength/Resistance Training

There is much more research supporting the cognitive benefits of aerobic exercise (exercise that maintains an elevated heart rate for an extended period of time) and of "motor training" (forms of exercise that require more complex motor movements) than there is on the benefits of strength or resistance training. However, a recent review article reports some evidence that strength or resistance training can bring about significant changes in the brain's prefrontal lobes (one part of the brain that is affected by ADHD) that improve executive functioning (our ability to organize, plan, and accomplish our goals).[27]

Making Exercise ADHD-Friendly

The older adults that I interviewed, both those with ADHD and those without, told me that getting regular, daily exercise was one of their biggest struggles. They knew how important it was, but couldn't seem to get themselves to regularly exercise. So what can make exercise a more regular, more natural part of your day?

- **Grab a minute of movement here and there.** A woman with ADHD told me that she now no longer feels impatient while she is waiting—waiting for the microwave to heat up her lunch, waiting for the coffeemaker to produce her morning coffee—because that is her cue to exercise. *"I use these moments that occur many times a day to do my stretches and even strengthening exercises. By the end of the day, I've done quite a bit."*

- **Make it social.** Find a neighbor for a regular morning or evening walk. Making it social means that your walk improves in a couple of ways. First, you'll be more consistent because you don't want to let your friend down. And second, this is a great way to have a daily social interaction, the importance of which I'll write about later in this chapter.

- **Get a dog!** Another woman with ADHD told me that it's her dog that gets her out to walk twice a day. *"If it weren't for my dog, I would find countless reasons why I needed to do something other than go for a walk. But my dog reminds me, and although I might neglect myself, I'm not going to neglect my dog."* Her dog provided the reminders and structure she needed to keep going. If you can't have your own dog due to living arrangements or some other issue, apply the suggestion above: find a neighbor or friend with a dog and go on walks with them.

- **Set a low bar.** A little bit of consistent exercise each day is better than an hour of exercise once or twice a week. Check out several online videos that guide you through a brief sequence of yoga poses or quick aerobic exercise. Set up your laptop or phone in a place where you can comfortably exercise and then grab a few minutes a couple of times a day. Two of my favorite quick and easy routines are these:

- **The 7-minute workout:** https://www.nytimes.com/guides /well/activity/the-7-minute-workout
- **Yoga for neck, shoulders, and upper back:** 15 minutes on YouTube—this one has over ten million views, so they must be doing something right!

ADHD-friendly ways to build exercise into your day:

- Join in an already existing activity—line dancing, square dancing, pickleball, and so on. All you need to do is show up!
- Make it small—if you feel like continuing after your brief workout, all the better, but if you start with small goals, you'll be more likely to do it.
- Make it social.
- Make it regular.

N NATURE

Over the course of the past 150 years, as our society shifted from agriculture to manufacturing, the lives of most of us have become more and more removed from the natural environments in which human beings have always lived. Recent research indicates that exposure to nature can improve health and cognitive functioning.

Why "green breaks" are so important: Research shows that our ADHD symptoms are lower and our general health improves by taking time to be outdoors in nature every day—ideally more than once a day. A "green break" is a great habit to get into as an alternative to heading to the kitchen to drink or eat something each time you need a break. There is a growing body of research on the brain benefits of spending time outdoors in nature.[28] The Japanese practice of "forest bathing" (*shinrin-yoku*), developed in the 1980s, entails walking quietly in a natural forest setting, observing nature, and soaking in the peace and quiet. Many studies have demonstrated the health benefits of forest bathing. We don't all have a forest nearby, so look for the nearest spot where you can "bathe" in nature. This might be a nearby park or even a walk in your neighborhood if you are fortunate enough to be surrounded by trees. In a busy day, being outside for fifteen minutes twice a day can be very healing to your cognitive functioning on an immediate basis and to your overall health on a long-term basis.

Nature helps with mental fatigue. Mental fatigue is real for everyone, but especially for adults with ADHD. Professors of psychology at the University of Michigan Rachel and Stephen Kaplan developed a theory about mental fatigue and recovery from mental fatigue. They talked about two different types of attention—"top-down" attention, what we often call "paying attention," attention that is directed and effortful, such as the type that is used to read, engage in conversation, or complete a task; and "bottom-up attention," which is a "softer" type of attention, attention that is not effortful and that is "drawn" by the natural environment. We might notice the leaves dancing in the breeze, a butterfly fluttering around flowers, or the smell of the fresh air.[29] This can be a restorative antidote to our "always on" culture.

Green breaks restore our ability to pay attention. When we are frequently interrupted while trying to pay attention—such as having to answer the phone or respond to a question while we need to concentrate—our attentional capacity is taxed even more. We have to redirect our attention to the phone or to the person asking the question and then redirect our attention yet again to return to the task at hand.

When you have ADHD, your attentional capacity is more easily depleted because your brain often "interrupts itself" through internal distractibility. For example, you might be reading a detailed document and then suddenly recall that you meant to call your doctor for a follow-up appointment. Your concentration is broken while you either write down a reminder to call the doctor or, perhaps, actually call the doctor. By this time, you may have difficulty returning to your original task. And if you do return to it, your attention capacity is doubly depleted—first by paying attention to your fleeting thought about calling the doctor, and then by the effort to get back to the complicated document you were reading. You may even need to reread a paragraph or two to recall what you'd been reading.

We have limited top-down attentional capacity, which is why we need a break, preferably green, from activities to restore our ability to pay attention in a way that requires effort. Listening to crickets or birds while sitting in the park is not an effortful activity. Listening to a lecture or reading important information requires top-down attention. Urban environments are not relaxing and restorative like natural environments because they frequently require effortful top-down attention to navigate—such as avoiding other pedestrians on a sidewalk or checking for cars before we cross the street. So, in urban environments, we are still depleting our directed or top-down attention capacity as we walk outside.

Leave your digital device behind as you head outside for a nature break. Habitual attention to our electronic devices completely negates the restorative aspects of natural environments. One study carefully measured attention capacity in a variety of settings—outside, but in a barren, treeless environment; outside in a very green natural setting; and outside in a green natural setting while engaging with a digital device. Of the three settings, the *only setting* that restored a person's ability to pay attention was being in a natural environment *without a digital device.*[30]

The benefits of green breaks are reduced, if not lost altogether, if we spend the time on one of our electronic devices while taking a green break. Going for a walk while talking on the phone, checking text messages, or listening to a podcast while wearing earbuds prevents us from truly "being there" in the natural setting. Our body may be there, but our mind is on the conversation, the text message, or the podcast.

The Kaplans also believed that exposure to nature was restorative only when the individual wanted to be in the natural setting and was not feeling internal pressure to attend to other responsibilities. In other words, if a friend drags you out to have lunch in a park, but you can't get your mind off some task that you "ought" to be doing, then the natural setting will not work its restorative magic.

ADHD-friendly ways to build green breaks into your day:

- Walk your dog before and after work.
- Grab a quick bite so that you have time to walk at lunchtime.
- Go outside for a few minutes when you take your break, rather than heading for a cup of coffee or a snack.

D DIET

We all know that it's important to eat a healthy diet—plenty of fruits and vegetables, lean protein, whole grains, and so on. But here's what you may not know:

- People with ADHD have a much harder time than others eating in a healthy way.
- When and what we eat can have a big impact on our cognitive functioning.

Healthy eating is a huge topic—one that I will only cover in very general terms, providing you with a few resources if you want to read in greater depth about a healthy diet. What's important for you, as an older adult with ADHD, is to understand why it's so difficult to consistently follow a healthy diet and what you can do about it.

ADHD Tendencies That Make Healthy Eating More Challenging

The following list highlights how ADHD can lead to poor eating habits, with more explanation to follow:

- Impulsivity
- Emotional reactivity that can lead to distress-driven eating
- Addiction tendencies
- A brain wired to seek short-term pleasure over long-term benefit
- Poor planning abilities that make it difficult to plan and prepare healthy meals
- Stimulation craving that is often satisfied through food
- Long-standing poor eating habits that are hard to break

Addiction Tendencies

Those with ADHD are more vulnerable to "hyperpalatable foods" due to addiction tendencies associated with ADHD. Processed and fast food has become so ingeniously engineered to appeal to our taste buds that a growing body of research draws many parallels between hyperpalatable foods and addictive drugs. The pleasure-seeking pathways of the brain that are activated by highly palatable foods overlap with pathways that are activated by drugs of abuse. And patterns of compulsive eating and "relapse" eating following dieting mimic similar patterns seen in people addicted to drugs.[31] There is still debate over whether you can truly be addicted to food, but the evidence of food addiction, specifically sugar addiction, is growing.[32] ADHD and substance abuse tendencies are highly heritable and tend to be found together. Brain studies have found that differences in the pathways related to cognitive control, to emotional control, and to "reward craving" are common in both ADHD and substance abuse.[33]

My client Tina has a story that exemplifies some of this. Tina's story is extreme, but many adults with ADHD struggle with binge eating patterns, and many report that just eating "that first cookie" or those first few chips triggers compulsive eating that may last until all the cookies or chips are gone.

Tina was a middle-aged woman with ADHD. She and her husband, Mark, had married late and had no children. Mark had a high-paying job and Tina elected not to work after they married. At the time she was referred to me for treatment, she reported that her eating patterns had taken complete control of her daily life. Try as she might, as each weekday morning wore on, Tina had increasingly strong compulsions to go out and buy sweets. (Her eating was much more restrained on weekends when Mark

*was home, as she didn't want him to see how frantically she ate.)
During the week, her self-control wore down by midmorning
and she began to make the rounds. She felt such overwhelming
shame at her eating patterns that she spread out her purchases
among many stores so that no one would see a shopping cart
piled high with sweets. She had a regular route, starting at a local
bakery, then to several local groceries, and finally to Dunkin' on
her way home. Many days, she couldn't wait and started wolfing
down sweets in the car. Once home, she ate frantically, even as
her stomach was full to bursting. Finally, she reported, she fell
into a "sugar coma," as she called it, feeling sick and exhausted.
Some days, her sugar overdose was so extreme that she spent the
afternoon in bed, unable to get up and interact with Mark when he
arrived home at suppertime. Mark was accustomed to preparing
his own evening meal because Tina was often in such a bad mental
and physical state by the end of the day.*

Tina's behavior surpasses "normal" binge eating. It had clearly
risen to the level very suggestive of a serious addiction. Sucrose acti-
vates specific receptors in the mouth, which ultimately results in the
release in the brain of dopamine—a neurotransmitter often referred
to as the "pleasure chemical." The rewarding effects of dopamine lead
us to seek more sugar to replicate the rewarding feeling. Importantly,
studies have shown that it is not the sweet taste that is driving the
behavior. Even if sucrose is administered into the bloodstream so that
no pleasurable taste is involved, the brain responds in the same way,
suddenly boosting the release of dopamine—the reward neurochemical. In fact, intense sweetness *surpasses* the effects of cocaine in terms
of internal rewards![34]

Eating Disorder Treatment and ADHD

Standard eating disorder treatment programs ignore the specific challenges of ADHD. Eating disorder programs operate from a central belief that eating disorders (both anorexia and bulimia nervosa and binge eating disorder) stem from deep-seated emotional struggles, including low self-esteem, anxiety, and depression. Although these factors can certainly play a strong role, especially in those without ADHD, most eating disorder programs ignore the ADHD tendencies and vulnerabilities that contribute to unhealthy eating patterns.

Almost universally, traditional eating disorder programs forbid people from taking their prescribed stimulant medications for ADHD while changing their eating habits.[35] They fear that those with eating disorders are misusing stimulants to suppress appetite. In great contrast to this approach, I encourage people with disordered eating patterns to take their stimulants because it will help them be more self-aware, focused, and less impulsive.

The Deck Is Stacked Against You by the Food Industry

Many, if not most, people with ADHD have a difficult time following healthy eating habits. In the developed world, we live in an age of food hyperavailability. Not only is it hyperavailable, it is also hyperpalatable. That "hyperpalatable" part is worth understanding. The food industry has gone out of its way, conducting an enormous amount of research, to make food as appealing as possible. Remember the ad for Lay's potato chips—*Bet you can't eat just one?* That's what the food industry is banking on, whether it's salty chips or sweet snacks. Sugar acts so much like an addictive drug that research documents a "sugar withdrawal" when we suddenly cut sugar out of our daily diet.[36] Sugar withdrawal can induce feelings of depression, anxiety, brain fog, cravings, headaches, fatigue, and dizziness.

Ways to reduce your sugar intake:

- Always try to eat sweets in combination with protein so that you aren't experiencing the more intense feelings that sugar in isolation can create.
- Cut down gradually. This will reduce the withdrawal symptoms.
- Brush your teeth after eating sweets. Getting the sweet taste out of your mouth will cut down on your desire to eat "just one more" cookie, candy, or other sweet.
- Consider eating ripe fruit, cut up into slices, as your dessert, with just a dollop of ice cream on top (instead of a bowl of ice cream with a little fruit on top).
- Purchase your favorite sweets in very small quantities.

Stop Losing the Food Fight is a short-term structured group that I have developed to help people with ADHD learn ADHD-friendly ways to develop a healthier relationship with food. In my group, our focus is not on the healthy foods that we all know we should eat. Instead, the focus is on what gets in the way of healthy eating when you have ADHD. Group members learned specific practices that you can try:

- Avoid "black-and-white thinking" that leads people to go from one extreme to another in their eating patterns.
- Understand "harm mitigation"—e.g., just because you've eaten three cookies doesn't mean you have to eat the whole box of them.
- Build habits that lead to gradual change. For example, start by simply changing your afternoon snack to something healthier— an apple, a handful of unsalted almonds, a hard-boiled egg.
- Avoid food triggers—such as food items you want to avoid or limit being in plain sight. We teach people not to keep foods in their home that they can't seem to resist.

- Learn simple, healthy ways to prepare dinner, rather than ordering carry-out.

- Break associations between activities and eating. For example, if you have a habit of eating while watching TV at night, start by breaking the association. Allow yourself to eat your evening snack, but not while watching TV. Make yourself walk into the kitchen, prepare the snack, and eat it at the kitchen table instead of while watching TV. This makes eating more "mindful," and eventually breaks the association between TV watching and eating.

- Avoid "mindless" eating by not engaging in any other activity while eating.

- Pursue enjoyable activities that don't involve eating.

- Get back to your healthy habits if you "fall off the wagon" and overeat or binge eat.

- Understand that you are starting on a lifelong path to develop a different relationship to food.

- Eat a protein-rich, low-fat, low-glycemic diet to stabilize blood sugar levels, providing your brain with a steady supply of energy. On a longer-term basis, a low-glycemic diet reduces inflammation associated with many chronic diseases. For more on the low-GI way of eating, see Appendix C, pages 311–313.

Micronutrients (Vitamins and Minerals)

This brief section is not meant to be an exhaustive discussion of the importance of micronutrients for optimal health and cognitive functioning. This is a large and complex topic. However, it is important to know that research has demonstrated that adults with ADHD, as well as family members of those adults, report an improvement in ADHD symptoms after taking prescribed micronutrients (multivitamins).[37] In a study of children with ADHD who took vitamin-mineral supplements, parents reported reduced ADHD symptoms, better attention and emotional regulation, and less aggression. These vitamin-mineral supplements did not improve hyperactivity and impulsivity, which are typically more effectively treated with stimulant medication.

Brain signaling also relies on such micronutrients as zinc, iron, and vitamin D. If levels of these three nutrients are deficient—as they often are in children and adults with ADHD—focus, attention, and impulse control will suffer.[38]

Recent studies document the importance of zinc,[39] iron,[40] fish oil (omega-3 fatty acids),[41] and magnesium[42] as supporting optimal cognitive functioning.

If you decide to use supplements, check with your health-care provider first to make sure there are no contraindications with any other medication you are taking and that the dosages of these supplements do not exceed their recommended level.

S SLEEP

Sleep is critical to good brain functioning. In fact, chronic sleep deprivation can give you a "double dose" of ADHD because it reduces the functioning of the prefrontal lobes, which is already compromised by ADHD. Furthermore, it has been discovered recently that one of the most important functions of sleep is to allow the cerebrospinal fluid to flow in and out of the brain, washing away waste proteins that are toxic to brain cells.[43] As an older adult, you should know that there is evidence that chronic sleep disturbance is related to cognitive decline and dementia.[44]

Sleep Issues Specific to Adults with ADHD

Delayed sleep phase syndrome, a pattern of having a dysregulated circadian rhythm, is very common among people with ADHD. Among adults, studies consistently report high rates of sleep problems, including sleep onset problems, restless sleep, and poor-quality, nonrestorative sleep.[45] Adults with combined-type ADHD are significantly more likely to experience insomnia (64.3 percent). Although there has been long-standing concern that taking stimulant medication may interfere with sleep, it has been demonstrated that adults taking stimulant medication for ADHD report lower rates of insomnia. Adults with ADHD and mood disorders, anxiety, personality disorder, and substance use disorder all report higher levels of insomnia.[46]

What's Getting in the Way of Falling Asleep?

Thinking about your worries? You may avoid going to bed because you can't quiet your mind. Many older adults shared with me that lying down in the dark, trying to fall asleep, is the time when all of their worries and concerns come to the foreground. To avoid this period of troubling rumination, they distract themselves by watching television, scrolling through social media, or doing some other activity until they finally fall asleep on the couch, shuffling back to the bedroom in the early-morning hours.

If this is your problem, get into bed, turn out the light, and try listening to calm music, a podcast, or recorded book (using your earbuds if you are sharing the bed). Turn the volume low and quietly listen as you fall asleep. If your ADHD brain has something calm and not too stimulating to focus on, you'll be more likely to fall asleep.

Needing time to yourself? Is avoiding going to bed your way of finding uninterrupted time for yourself without having to attend to the needs of others in the household? If your spouse is in poor health and needs caretaking, late-night hours may feel like your only respite from being on duty.

If this is your problem, look for ways to find "me time" during the day. Staying up late may seem like the easiest way to find time to yourself, but you're risking your health by falling into this pattern. Late-night eating and shorter sleep hours are often the result.

Create a calm space in your house where you go to be alone to read, pursue a hobby, or call a friend. Consider taking a couple of daily walks each day—they will provide exposure to nature and exercise along with a break from your caretaking routines.

Is staying up late a guilty pleasure? During the day, do you feel unable to take time to simply relax and entertain yourself? Do you pressure yourself to take care of various tasks during the day, but give yourself a break from self-blame late at night? Does staying up too late give you a few hours when you give yourself a "pass" from worrying about (and often avoiding) the life management tasks pressing upon you during the day? Does nighttime give you a chance to stop recriminating yourself for a few hours?

Instead of sleep-depriving yourself to create guilt-free time, try rewarding yourself for getting unappealing tasks done by giving yourself "me time" during the day. For example:

- Reward yourself after running errands by stopping by a local café for a cup of coffee or tea and a few moments of relaxation.

- Create a "me space" at home where you can read, pursue a hobby, or talk on the phone with a friend or family member. It can be a room of your own, if you have the space, or even just a favorite chair that you reserve for "me time."

Are you avoiding conflict with your spouse or partner by going to bed later? Some couples have a tacit agreement to keep their distance from each other. "He snores." "She wants to keep the light on too late." "We like to watch different shows on TV." For whatever reason, one spouse stays up late while the other spouse heads to bed.

Staying up late, falling asleep on the couch watching TV, and keeping an irregular bedtime will all set you up for less restorative sleep. If you think that relationship issues contribute to this pattern, this would be a good topic to discuss in ADHD-focused marriage counseling (see Chapter 11).

Do either you or your spouse have chronic pain? Many older adults experience sleep difficulties due to chronic pain, sleep apnea, snoring, restless leg syndrome, muscle cramps, and so on. Maybe it's time to set up comfortable separate bedrooms for yourself and your partner, rather than staying up too late and falling asleep in your chair or on the couch.

Tools for ADHD Adults to Build Healthier Sleep Habits

Blue-blocking glasses to counteract the negative effects of screen time

Although many professionals suggest "no screen time" for an hour before bedtime, few adults are willing to forgo their evening screen-time habits, whether it's TV, laptop, iPad, or smartphone. Instead of giving up prebedtime screen time, get yourself a pair of "blue-blocking" glasses. If you wear reading glasses, blue-blocking glasses can be worn over them to block out the blue light emitted by your screens that interferes with sleep.

Melatonin

Per the Mayo Clinic website, "Melatonin is a hormone in your body that plays a role in sleep. The production and release of melatonin in the brain is connected to time of day, increasing when it's dark and decreasing when it's light. Melatonin production declines with age.

"Melatonin is also available as a supplement, typically as an oral tablet or capsule. Most melatonin supplements are made in a lab."[47]

It's important to take this earlier in the evening, to allow time for it to work naturally, building up the hormones that induce sleep naturally. A lower dose (3 mg) taken two or more hours before bed is much more effective than a higher dose taken at bedtime.

Note: Be sure to check with your health-care provider before starting any supplements to make sure they are safe for you and are not contraindicated with any of your medications.

Oral lavender oil

Oral lavender oil preparation (80 mg/day) showed a significant beneficial influence on quality and duration of sleep and improved general mental and physical health without causing any unwanted sedative or other drug-specific effects in 221 patients suffering from subsyndromal (mixed) anxiety disorder.[48]

Note: When you purchase lavender oil, be sure to get food grade, NOT the essential oil you rub on your skin.

Also, be sure to check with your health-care provider before starting any supplements to make sure they are safe for you and are not contraindicated with any of your medications.

Topical essential oils

While I suggest taking lavender oil internally, essential oils are also effective topically (on the skin). A mixture of essential oils that includes lavender, basil, juniper, and sweet marjoram is shown to reduce sleep disturbance and improve overall well-being in older patients.[49]

CBD oil

CBD oil has begun to be recommended by physicians who practice integrative medicine. There are initial research projects to suggest that CBD oil in doses from 25 to 175 mL per day are effective in reducing anxiety and improving sleep. As is true for all substances that fall into the "alternative medicine" category, it is critical to purchase CBD oil from a reputable source. Preliminary studies indicate that CBD oil is safe and effective, and does not produce negative side effects.[50]

Note: Be sure to check with your health-care provider before starting any supplements to make sure they are safe for you and are not contraindicated with any of your medications.

Sleepytime tea (chamomile tea)

If you still can't fall asleep, try drinking sleepytime tea (one that contains chamomile), or drinking a glass of warm milk flavored with real vanilla and a teaspoon of sugar.

Meditation recordings

Meditation recordings can also be sleep inducing. Try MindWorks Press's "Brain Train" recording available from Amazon. Countless meditation apps and recordings designed to induce sleep can be found on the internet. Here's a list to start your exploration of good meditation recordings: "20 of the Best Guided Meditations for Sleep and Insomnia" at https://www.lifehack.org/844530/best-guided-meditation-for-sleep.

Reduce your caffeine intake

Think about your caffeine intake (coffee, tea, some sodas, chocolate). Caffeine can stay in the system for a long time. Try to limit caffeine to breakfast each day; at the very least, try to stop caffeine intake after lunch.

Regular daily exercise

Regular, daily exercise is an important and healthful way to promote good sleep. But be sure not to exercise right before bed. Exercise either in the morning, at noon, or early evening after work.

Prepare Yourself to Fall Asleep

There are simple steps you can take to wind your day down and set yourself up for a good night's sleep:

- Create a bedtime routine that you look forward to. From earliest childhood, many of us associate "bedtime" with stopping the pleasurable activities we're engaged in. Instead, build up positive associations with bedtime, such as a warm bath, a cup of chamomile tea, reading in bed, or wearing blue-blocking glasses to spend time online without stopping your body's natural production of melatonin.
- Falling asleep takes time—you can't just flip a switch.
- Be sure to allow time for "getting ready" for bed.
- Take a shower or bath—going from the warmth of a bath or shower to bed cools your body, which is sleep inducing.
- Develop a brief routine of slow stretches before you get into bed. Stretching is another way to signal to your body that it's time for relaxation and sleep.
- Sleep in a cool room (between 60 and 67 degrees Fahrenheit).
- Block out distracting sounds—there are many "white-noise" sounds you can play on an iPad or smartphone, such as the

sound of rain or of the ocean, which are calming and block out other sounds that may distract you from sleep.

- Sleep in a dark room. If you leave a nightlight on because you typically need to go to the bathroom in the middle of the night, consider keeping a small flashlight or using the light on your smartphone to guide your steps to the bathroom so that the room can remain completely dark while you're in bed.

- Give yourself forty-five minutes from getting into bed to falling asleep.

- Get into bed eight hours before you plan to get up the next day.

- Make bedtime a regular time. If you lose track of time, set a reminder to start your bedtime routine.

A Good Morning Routine Contributes to a Good Bedtime Routine

Get up at the same time each morning, even if you haven't had enough sleep. Sleeping late will only continue your night-owl pattern. A brief nap (twenty to thirty minutes) later in the day is key if you're very tired, but not after four p.m.

Take your stimulant forty-five minutes before you need to get up. If waking up is hard, try setting your alarm forty-five minutes before get-up time (or set two alarms). Take your stimulant medication then and go back to sleep. By the time your alarm rings at your desired rising time, the medication will be in your system and you'll feel more energetic and alert.

When to Seek a Medical Consultation for Sleep Problems

If you've tried all of these consistently for a period of three weeks and sleep still evades you, it's time for a medical consultation with your health-care provider.

S SOCIAL CONNECTIONS

Many studies have shown the importance of social connections and support in maintaining both mental and physical health.[51] In fact, social connections are so critical to the well-being of older adults with ADHD that I devote the following chapter to this topic. Here, I will simply offer the highlights of the powerful links between social connections, physical well-being, and cognitive functioning.

- Human beings are fundamentally social creatures that rely upon social interactions with other humans for basic well-being. Solitary confinement, the removal of all social interactions, is the most powerful punishment meted out in a prison environment. Babies deprived of physical touch fail to thrive. We need to be literally "in touch" with one another.

- Social skill deficits and difficulty organizing and maintaining social contacts with others often result in social isolation for older adults with ADHD.

- Being around other people helps older adults with ADHD structure their day and be more aware of time. When we live with others, we tend to share meals, or at least receive cues that mealtimes have arrived. Likewise, if we live with others who have a more regulated day in terms of wake-up time and bedtime, we are more likely to regulate our wake/sleep cycle as well.

- Social isolation can lead to an increase in problematic ADHD tendencies, such as disorder, messiness, lack of meal planning, and difficulty in planning and executing projects.

Chapter 10 provides much more detail on the importance of social support networks and offers practical steps on how to build them.

Think You Don't Have Time for All of These Brain-Healthy Daily Habits?

"Habit stacking" is a way to make and keep new habits. The phrase "habit stacking" was coined by *Wall Street Journal* best-selling author S. J. Scott. In his book *Habit Stacking: 127 Small Changes to Improve Your Health, Wealth, and Happiness (Most Are Five Minutes or Less)*, he proposes that you "build routines around habits that don't require effort" since "small wins build momentum because they're easy to remember and complete."[52]

Here are some habit-stacking examples:

- Walking your dog in a leafy green natural environment provides both exercise and exposure to nature.
- Stopping to chat with a friend somewhere along your walk adds a third healthy habit—social connections.
- Likewise, exercising with a friend accomplishes two important daily health habits, exercise and social connection.
- Group meditation, even if online, provides the calming and focusing benefits of meditation while also giving us a feeling of connection to others in the group.

Don't try to change everything at once, then feel discouraged and quit. Start one healthy habit at a time and work on it until it becomes a regular part of your day. And build these habits strategically. For example, use your green break/exercise break as a brain break when you can't concentrate any longer. Instead of heading to the kitchen for a snack or to social media, head outside, take a walk, and clear your head.

KEY TAKEAWAYS FROM THIS CHAPTER

✔ Brain-healthy daily habits can have a large, positive effect on your ADHD symptoms.

✔ MENDSS is an acronym to help you remember healthy habits to improve all aspects of brain function.

- ○ **Mindfulness/Mindful Meditation/Stress Reduction**
- ○ **Exercise**
- ○ **Nature**
- ○ **Diet**
- ○ **Sleep**
- ○ **Social** connections

✔ You don't have to follow healthy daily habits perfectly to achieve a real benefit.

Getting Connected, Staying Connected

The importance of social support networks and how to build them

L oneliness and isolation affect all older adults, not just those with ADHD. The factors that can lead to isolation are numerous. In this chapter, I will share stories of older adults with ADHD who have struggled with social isolation, but my focus is to help you find ways to counteract isolation as you grow older. As I tell many of my older clients, we need to actively engage in "additions" to our social world to counteract the inevitable "subtractions" that occur with aging.

Social "Subtractions"

By the time we reach our retirement years, we may have an ever-shrinking social group as friends move away or die; from cognitive decline, in either ourselves or our friends, that makes socializing increasingly difficult; from mobility problems that limit our ability to go out and be around others; and from the loss of social roles that provide built-in social contacts. For example, work-related relationships fade away after retirement and even our involvement as grandparents tends to lessen as grandchildren grow older and more independent.

Social "Additions"

To counteract inevitable social "subtractions," we need to consciously add activities, pursue new friendships, and engage in pursuits that involve us in the lives of others and in our community. Here are some ideas for making "additions" in our lives:

- **Join a walking group or find a walking buddy.** Walking is much more social than running, allowing plenty of time each day to socialize as you exercise. Having a walking buddy is very ADHD-friendly in several ways: (1) it provides daily exercise that promotes better mood and cognition; (2) it creates a daily dose of "nature," which I wrote about in the last chapter as a health-promoting, stress-reducing activity; (3) it provides you with daily socializing; and (4) if you are someone who doesn't like the pressure of straightening up your home to invite friends inside, it doesn't require any preparation other than putting on your walking shoes!

- **Play a sport with other seniors.** Any sport counts, but pickleball is a great example. It has become the fastest-growing sport in the US, with seniors leading the charge. Many communities have transformed rarely used tennis courts into pickleball courts and it has become a great way to exercise and meet others in your same age group.

- **Form a monthly dinner group at a local restaurant.** Many older adults with ADHD do not relish the effort required to invite people into their home because it requires so much preparation and planning. Instead, find a public meeting place. In my area I have noticed a group of seniors who meet regularly at the local McDonald's for breakfast. A highly affordable and convenient way to see friends regularly.

- **Get involved in your local senior center.** Most of their activities are low cost or no cost and provide an excellent way to get to know others your age who share your interests.

- **Move to a place inhabited by other seniors.** One woman with ADHD whom I saw in therapy told me that after retiring from her very busy career as a journalist, she had become lonely. Her city apartment, chosen due to its proximity to her work, no longer met her needs. Most of her neighbors were busy, younger professionals. She decided to move to an apartment building farther from the center of the city, where many retired adults lived. She happily reported to me a few months after her move that she had the busiest social life she'd ever enjoyed. People reached out to one another, inviting neighbors to have lunch at a nearby restaurant, go to a nearby movie theater, or play bridge at the tables in the building's social area on the ground floor.

Research shows that a sense of well-being in later years is strongly tied to one's social connections, family involvement, and volunteer work that provides a sense of purpose and belonging in the community.[1]

Those with ADHD have personalities ranging from deeply introverted to extremely extroverted. People on the extroverted end of the social continuum can be socially adept, talkative, engaging, and charming. Many of these individuals with ADHD can be found in sales, politics, and the entertainment industry. James Carville, a highly effective and very colorful political consultant dubbed the "Ragin' Cajun," is an example of someone with ADHD who is a great social connector. Fearless, challenging, funny, and engaging, he is so hyperactive and hypertalkative that his diagnosis was prompted by a physician who approached him in an airport, told him he'd been observing him, and shared that he felt strongly that Carville had ADHD. The diagnosis was confirmed. Subsequently, Carville has become a fierce advocate for those with ADHD.

In great contrast to James Carville's experience, I want to share a few comments written by Elizabeth, a middle-aged woman with ADHD who struggled with making social connections.

> "I was constantly blurting things out, speaking out of turn when I was in elementary school. I just didn't know how to have a conversation, didn't know how to follow what others were saying, and didn't know when it was my turn to talk. This still happens to me as an adult.
>
> "I know that I've hurt people because I will randomly insert something into the conversation, something that is on my mind, rather than responding to what the person has just told me. Also, I don't know how to keep the conversation on a socially appropriate level. For example, when someone says, 'How are you?' I don't know the appropriate thing to say and sometimes launch into an inappropriately long response instead of responding with a pleasantry such as, 'I'm fine. Good to see you.'
>
> "Other women sometimes feel put off by my hyperenergy and enthusiasm. I tell people I'll do something and then not follow through, so they see me as unreliable. I have never been able to keep in touch with friends on a long-term basis because it takes remembering to call them or to email them. I'm always caught up in what's happening at the moment. And, I'm always anxious. For example, even though I work with a very nice group of people, I worry that they hate me or resent me because of my ADHD screw-ups.

"The friends I do have all have ADHD. They 'get' me and I 'get' them. They overlook my weird changes of direction in a conversation or the fact that I space out and miss what they've been telling me. I really try to stay focused on what the other people are saying, and I work hard to be 'appropriate,' but eventually my ADHD pops out and I say something completely unrelated to the conversation. I try so hard, and I am so glad that I have found a few people that truly do forgive me for my social mistakes and understand that I really do care about them, even when I seem tuned out or insensitive."

Elizabeth writes from the perspective of an adult who missed the benefits of receiving help for her social skills challenges when she was growing up. Many reading this book may have experienced similarly crushing social experiences and didn't have the opportunity to know about their ADHD and how it impacted their interactions with others until much later in life.

Social Skills and Social Connections

Stephen Hinshaw, PhD, a highly regarded ADHD researcher at UC Berkeley, described the girls with ADHD that he studied as either "socially rejected" (the hyperactive/impulsive girls) or "socially neglected" (the shy, inattentive girls).[2] Social skills impairments can lead to low self-esteem, social withdrawal, and even self-harm. It's so important to look for others who accept your ADHD foibles and appreciate you for your good qualities.

Here's what some older adults with ADHD say about their social struggles:

"Every time you don't notice something or forget something, a lot of people take it as a personal slight and I ended up feeling

like an inconsiderate person. I was unhappy, drank too much, and craved letting go of responsibility. It was so hard to be what everyone expected me to be. When I drank, I felt better, but I was a fundamentally irresponsible, unreliable, untrustworthy person."

"It's hard to make new friends at my age. Work was a very social place, but once I retired, I lost touch with those people. I'm not the best at staying in touch or at making new friends."

"I'm a very fast talker. It's hard for people to understand me sometimes. If I don't take my meds, I can be untactful, rude, and impatient."

"Now that I am retired and a widow I looked for social connections at my local senior center. You would think that I would find acceptance there, but that's not what happened. I joined a book group, but the other women were clearly not comfortable with me because I interrupt and talk too fast. And when I volunteered to help organize an event at the senior center, the other women pulled away from me. They already had their own little group and they were frustrated with me if I arrived a little late for a meeting or forgot to take care of something. I guess I just don't know how to get along in a group."

"I've never been able to get along in any close relationship. My ex-wife said I'm too focused on what I want to do and not focused on the needs of other people."

"When I don't take my meds, I'm very irritable with other people."

"I tend to be impulsive and angry, hot-tempered and sarcastic with people when I'm feeling stressed."

"I don't really have a social life. I go to church, have a men's group once a month. I'm fine with that."

What's Gender Got to Do with It?

A number of studies of adolescents with ADHD suggest that social struggles and social rejection are a greater issue for girls than for boys.[3] Whereas adolescent girls report significant unhappiness in relation to peer rejection, adolescent boys do not report feeling socially rejected or unhappy about their limited social life.[4] Parents, teachers, and peers describe these boys with ADHD as being rejected, not included, and having fewer friends and fewer social activities in comparison to boys without ADHD,[5] but the boys themselves do not describe themselves as socially excluded. This is in marked contrast to girls with ADHD, who crave social acceptance and inclusion but can't seem to achieve it.

While those studies were on children, my small and very unscientific survey of older men and women with ADHD reflects a similar pattern. Men reported issues such as pushing people away with anger, irritability, and impatience and, in general, being less troubled by having a limited social life. Women, on the other hand, report anxiety, depression, and regret about not fitting in.

While there may be some gender differences in the social struggles of men and women with ADHD, there is a great deal of overlap. Although there is certainly a significant and still evolving change in the social roles of males and females, most older adults today grew up in a time when "boys will be boys," expected to be rough-and-tumble, settled their differences with verbal and physical aggression, whereas girls were expected to be "sugar and spice and everything nice."

Just as is true for many women with ADHD, certainly some men also suffer greatly due to their social isolation. Doug shared his story with me:

> *"My social life is severely constrained by my finances and living conditions. It's been this way for a long time. My closest friends live far away. I talk to them on the phone and communicate via*

email and text messages. Occasionally, I see them when they travel to my area. Entertaining at home is out of the question. I live in a crowded two-bedroom apartment without appropriate furniture. I attend a social group at church, but haven't met anyone there that might become a friend. I also attend the monthly social gathering organized by my alma mater and have made one friend there. My other friend is about to move away after a two-year training stint and I hope to keep in touch with him."

Doug is "twice exceptional." He not only has ADHD but is also very intellectually gifted. Like many twice-exceptional adults, he has not been able to keep up with his very bright neurotypical peers professionally due to his untreated ADHD. At the same time, his strongly intellectual interests make it difficult for him to meet others who share his "universe." Doug has made many of the "right moves." He attends a church social group, his alma mater's social gatherings, and, when he could afford to, weekly swing-dance classes. Given his twice-exceptionality, Doug needs ways to connect with other highly intelligent people and might find it easier to meet like-minded friends through Meetup groups organized to discuss topics of interest to him.

Leo's story shares many features with Doug's. He is very bright, an engineer by training, but has experienced lifelong difficulties with making friends. Although he has been married for over forty years, his wife has been in a nursing home for a dozen years, making his loneliness and isolation even greater.

"I have concluded that either you have it or you don't have it [social skills]; as for making friends, I think that most people with ADHD don't have it. To make friends, it has to come naturally. If it doesn't come naturally, you're out of luck. Recently, it was so clear to me about my lack of friends. I had outpatient surgery and needed someone to accompany me and take me home. There was no one I felt comfortable calling. I know some people, but not well

enough. It would have felt like an imposition to ask anyone to do this for me. I had to call a taxi."

Helping Older Adults with ADHD Move Out Of Dangerous Social Isolation

Many older adults with ADHD who live alone are more at risk for leading chaotic, dysregulated lives that make it difficult to build or maintain social connections. With active support and intervention, both Edgar and Marcia were rescued from isolated living situations and are on the road to building a much more socially connected life.

Edgar was a scientist in his sixties, still working, but edging toward retirement. He had been briefly married and had a son in his late thirties who lived in New York City and only rarely came to visit. His wife had divorced him after ten years or so of marriage due to his emotional disconnectedness and disorderly living patterns. Edgar had been alone ever since the divorce, leading an isolated life of going to work at a government science lab five days a week and spending weekends alone in his apartment. He was a man with many interests, highly intelligent, but with no one to talk to. Finally, he began attending a nearby Unitarian church where, to his surprise, he began to meet people he enjoyed. Over the course of the next year, he joined a group at the church that met regularly and felt increasingly comfortable attending the social events at church.

Marcia was a highly intelligent woman married to a much older man. Both she and her husband had ADHD and shared a chaotic home environment filled in every nook and cranny by objects that they collected on their travels, by items related to their numerous interests and hobbies, and by anything that caught Marcia's eye. In addition to having ADHD, Marcia was a hoarder (a pattern that I discussed earlier in Chapter 8 about hoarders working with a coach). Her husband passed away and Marcia's health began to fail. All alone in the large home she had shared for many years with her husband, her world shrank until she was living in two rooms. Marcia became increasingly despondent and contacted a therapist she had seen many years earlier. At her therapist's suggestion, Marcia made arrangements to move from her home to an apartment in a very pleasant continuing-care facility a few miles away. Marcia gradually became acquainted with others in her facility. She had a small group to eat the evening meal with and a friend who became her daily walking partner. Living in a facility that provided built-in activities and the company of others helped her come out of her shell and also helped her build much healthier daily habits. She was exercising, sleeping more normal hours, eating healthy food, and socializing. The structure and emotional support provided by the retirement community helped her build a new social world.

Quite a few of the adults I interviewed had been able to create or maintain healthy social connections as they aged despite their ADHD. In the rest of this chapter, I address the social needs and challenges of the broad swath of older adults with ADHD who fall in the middle—those who need and want a social life but struggle to maintain a social support network.

What ADHD Tendencies Get in the Way of Making Good Social Connections?

One study of adults with ADHD showed that they had significantly fewer social contacts.[6] Several factors often related to ADHD may be at play in those who have difficulty making and maintaining social contacts:

- **Executive functioning (EF) skill deficits**—First, initiating and maintaining social contacts requires a set of executive functioning skills that are often lacking in those with ADHD. EF skills are needed to keep track of phone numbers and addresses, to initiate social contacts, to make plans, to remember plans, to show up on time, and to control a tendency to talk too much and to interrupt.

- **Distractibility**—You may find yourself looking away frequently from someone who is speaking to you because you are distracted by something going on behind or beside the speaker. One solution I often recommend, especially in a distracting restaurant environment, is to select a seat where you are facing the wall rather than facing the room, to cut down on visual distraction.

- **Inattention** can lead people with ADHD to have difficulty following a conversation and recalling what's been said. You may be distracted by things you hear, things you see, or just things you think about. Listening and then repeating back what you've heard can keep you more focused on the conversation. For example, if a neighbor who you encounter mentions that their grandchildren will be visiting, you could respond, "Oh, your grandchildren are visiting next week? How old are they?" Repeating what the other person has said shows you've been listening, and asking a question related to their comment shows interest.

- **Unreliable time awareness** can lead people to repeatedly show up late, annoying and eventually losing friends. Humor and apologies can go a long way. As you become closer to people, it can help to explain how easily you lose track of time and ask them to text you if they are waiting for you.

- **Feelings of restlessness**—If you feel restless when you are sitting talking to people, look for ways to be more active while socializing. For example, go for a walk, play golf, or engage in an activity while socializing.

- **Forgetfulness**—You may forget to send a thank-you note or email, or you may forget that it is "your turn" to invite a friend to do something with you. I always recommend that you "do it now or write it down." In other words, send your friend a thank-you text message or invitation the moment you think of it. Or write yourself a note and take care of it as soon as possible. You don't want friends to think you don't care about them when it's your ADHD forgetfulness that's getting in the way.

- **Interrupting**—Interrupting is fueled by both impulsivity and the fear that "if I don't say it now, I'll forget what I wanted to say." Impulsivity can also lead you to go off-topic, suddenly changing the subject of the conversation to something that has just popped into your head, giving your friends the misimpression that you aren't interested in what they had to say. As one woman told me, "I have a lot of friends because I'm a good listener." Keep in mind that saying something that pops into your mind is less important than showing interest in a friend or neighbor who is talking to you. If the thought that has occurred to you is important to tell your friend, apologize for the change of topic, and tell them that you wanted to be sure not to forget to share the information that occurred to you.

- **Talking too much**—There is a tendency among more talkative adults with ADHD to become so caught up in what they are saying that they miss the social cues indicating that the person they are talking to has lost interest in their topic. Again, humor can go a long way. "Here I go again! Just tell me to shut up if I talk too long!"

Maybe you find yourself identifying with some of these issues. The good news is that awareness can help you find ways to bolster your ability to foster social connections.

Relationships with Family Members

When there is intergenerational undiagnosed ADHD, conflictual and even estranged family relationships are not uncommon. A group of argumentative, short-tempered, easily offended, and sometimes alcoholic family members can be a recipe for difficult family interactions. This is not just anecdotal; researchers have also found that adults with ADHD tend to have more negative interactions with family members.[7]

Sometimes families with intergenerational ADHD experience conflict for the opposite reason: too much involvement. One man I interviewed told me how concerned he was that his son, in his forties, married with a child, had been fired from his job. In this family, conflicts developed between the daughter-in-law and her father-in-law, who she felt was inappropriately interfering in their life. She made it clear that she didn't want her in-laws to visit very often and criticized her husband for going to his father for advice.

Happy and Socially Connected Adults with ADHD

Whereas many of the adults I interviewed had a limited social life and little family connection, others told me that these later years were some of the happiest in their lives. What were they doing right?

> Bonnie, who has lived and worked in the Boston area for most of her adult life, told me that her retirement years have been the happiest. She had married, divorced when her kids were half-grown, and worked in a variety of jobs that she found quite stressful. Bonnie's two children were diagnosed with ADHD. She suspected ADHD in herself, but, like so many women, prioritized her children's needs over her own. She finally was diagnosed with ADHD in her fifties and found that medication was helpful in functioning better at work, which was largely administrative—work that is typically a poor match for those with ADHD. Her last job was especially difficult due to a critical supervisor with poor management skills. In retirement, Bonnie told me with a happy sigh, "I am free to do what I want." She actively volunteers at a senior center and also writes for its monthly newsletter. The job stress is gone and her children and grandchildren all live in the general area. Bonnie

*spends one day a week taking care of a young granddaughter
to help her hard-working daughter. During her working years,
Bonnie was able to scrape by financially, and managed to help
her two children get through college. Now, she lives in subsidized
senior housing and subsists on a very modest retirement income.
Although she doesn't have the money to travel, go to nice
restaurants, or buy tickets to cultural events, she revels in her
connections in the community. She has made friends in her senior
housing facility, attends church regularly, sees her family often, and
feels that she is making a valuable contribution to her community
through her volunteer work. "I always felt under so much pressure
during the years I was working. Now, I can cut back on activities
when I need to. It's wonderful to have my friends and family
nearby." Bonnie has been able to manage her ADHD in a way that
allows her to make and maintain social relationships. She goes out
into the world each day feeling connected and useful, helping her
family and older seniors at the local senior daycare center.*

*Grace also describes her retirement years as her happiest.
When her two daughters settled in the same area, she and her
husband made the decision to move near them to be close to their
grandchildren as they grew up. She and her husband are actively
engaged in caring for their young grandchildren on weekdays.
They pick the kids up from school and bring them to their home to
spend the afternoon while their two daughters pursue their equally
demanding careers. "My husband and I are more connected
now. When our kids were growing up, he was working so hard
to support the family and I was busy running the household and
raising the kids. We didn't have much time for each other. Now, we
take it easy, spending the mornings together taking walks, taking
care of the yard and garden, which we both enjoy, and then pick
up the grandkids in the middle of the afternoon. My husband is so
patient with them and helps them with their homework, something*

he never had time to do with our kids. On weekends, we pursue
our artistic interests. Dan is a potter and loves spending time in
his studio. I love to make jewelry. We are a happy pair."

All the people who described their later years as happy ones
were connected to their community, to friends, and to family. Some
women were living alone but very involved with children and grandchildren. Other men and women described their marriage as their
saving grace—the "happily ever after" couples you'll read about
in Chapter 11. In all cases, it seems to be the combination of having
strong relationships with others while feeling under much less pressure now that working years are behind them.

What Can You Do If You Don't Have Enough Satisfying Social Connections?

Here are some guidelines based on my interviews with the most content older adults with ADHD.

Understand the Importance of "Feeding" Your Social Self

Some of the unhappiest individuals I came to know had retreated
into social isolation, focusing their lives on avoiding negative social
interactions rather than on developing positive ones. They had given
up: *"I'm tired of trying, tired of getting hurt."* It can be difficult to overcome, but practicing awareness of your tendencies to retreat can help
you get back on track in making and maintaining friendships.

Remember That It's Not Too Late to Build Better Social Skills

At my clinic, we teach social skills to people of all ages. Here are some
of the most common comments that people make about their difficulties with social interactions:

- **I feel too shy and don't want to embarrass myself by saying something "dumb."** If you are an anxious conversationalist, it can help to prepare in advance a few topics of conversation to bring up. Also, keep in mind that being a good listener may be even better than being a good conversationalist.

- **I talk and/or interrupt too much.** Don't be shy about apologizing. "I know I sometimes talk too much. Please interrupt me if I go on too long." Joke about yourself. "Okay, I'm going to shut my big mouth now and give everyone else a chance to talk!" People will be a lot more tolerant if they know that you are aware of your patterns and are trying hard to change them.

- **I'm late for everything**. Again, apologies are in order, but so are efforts to change your patterns so that you don't always keep people waiting. Working with a coach can be helpful. Also, planning to be early can help.

- **I'm "too honest."** Being "honest" is another way of saying, "I speak before I think." Young children are "too honest" for the same reason. They haven't yet learned that you shouldn't say everything that you think. Stimulant medication and mindfulness meditation can both give you a little "space" between your internal thoughts and your decision to say those thoughts out loud.

- **I never know what to say.** Keep in mind that some of the best conversationalists are good listeners. You don't have to be the life of the party or the most informed person in the room. Being interested and asking questions is always appreciated.

- **I can't keep up with group conversations.** Many with ADHD, especially women, feel self-conscious due to the pace of verbal interaction. If this is true for you, it may be best to arrange for one-on-one conversations.

- **My feelings get hurt easily.** This is a common problem, especially for women with ADHD. It's a good topic to work on in therapy. It's likely that you are expecting to be rejected or that you are taking it personally when someone disagrees with you.

- **People usually annoy me.** While you may find yourself irritated by basic social interactions, take some time to think carefully about the situations in which you feel annoyed and the social situations that you enjoy.

- **I can be really rigid about things.** Sometimes, people with ADHD overcompensate by creating very rigid rules for themselves. When you are speaking with others whose ideas are different from your own, it's important not to fall into challenging or criticizing them because they differ from you.

- **I have no idea what the problem is.** Poor social awareness is an issue for some with ADHD. If this is true of you, it might be helpful to ask for feedback from someone you trust. "What am I doing that turns people off?" This is also a good topic to explore in therapy.

There is no single answer. We all have different social needs. Some adults with ADHD have learned that group interactions are difficult for them. It's too hard to follow the "bouncing ball" of the group conversation. For them, cultivating one-on-one relationships will probably work best. Some are most comfortable when social life turns around a common activity or interest. That way, there is always something in common to talk about. For still others, they are more socially confident when they are serving others, being useful. These people volunteer and play a helpful role in some aspect of their community.

Working in individual counseling, individual coaching, or support groups, you can gradually identify and work on issues that have always gotten in the way when socializing.

Join a Community

Many people rely upon their place of worship to provide the majority of their social connections. Even if you have not been active in your church, temple, or mosque earlier, you may find that it provides a feeling of belonging that becomes increasingly important now that you no longer have a workplace group to socialize with regularly.

Look for Groups That Share Your Interests

The good thing about book groups, photography groups, bridge groups, and so on is that you don't have to plan and organize them. All you need to do is show up. Social interactions on any level are good for our mental and physical health.

Look for Your "Tribe"

So many adults with ADHD described always feeling "different" or being "an outsider" throughout their lives. In retirement years, you have more time to look for your "tribe"—the people with whom you share interests and values and with whom you feel at home. For many, that "tribe" is other people with ADHD. It's quite striking at national and regional ADHD conventions to find people talking with each other with great animation. "I know just what you mean! You're describing my life!"

If you are fortunate enough to live in a community that has a CHADD (https://chadd.org) group, attend their monthly meetings to advocate for the formation of a senior support group. The number of seniors with ADHD is growing rapidly, but CHADD will continue to focus more on parents and kids impacted by ADHD unless more seniors attend the meetings and make their needs known.

Make It a Daily Habit to Reach Out to Someone

This is one of the most important "healthy daily habits" mentioned in Chapter 9. The contact doesn't have to be complicated or time-consuming—a quick text to share a humorous comment or YouTube video tells someone that you are thinking about them. More and more older adults make postings on their Facebook page, but while these allow people who are interested to know what you've been up to, they don't create a direct connection. "Liking" something on Facebook is a very bland and impersonal way to "reach out and touch someone." A direct, one-to-one text or email is much more personal and likely to build or maintain a friendship. So, every day, reach out to someone—friend or family—by text, email, phone call, or actual in-person time.

Social connections are a basic human need; retreating into solitude will only lead to depression and eventually to poor health. There are many ways that you can build a stronger social support network. Look for like-minded people, for activities and gatherings that you don't have to organize yourself, and for support that can help you improve your social skills. If you are only going to pick one good habit to develop, building a social support network is the most important one to select. Older people with meaningful connections to friends and family lead healthier, happier, longer lives.

KEY TAKEAWAYS FROM THIS CHAPTER

- ✔ Social connections are critical to good functioning in our later years. We have different levels of social needs, but living in social isolation tends to lead to depression and an increase in ADHD challenges.

- ✔ ADHD patterns can easily be misinterpreted by those without ADHD. A humorous acknowledgment and apology for your forgetfulness, lateness, or tendency to interrupt can go a long way.

✔ Actively look for groups or organizations that can provide a built-in social network.

✔ Look for your "tribe" of fellow ADHDers—in a local support group or even an online support group.

✔ Be sure to "add" connections to new people in your life to counterbalance the inevitable "subtractions" of people from your life as they move away, suffer from poor health that prevents socializing, or pass away.

Marriage and ADHD in Older Couples

Building empathy, connection, and collaboration

Coauthored by Melissa Orlov

I invited my friend and colleague Melissa Orlov, a top expert on ADHD and marriage, to coauthor this chapter. Her online class for couples has been a wonderful resource, providing couples with a greater understanding of how ADHD impacts relationships and offering them very straightforward advice to help them navigate the particular challenges that ADHD can bring to a relationship. I especially appreciate her balanced view of couples impacted by ADHD. She does not pathologize the ADHD partner as needing to be "fixed," but instead guides both partners toward compromise and collaboration.

The following combines my experience over the years while working with couples along with some of the very useful advice that Melissa Orlov provides in her book, *The ADHD Effect on Marriage: Understand and Rebuild Your Relationship in Six Steps*.[1]

Common problematic patterns in couples impacted by ADHD

- **Defining ADHD as "abnormal" and a "defect"**—Many, even most, couples become embroiled in the "I'm 'normal' and you have a disorder" game. These partners don't see ADHD as a series of traits that can be negative in some situations and very positive in many others. Instead, they focus only on the negative. No strong marriage can be built upon a foundational belief that one partner is the way that people "should be" while the other partner is deficient.

- **"It's *you* who needs to change"**—Yes, many ADHD traits may cause difficulties. The spouse with ADHD needs to commit to understanding and making every effort to change problematic behaviors; but it's not only the ADHD spouse who needs to change behaviors. Nagging, blaming, feeling superior, and having frequent angry reactions are behaviors that the non-ADHD spouse needs to change if partners are going to collaborate on building a stronger, more loving relationship.

- **Diminishment and judging**—"I'm in charge/you're a failure" comments (such as "How many times do I have to ask you to take care of something before you finally do it!") can diminish the ADHD partner.

- **Criticism and blaming**—Often, the ADHD spouse feels constantly picked on. People with ADHD frequently marry someone who is more focused and organized. What may feel like a good balance in the beginning—"I'm fun and spontaneous, you're focused and orderly"—can soon begin to feel toxic, especially after kids arrive and there is so much more to take care of.

- **Markedly different "speeds" or energy levels**—Sometimes the ADHD partner is restless, high energy, and stimulation seeking, whereas their spouse is slower, more cautious, and desires to do one thing at a time. In ADHD marriages that work, the couple comes to terms with these differences, and each lets the other be him- or herself.

- **Impulsive vs careful**—Both traits have positive and negative aspects. The more impulsive spouse with ADHD can come up with a plan on the spur of the moment and can sometimes prod their spouse to take a chance and get out of their rut. Impulses can be exciting and breathe life into a relationship, as long as they are not "dangerous" impulses, such as making large purchases that are not affordable, or quitting a job in frustration with no other employment on the horizon. Careful spouses can help couples plan for, and secure, their future.

- **Different relationships with the experience of time**—For many with ADHD, the time is always "now" and anything that needs to be done in the future, even if the "future" is only a few hours away, doesn't need to be addressed. People with ADHD can throw themselves into an immediate project because it suddenly comes up on their radar but are less likely to plan ahead and prepare for future deadlines before they arrive. There is often conflict between a non-ADHD spouse who always wants to arrive early (or even on time) for an event and an ADHD spouse who believes it's not necessary, in fact a waste of time, to arrive so early.

- **Feelings of being ignored**—Non-ADHD spouses often feel ignored because their spouse is either hyperfocused on some activity or distracted by their own thoughts. In addition, some ADHD adults may verbally agree upon a plan to avoid conflict with their spouse when, in fact, they disagree. Later, when they don't follow through on their "agreement," the non-ADHD partner feels ignored.

How do ADHD traits impact a marriage?

- **Misinterpreting your ADHD spouse**—It's so important for the non-ADHD spouse not to view every interaction only from their own viewpoint. The non-ADHD spouse may frequently feel hurt and angry because they interpret negative behaviors as intentional. "If I did that [interrupt, never finish something you've asked me to do, forget what you said, only half listen, get home late repeatedly], it would be because I just didn't care how I impacted you. So, you must not care about me because you keep doing these things." Often, it's just that ADHD symptoms are present and the behavior is not a reflection of not caring about their partner's feelings.

- **Developing a parent-child relationship**—Many non-ADHD spouses feel that they must always be in charge, doing more than their share, always frustrated and feeling less and less respect for their spouse. Many joke about having three kids in the house: my son, my daughter, and my husband/wife with ADHD.

- **Withdrawal and eventual departure**—There is a common pattern of non-ADHD spouses withdrawing into work instead of participating in a true partnership.

- **Chore wars**—Especially when there are kids in the household, there is always more to do than there is time to do it. Chore wars begin and escalate when there is no careful problem-solving to determine which spouse is best at what, who is responsible for what, and whether money needs to be spent to pay for some chores to be done by others.

- **Escape patterns**—Many couples fall into a destructive pattern of the "criticized spouse" trying to escape what feels like a constant barrage of criticism, while the "critical spouse" feels unloved and ignored.

- **One side of the ADHD coin: denying that ADHD matters**—In some marriages, the more dominant partner has ADHD, feels comfortable with who they are and how they behave, and mocks the non-ADHD spouse for their need for order and timeliness. "Relax! What's the big deal?" This is one side of the ADHD coin.

- **The flip side of the ADHD coin: insisting that the "right" way to be is orderly, organized, and on time all the time**—On the flip side of the ADHD coin, the dominant partner does not have ADHD and engages in constant nagging and criticism, making their spouse feel that nothing they do is good enough.

> The blame game only leads to anger and defensiveness.

The "Blame Game" Only Leads to Anger and Defensiveness

So, what's to be done about resolving these differences and getting back in touch with why you two fell in love with each other?

Melissa Orlov, in her book *The ADHD Effect on Marriage: Understand and Rebuild Your Relationship in Six Steps*, outlines an online course that she has created for married couples impacted by ADHD. These steps are very applicable to any committed relationship that is impacted by one partner having ADHD. She does not directly address same-sex couples, unmarried couples, or couples in which both partners are affected by ADHD, but in my view, her approach can be very helpful for any adult couple in a committed relationship that is impacted by ADHD.

Put Yourself in Your Partner's Shoes

Feeling empathy isn't always easy, especially empathizing with a spouse toward whom you feel anger and resentment. But if your goal is to rebuild your marriage, it's crucial to be able to put yourself in your spouse's shoes—to see the world from their point of view rather than deciding that they are "wrong" to be the way they are.

Identify Emotions That Are Getting in the Way of Resolving Problems

The emotions that block constructive problem-solving include the following:

- **Fear of failure**—"If I try and fail, she/he will only become more angry."
- **Chronic anger**—"I'm so angry and frustrated, I can't see anything positive in him/her."
- **Denial**—"It's not so bad. There is nothing really wrong. He/she is just in a bad mood."
- **Hopelessness**—"I've tried and tried; nothing is good enough."

Get Involved in Couples' Therapy That Includes Both Partners

Remember, change needs to occur in both partners. An effective couples' therapist can help couples move away from blame, accusations, and resentment and toward constructive problem-solving, clear communication, and empathetic listening so that each can understand the other's point of view and make changes in response to their new understanding.

Focus on Improving Communication

A good couples' therapist can help couples to communicate how they feel and what they want from their partner in a way that is mutual and caring. When one spouse feels "heard," they are much more likely to listen and respond constructively, "hearing" their spouse in return. If you do not have access to a couples' counselor, or if the cost of professional couples' counseling is outside your budget, look for a "cocounseling" group in your community. Cocounseling groups offer classes to teach new members how to cocounsel each other. You and your spouse can participate in cocounseling, helping both of you learn better listening and communication skills.

Set Boundaries in the Relationship

No strong relationship is built upon an expectation that one partner will sacrifice their basic core needs to accommodate the other's needs. Of course, compromises are made in all healthy, caring relationships. But if you or your partner feels that they are expected to deny core aspects of themselves to satisfy the other's expectations, the relationship will become unhealthy and increasingly unhappy over time.

Don't Let a Loving Relationship Turn into a "Partnership" Defined by Duties and Responsibilities

Life is full of responsibilities, and successful couples share in fulfilling those responsibilities in a balanced way. But many couples let their romantic relationship fall by the wayside as life's demands take center stage, especially during child-rearing years. It's important to hang on to the things that attracted the two of you, that led you to fall in love and decide to spend your lives together. Sometimes, to recapture those feelings, it's important to be intentional in making time to be together; for example, establishing a "date night" in which you and your partner go out for the evening to reconnect and enjoy each other, or planning long weekends away from the normal flow of day-to-day life.

For *much* more information about how marriage is impacted by ADHD and how to strengthen and rebuild your relationship, I strongly encourage you to read Melissa Orlov's book *The ADHD Effect on Marriage: Understand and Rebuild Your Relationship in Six Steps.*

What Can Be Done to Help Older Couples Impacted by ADHD?

Many couples impacted by ADHD develop unhealthy patterns of interacting with each other over their years together. Research suggests that more than half of relationships affected by ADHD are troubled. Not all relationships that involve ADHD are struggling, but retirement can add pressure for couples that have been doing well. This is in part because, after the retirement of one or both partners, couples typically spend more time together, and this has the potential to exacerbate issues that had previously been set aside during years focused on work demands and raising children.

But while retirement may add pressure, the first order of business is to make sure that a couple interacts in healthy, productive, and respectful ways. Further, "right-sizing" expectations can help couples adjust to their new, retired lives more quickly.

Understanding the Impact of ADHD Helps Troubled Couples Get It Right

Moe and Mike now are both retired. Moe was previously in finance and looked forward to getting more time to just do what she wanted. Mike, who has ADHD, was a popular professor. The couple was struggling with anger in their relationship before their retirements. Mike's way of dealing with the anger was to hide in his hobby room for many hours, staying clear of his wife. With retirement, she expected to see more of him, so his frequent disappearances "down his rabbit hole" added to her frustration. They both felt lonelier in their retirement than they had expected. Moe felt lonely because of Mike's regular disappearances; and Mike, because he missed the socializing he had had while teaching.

The first thing that this couple needed to do was learn more about the specific impacts of ADHD in their relationship. In their case, the anger that Moe felt was from two primary sources. The first was a deep-seated anger she had carried with her from cruel interactions with her mother as she was growing up. The second was from her long-standing resentment that she had had to take on more than her share of responsibilities in her relationship with Mike, and that he had emotionally avoided her for years.

They, like many other couples impacted by ADHD, had developed a parent-child dynamic—a pattern of interaction where non-ADHD partners end up overperforming as they try to compensate for inconsistency brought about by undermanaged ADHD symptoms of their spouse. The ADHD partner promises to do things but then often doesn't follow through. Non-ADHD partners take control as a way to move their lives forward, and end up in a "parental" role, reminding, setting priorities, organizing, and taking on the lion's share of household responsibilities. This generates a great deal of frustration, resentment, and chronic anger in the non-ADHD partner (as they feel they are doing too much) and in the ADHD partner (as that partner feels controlled and unimportant). ADHD partners who are not adequately managing ADHD symptoms, as Mike had not been, underperform in the parent-child dynamic, and over the years tend to either respond defensively to their partner's growing frustration or by retreating, as Mike had, to avoid their partner's demands altogether.

To successfully navigate their retirement, Moe and Mike had a good deal of work to do to change the unhealthy interaction patterns they had developed and better manage their emotions. Most important, they needed to move out of the parent-child dynamic if they were going to be happy together.

They started by finding out much more about adult ADHD and its impact. It helped Moe understand that Mike still loved her and his responses to her requests weren't personal; rather, they were the result of both undermanaged ADHD and his inability to deal with the shame he felt when his lack of follow-through led to disappointing her. Mike's first task, then, was to learn to better manage his ADHD timeliness and project completion. He installed a whiteboard in the kitchen that he would see regularly, and created a daily routine that included reviewing what he had to do that day and checking off each task as he completed it. He also added exercise to his daily routine (a known treatment for ADHD) and medication. Because he didn't function as well in retirement as he had when teaching had provided a routine, Mike created a daily routine that would help him remain productive.

Next, Moe and Mike worked on addressing the roots of the anger in their relationship and practiced new, more structured ways of communicating their concerns to each other that would be less likely to trigger anger or feelings of shame. Although she had been avoiding thinking about her mother for many years, Moe took on the task of exploring her anger at her mother as well as that toward her husband and made excellent progress in that area.

Once their interactions were less likely to be overtaken by strong, negative emotions, Moe and Mike started building connections with each other and addressing their loneliness. It's one thing to *eliminate* problems, but to have a relationship that they really enjoy, couples also have to *add* things that bring them joy and connection. As the only man in his swim class, Mike found he enjoyed the attention he got, which helped replace the attention that he missed from his teaching days. Together, the couple decided to rebuild their bridge-playing skills and began playing regularly with a bridge club. Both are much happier with their newfound time together and their blossoming social life. As a bonus, that happiness led to a sense of generosity, and both are now becoming active in volunteer organizations in which they believe, adding to their sense of purpose.

Once Moe and Mike were able to confront their own feelings and contributions to their marriage problems, they could stop blaming each other and take responsibility for improving their own behaviors. This allowed them to address long-standing anger issues, lessen parent-child dynamics, and finally step away from hurtful interactions they were having. They could rebuild the friendship and love they so longed for.

Navigating Differences in Expectations at Retirement

John and Lori had a bumpy path into retirement, as well as a rocky relationship. They had had a nine-year stretch in the middle part of their marriage during which they were living separately because they could not deal with the parent-child dynamics that had built up in their relationship. But then, at a son's football game, they realized they genuinely missed each other and decided to repair and strengthen their marriage. To everyone's surprise, they got back together again and did a good job of growing their love and empathy.

Several years after reuniting, they discovered that closing in on retirement had put new stressors on their love. Lori really liked her job working with animals and felt anxious about no longer having the satisfaction and routine she got daily from work. Routine was one of her main ways of managing her ADHD. John, on the other hand, had nurtured a dream of moving to the West Coast and experiencing the freedom and joy of living more of his life outdoors. Their two visions of retirement could not have been more different, and their disagreements were magnified by Lori's anxiety.

In couples' counseling, Lori opened up about her habit of hiding her anxieties from John because she was embarrassed. She also felt anxious that John might judge her if she shared her feelings. As a result, the anxiety would build up, feeding on itself and making the world (and their relationship) look much more threatening than it really was.

With help from their marriage counselor, Lori began to share her anxieties much earlier so that they could dissipate in the presence of John's affection. They developed a simple routine. Each evening they would sit together and finish the sentence "The most important thing you need to know about me today is…" This provided an opportunity to become closer by sharing successes, hopes, fears… and anxieties.

Soon after they adopted this routine Lori realized that many of her anxieties had been due to a pattern of catastrophizing rather than based in reality. She grew to understand that John, true to his word, was genuinely empathetic to Lori's feelings. This simple exercise helped them become closer, more relaxed, and more trusting of each other.

As for whether to move west, fate stepped in to help them make the decision. Lori had a serious car accident and John helped with her recovery. Then, John was diagnosed with a life-threatening condition that he recovered from with Lori's support. Forced to confront their own mortality, they realized how lucky they were to still be together. They are now both fully retired and thoroughly enjoying exploring a new life out west, grateful they are around to do so. And they still use the "most important thing" routine daily to build emotional closeness and enrich their time together.

When One Partner Retires While Their Spouse Continues to Work

Ami and Dan also had conflicting expectations about retirement. In their case, it had to do with Dan's retiring while Ami continued to work. Dan, who has ADHD, retired before Ami did and gleefully hyperfocused on his favorite hobby. Ami, still working full-time, felt Dan should spend some of his time picking up some of the household responsibilities that she had traditionally shouldered.

At first, Dan agreed to do so. But the reality was that he wasn't very interested in doing household tasks and his reward-focused

ADHD brain kept finding more interesting things upon which to focus. Finally, after Ami became increasingly agitated by Dan's lack of follow-through on his promises, he admitted that he had no desire to take on tasks that he had not previously had to do.

One of the challenges for many adults in their relationships is realizing that one cannot "make" a partner do something that partner doesn't wish to do. No matter how much Ami wanted (or asked for) Dan's assistance, it was up to Dan to determine how he would spend his time. If Dan continued to refuse to do the work, even after Ami made her case for why she felt he should be more involved, there wasn't much she could do.

Retirement can change someone's expectations, as it did for Ami, and couples must constructively deal with the reality of each partner's opinions and actions in the face of those expectations. Ami could have become bitter about Dan's attitude. Instead, she chose to admit he had worked hard for many years, even if it wasn't at chores. He did deserve some downtime and had a right to do whatever he wanted to do. But Ami had also worked hard, and she deserved some downtime too. So, she hired some basic help with cleaning, freeing up several hours a week. She got Dan to agree to take charge of two tasks that he didn't object to but that she particularly disliked. And she convinced him that just as he has a right to choose what not to do, so does she. Although he had previously balked when she approached the topic of getting help, he acknowledged her point of view and stopped resisting. With newfound free time, Ami gave herself permission to do some fun things, rather than just fill in with more chores.

The result is that they are both happier and have successfully adjusted to their new status with one of them retired while the other is still working. Their breakthrough came when they realized that no one partner gets to set the agenda for the other. They both have free will and a right to make their own choices.

Lack of Structure in Retirement and Taking Charge

Dinesh and Amara have been married for forty-five years, but their marriage has been difficult enough that they have been in counseling much of that time. They now understand that ADHD and responses to ADHD have played a big role in their conflicts. Dinesh's ADHD is severe, but the couple enjoyed raising their daughters together as it gave them a shared purpose. Now that their daughters are grown and out of the house, the couple doesn't seem to have much in common and Amara is rethinking her life. On her down days, Amara thinks about divorce and Dinesh's less-than-perfectly-managed ADHD. She worries about whether he "will have my back if I get sick someday."

On her better days, Amara is less negative. "I really do love my husband. And while things will never be perfect between us, I don't really wish to leave. Nor do I wish to expend all the energy needed to start over again. So, I prefer to stay and do what is needed to be happier."

At age sixty-eight, Dinesh would like to retire but money is tight. Dinesh hasn't spent much time thinking about retirement, saving money, or planning what a transition to retirement might look like. He simultaneously imagines a happy retirement and fears what having large blocks of time and less obvious purpose may feel like. He doesn't voice these concerns often. Mostly, he feels uneasy that money might run out or that he will miss work. He also worries about Amara's continued feelings of discontent.

Amara, true to her word, decided that the key to staying in this relationship was to take charge of her own happiness. She joined a support group that, over the course of the year, helped her learn how to balance her independence and her relationship with Dinesh. She decided to keep working, even though she is in her midseventies, because she enjoys her work and she also likes the additional security it gives her. She is committed to staying with Dinesh, and encouraged him to get additional support for his ADHD, while realizing she wasn't in control of that. She is working on reengaging with one of her children who had become estranged.

In short, Amara took control of her own happiness while not abandoning Dinesh in the process. This has provided the kind of control over her own life and happiness that feels satisfying, while taking pressure off the relationship. Amara has come to terms with the idea that not everything will be perfect while not sacrificing her happiness to do so. Her reassessment of what she wanted in her life helped her chart a more joyful and purposeful course.

Your ADHD Is Getting on My Nerves!

Michael and Helen have been married for over forty-five years. Each had a successful professional career, and they raised two children together. Throughout the marriage, although they shared many core values, they went through life as polar opposites. Helen was anxious and a perfectionist, hard-working and very conscious of her position in their community. Michael was a "people person" and loved to get caught up in conversation with nearly anyone he encountered, a pattern that was a great frustration to Helen. He was caught up in the moment while she wanted to keep the trains running on time. In retirement, Michael's ADHD patterns seemed to irritate Helen more than ever. The more time they spent together, the more she became frustrated with his messiness and lateness. Her anger was often simmering as she waited for him to get in the car to go to a planned event. He was perfectly okay with arriving a few minutes late; Helen always wanted to be early. As Helen's anger and frustration grew, they decided to seek out ADHD-focused couples' therapy. Because each of them was reflective and self-aware, they were able to make good use of the therapy. Helen agreed that Michael could "keep his mess in the family room" so long as he picked up his belongings in the other common areas of the house. Michael agreed to be more time aware, as he came to accept how important this was to Helen.

Over the course of a year, they grew closer, more understanding and tolerant of each other's quirks and foibles. They had always had a strong commitment to their marriage, but finally, in their later years, they were actually enjoying their time together.

Each of these couples engaged in ADHD-focused couples' counseling and was able to understand each other better, to solve problems rather than holding grudges, and to learn to focus on the positive and to not try to control each other.

What Happens When Both Partners Have ADHD?

Sometimes, two people with ADHD find each other and fall in love. "Finally, someone who understands me!"

Marty and Robin

Marty and Robin each had ADHD, and each was long divorced when they met in a small artsy community in Northern California. Their earlier marriages had also been to spouses with ADHD, but the pressures of raising challenging children had been more than could be managed. Their marriages had split apart and each had gone through difficult years of raising children as single parents. Once the children had left the nest, both Marty and Robin decided to move to a community better suited to their needs. Each wanted a simpler life in a community of fellow artists. Robin painted and made beautiful beaded jewelry. Marty had always worked as a small-scale developer, but he cut down on these sorts of jobs to allow time to fulfill his dream of making beautiful handcrafted furniture. Marty and Robin found each other after the high-stress child-rearing years were behind them. Each was pursuing a dream to live a simpler, more artistic life. They had met in a community of people who all prioritized quality of life rather than quantity of income and belongings. Neither Marty nor Robin stuck to regular routines. They each had workshops attached to the simple rustic home that Marty had built for himself. They managed the downside of their ADHD by creating a lifestyle that didn't require them to be focused, timely, or organized. Robin happily shed her previous role as homemaker and reveled in her more authentic sense of self as an artist and "free spirit."

Tina and Rick

Tina's marriage to Rick was another successful match between two adults with ADHD, but quite different from Marty and Robin's marriage. Tina had grown up in a very dysfunctional household. Her father had died when she was in high school and her relationship with her mother was far from calm. She described her first marriage as a "desperation move" that she made as a teenager. During her senior year in high school, her alcoholic mother announced that she was moving back home to the Midwest. Mom proclaimed that Tina must either marry her high school boyfriend or move with her mother. Tina chose the first option and the marriage lasted barely a year. Tina, only nineteen, divorced and underemployed, moved to be with her mother, an arrangement that was fraught with conflict. Tired of working minimum-wage jobs, Tina decided to go to cosmetology school. Soon after graduation, and unhappy living with her mother, she impulsively married a young man who was into drugs, alcohol, and "wild behavior," telling herself that he would settle down. It soon became clear that he had no interest in changing. She left her second bad marriage and decided to strike out on her own. As a hairstylist, she could finally afford her own place.

Tina gradually built a successful hair salon. She happened to meet her third husband in a restaurant across the street from her salon. Unlike her immature first husband and her highly dysfunctional second husband, Tom was smart, ambitious, and interested in business and real estate. Their interests and energy level were a good match and they have had a long, successful career managing hotels and restaurants. "We were partners and I didn't have to just sit home." Together they raised a son and a daughter. Tina reports that all four of her family members—she, her husband, and their two children—have ADHD, and all of them are doing well, the son and daughter also working in the family businesses.

The keys to success in a marriage when both partners have ADHD is to remember the following:

- **KISS—Keep It Simple, Sweetheart.** When both partners have ADHD, the more your life is simple and streamlined, the less challenging it will be; a larger house may seem appealing, but a smaller home is much easier to take care of; socialize with friends outside of your home—that way there's no pressure to cook, clean, or decorate for company.

- **Add the structure and support that you need.** When you *both* have ADHD, there may be things that neither you nor your partner is good at—such things as organizing paperwork, paying bills, filing income tax returns, maintaining order around the house, doing laundry, and meal planning and preparation. Many couples decide to "outsource" as much of these "life management" tasks as possible—hiring a bookkeeper and accountant, spending more money on cleaning services, and eating in restaurants or ordering carry-out much of the time. Consider "outsourcing" difficult tasks to friends and relatives on a barter basis, such as offering to do something you are good at in exchange for your friend or relative helping out with tasks that are particularly difficult for you.

- **Plant yourself in the right place.** In other words, instead of just trying to "fix" yourself, think about the environment that would allow you to function at your best and try to find it. This might mean distancing yourself from particularly critical friends or relatives; it might mean joining organizations that focus on your particular gifts or interests.

So, Here We Are All These Years Later

You may be still married to your spouse but are having difficulty adjusting to life changes such as retirement, financial issues, health problems, and increasing social isolation. Or you may be married for a second or even third time. When one or both of you has ADHD, the keys to a happy marriage late in life are understanding and acceptance, but sometimes that's easier said than done.

Life Gets Easier Once the Kids Are Grown!

Hillary and Brian had spent a good deal of their thirty-three-year marriage in conflict around ADHD issues and responses to ADHD issues. Once they found out about the impact ADHD was having on their relationship, they worked together to help improve their partnership. Still, the pressures of raising kids, work, and life kept them in conflict more than they wanted.

Seven years ago, after their youngest child was finally "launched," they discovered the freedom of having fewer responsibilities, and the ability to start acting upon some of their dreams together. They started traveling more, spending more time with friends, relaxing in the evenings instead of planning the next day's activities. They finally had the freedom to move to a smaller home in a warmer climate so they could be outdoors more of the year and have fewer home responsibilities. They also had fewer chores since fewer people were living there.

Finally, after many years of hard work, their relationship was simplified enough that they could really start to nurture the affection that had always been there for them but had been masked by the stressors of everyday life.

Getting Along by Staying Apart

Less is more

Maria joked, "I'd probably kill my husband if we were around each other all the time." While she said this with humor, she also clearly meant that the secret to her long marriage to Mark was the fact that they spent extended periods of time away from one another. They had the good fortune to own not just their home but also a small vacation cabin a few hours' drive away. This couple readily admitted that they accommodated the great differences in needs, interests, and activity level by spending weeks, sometimes even several months, living in their separate residences before coming back together again.

Your place or mine?

Carol and Ed met and married in their sixties. Ed had ADHD and had been long divorced from his first wife. Carol was recently widowed. They lived in the same large retirement community, but their paths hadn't crossed until they met at a social gathering organized by their condo association. After an initial flurry of romance and excitement, both Carol and Ed settled back into their very different routines. Ed was a night owl and loved to keep the sports network playing on his wide-screen TV most of the day. Carol was an early bird and enjoyed the peace and quiet of sitting on her balcony in the morning, sipping her morning coffee and listening to the birds. They loved each other and were very grateful for the companionship that their relationship gave them. They married and moved into Carol's larger condo. Within weeks, their frustrations began to mount. Carol was neat and tidy; Ed left things strewn around the condo. Carol wanted the TV off except in the evenings. Ed felt frequently nagged to pick up after himself. Carol explained to me, "It may sound unconventional, but Ed and I decided to live in our separate apartments during the day. We always eat dinner together at my place; we go out and socialize as a couple, and we love to travel together. But we don't love living together 24/7."

After All This Time, I'm Resigned

Other people spoke of their long-term marriage with resignation.

"We don't have much in common, but we've learned to lead fairly separate lives in the same house." Richard explained that his wife, who had ADHD, was a nonstop talker. If she wasn't talking to him, she was on the phone with someone. He reported that over the years, they had learned to live apart in the same house. He lived mostly on the basement level, where he had a large den to watch TV and a home office where he continued to work part-time. "We eat dinner together and sometimes watch a show in the evening while we eat, but my wife goes to bed much earlier than I do and

I often fall asleep on the couch watching television." They had separate friend groups—Richard played golf and poker with "the guys"; Ellen played bridge with her women friends and met them for lunch and shopping. Together, they enjoyed time with their grandchildren. Not a close relationship, but they had learned to make it work.

Adjusting to Big Changes Related to Retirement

When Marriage and Retirement Collide

Regardless of whether your marriage is conflictual or peaceful and harmonious, or something in between, life changes in our later years always pose challenges and require adjustments. These changes may include health issues; cognitive decline; geographic changes, such as downsizing; moving to warmer weather or to be closer to family. The move from working full-time to full retirement is another big change that often requires adjustments on the part of both partners.

Some marriages hit a very rocky patch as the couple transitions to retirement. A couple may have adjusted to one another reasonably well when work occupied most of their waking hours. But in retirement, routines are disrupted and some couples realize that they no longer have shared goals and desire very different lifestyles.

I Don't Want a Divorce, but I Don't Want to Live Together Either

Ron and Cheryl had developed increasingly separate lives in the years after their children left home. Rather than going through a messy, painful divorce, Cheryl suggested an alternative path. They wanted to retain the shared family holidays and celebrations and to enjoy family visits and time with their grandchildren. What Cheryl didn't want was to continue to live together in a way that caused daily irritation and resentment between them. She came up with a creative solution that worked out for both of them.

Ron was a smart guy who always liked to read about a variety of topics and missed having people at work with whom he could talk over lunch. His long marriage had ruptured after he retired. His wife, Cheryl, had very different interests than Ron and found that she was less and less tolerant of his relative messiness and lack of structure. Within a year after his retirement, she told Ron that although she didn't want a divorce, she no longer wanted to live with Ron. They could share holiday celebrations and time with family, but she no longer wanted to share living space and try to cobble a life together that didn't quite fit well for either of them.

Ron moved out into his own apartment and, to his surprise, instead of feeling lost or rejected, he began to spread his wings. For the first time, he could fully explore his own interests rather than catering to his wife's interests in going antiquing on weekends. He could do things his own way at home, without worrying about criticism or conflict. And they weren't divorced. They often got together on the weekend for lunch or brunch and found that they enjoyed each other's company more when their days weren't filled with frustration and conflict.

His wife had never shared his intellectual interests. Ron began searching for ways to find others who loved to talk about philosophy, history, science, and politics. He formed a men's group at his church, billing it as a "Senior Think Tank." To his great delight, he got to know a number of men he'd never met before who also belonged to his church. Then, Ron branched out to form another group, "The Armchair Philosophers," and met even more people he enjoyed. He and Cheryl decided that they now had the best of both worlds.

Satisfying Marriages among Older Couples Impacted by ADHD

We've all heard the discouraging statistics about marriage and ADHD—that the divorce rate among adults with ADHD is much higher and that mothers of children with ADHD are more likely to be divorced. Several excellent books have been written on marriage and ADHD describing dysfunctional parent-child relationships that often develop between a non-ADHD spouse and their ADHD partner.[2] But that's not the whole story. Among the older adults with ADHD I have talked to, quite a few of them described their marriage, typically a second marriage entered into when they were more mature, as a very happy relationship.

Rick and Kate

Rick, like Ron, has a graduate degree. He was married twice before meeting Kate, his wife of thirty-three years. Rick's first two marriages were very conflictual. His memory of his first marriage is murky—"No kids, thank God! I'm told by friends that we fought constantly." Three years after his first divorce, he married again— "Not my idea, but the woman I was dating wanted kids and I went along with it." This also highly conflictual marriage, which ended in divorce nine years later, produced two sons with ADHD. So far in Rick's narrative, his life sounds stereotypical. He has two sons with ADHD from his second marriage, and both marriages were relatively brief with high conflict. Ron is now very happily married to Kate, a marriage he describes as a marriage of opposites. "I'm still very ADD, she was diagnosed with OCD." Our kitchen table tells the story—my end is messy and covered with stuff, her end is tidy and organized. I can still be irritable and grumpy, but she is so tolerant, sometimes too tolerant. Kate is very patient. She knows I have trouble being on time. She just brings a book and reads until I am ready. Ron describes his marriage to Kate as "the best thing that ever happened to me."

Diane and Evan

After a brief, unhappy first marriage, Diane met her second husband while she was in graduate school, and they married soon thereafter. Evan was twelve years older, a widower with three children. Diane soon gave birth to a son. Evan was a successful businessman. Because the family was not reliant upon her income, she had the freedom to pursue graduate education, serve on the boards of several nonprofits, and become trained as an ADHD coach. Diane's extensive education about ADHD provided her with many insights and solutions to minimize the impact of ADHD on her marriage. Evan adored Diane and felt so grateful that she had come into his life to help him raise his three children. Their child together became the family glue as everyone adored Charlie, who grew up showered with attention from his parents and three much older siblings. Their marriage worked due to the deep emotional bond that Diane and Evan enjoyed, but also because the marriage provided Diane with financial security and the reduced stress provided by household help, a supportive husband, and no need for Diane to work while raising the children. While many women with ADHD find themselves divorced and working full-time as single parents, Diane's experience was quite the opposite. The emotional and financial support she experienced helped greatly to reduce the impact of her ADHD on her marriage.

Anais

Anais was married for only a few months as a young woman. When her husband became violent during an argument, she filed for divorce and remained single until she was in her early forties. At that point, she met her second husband, to whom she's been married for over thirty years. Her first husband was immature, angry, and focused on his own needs, whereas her current husband has been loving, patient, and supportive from the start. Now in her seventies, she is becoming increasingly anxious about the prospect of being left a lonely widow. She relies upon her husband to take care of all the finances and paperwork, tasks that have always been difficult for her. But even more than being her "organizing principle," he is her closest friend and support. Anais continues to work part-time as an art instructor and editor. One of her greatest pleasures is to make beaded jewelry in the evenings while her husband sits nearby reading aloud to her. They are in sync, loving and supportive of each other.

Gina

Like so many people with ADHD, Gina married impulsively at a very young age. She thought that she and her first husband were "soul mates," but after a number of years of marriage, her husband got caught up in the "free love" time in California and started having extramarital affairs. In reaction, Gina eventually had an affair with a neighbor, by whom she became accidentally pregnant. Bret, the father of the baby, wanted to be with her and raise the baby together. They have been together ever since, over thirty years. They now have two daughters and are very happily involved in helping raise their grandchildren. Gina and Bret have built a very mutually supportive relationship in which they encourage each other to pursue their interests. Gina has never made much money, focusing more on her interests and on being a mother. Bret, however, has been more financially successful. As Gina puts it, "Bret and I are the happy pair. Every year we are more and more grateful to be with each other. I used to get really mad at him, but I don't do that anymore, thanks to therapy, mindfulness, and AA. He even helps me get out the door when I'm disorganized—he's a great guy."

What Do These Long and Happy Marriages Have in Common?

The similarities in these happy marriages are that they all involve patience, understanding, and support of each other's needs. In every case, they were second (or third) marriages to a more suitable partner—a partner who was tolerant of ADHD foibles, who was supportive of their spouse's needs, and who focused on the positive.

KEY TAKEAWAYS FROM THIS CHAPTER

✔ ADHD adds extra challenges as a couple makes the major life transition into retirement.

✔ Specialized couples' coaching or counseling can be very helpful to assist the ADHD and non-ADHD spouses to better understand each other's needs.

✔ Couples impacted by ADHD can improve their relationship by practicing the following:

  ○ Working hard to understand their partner's point of view

  ○ Improving communication patterns by truly listening to each other

- ○ Reintroducing moments of connection, fun, and romance into a relationship that may have become distant and conflictual

✔ Simplifying their lifestyle and "right-sizing" their expectations of each other can help couples reduce marital stress.

✔ A long and satisfying second (or third) marriage occurs more often than might be expected.

The Long and Winding Road

Parenting experiences of older adults with ADHD

arenthood is one of the biggest challenges that anyone can under-
take, and the challenge is that much greater if you are an adult
with ADHD whose child has ADHD. In this chapter, I will share
the experiences of older adults with ADHD who are still involved,
for better or for worse, in helping their adult children emotionally,
financially, or both. These young adults with ADHD "fail to launch"
into independent lives because they feel anxious, overwhelmed, and
unprepared for adulthood.

I will also share stories of parents who haven't learned to establish boundaries and who develop a codependent relationship with
their adult child that hampers them from developing the confidence
needed to solve problems and manage their lives independently.
I will also share stories of young adults who are *unable* to launch
into independent adulthood due to inborn or acquired disabilities
that will require some level of ongoing support throughout their
lives.

Most older adults with ADHD today did not have the benefit of understanding their own ADHD as they were raising their children. Some of them were fortunate enough to identify their child's ADHD early in life and provide them with the treatment and support that they needed. But many others simply did the best they could, not understanding how their own ADHD and their child's ADHD were contributing to their daily struggles. Many parents worked hard to hold down a job and raise their child without understanding that they and their child both had a treatable disorder. Today, many of these parents are still involved in helping their now adult child with ADHD.

Our parenting experiences differ because the ADHD children we raise are highly varied. For example, it's much easier to raise a child with inattentive ADHD who is quiet and compliant and anxious about school, compared to raising a child who is defiant, oppositional, and impulsive, and who has little interest in school. Likewise, parenting is more difficult if you struggle with depression, anxiety, and poor emotional regulation. You and your adult child will also be affected by how much support you had as you raised your children. In sum, it's complicated, with a great deal of variation in parenting experiences.

Parental Regret and Renewal

Late diagnosis of ADHD almost inevitably results in some feelings of regret—for our own lost chances, but also regrets as parents. A number of older parents expressed regret for the way they related to their children as they were growing up.

> *"Parenting was entirely too much for me. I only had one child. I could barely manage that. Looking back, I realize that a lot of my struggle with my daughter was due to my anxiety. I always felt more in control in my professional life than in my personal life."*

This mother's experience reflects that of many women who have told me that they can manage to stay more focused and organized at work but have "very little left" when they get home from work.

> "My three kids all have ADHD, but they are doing well. They weren't doing so well when they were home and I was a mom with ADHD. I have apologized to them for not giving them what they needed."

> "It was always hard for me to juggle home and work life. Then, I was coming into menopause when my older daughter was in puberty. I was emotionally impulsive and she had mood swings. Looking back, I realize that I was verbally abusive to her for years. In high school, we were repeatedly on suicide watch with her. Then, I read an article about stimulant medication helping reduce emotional outbursts and it just changed everything."

This pattern of mothers and daughters whose hormonal fluctuations lead to intense, emotional interactions with each other is very common. Unfortunately, little has been written about this phenomenon when both mothers and daughters with ADHD are impacted by hormonal fluctuations and what can help.

The following is the experience of a father with ADHD looking back on the stormy relationship he had with his teenage daughter.

> "My daughter was a 'pretty tough child.' No one wanted to label her (this was in the years before there was more recognition of girls with ADHD). She had issues at school, issues with the law, relationship issues. Her mother and I could never agree on how to parent her. Her mom never wanted to make her responsible for her actions. As a teen, she went to a psychologist that told her she 'didn't believe in ADD.' I was very hard on her and things got pretty bad.

"My big breakthrough with my daughter came later when she was an adult and she finally agreed that she has ADHD. She takes medication now. And I explain to her that while I can be very short with her, she is also short with me. Now, I'm no longer angry when she is coming over and then changes her mind at the last minute. We can enjoy each other and play music together now."

This father has experienced intergenerational healing. Now, both he and his daughter can admit fault and can forgive each other for their shortcomings related to ADHD.

Parental Regrets and a Healing Do-Over

Linda, now in her sixties, reported that her eldest daughter, Tina, who had ADHD, was incredibly difficult as a teen—impulsive, defiant, and much more interested in boys than schoolwork. At sixteen, Tina became pregnant. The family had strong religious and family values and decided to formally adopt Tina's baby. Looking back at her experiences with Tina during her adolescent years, Linda voices regret. "Maybe if we had known that we both had ADHD we could have gotten some help and things might have been different."

As an older mother with more understanding of ADHD, Linda's experience in raising her granddaughter was much smoother. The granddaughter was evaluated at an early age for ADHD, started taking medication, received coaching and educational support, and was able to go to college after high school.

Linda feels as if she had a "do-over" as a mom. She was a very different mother, calmer and more patient, while raising her granddaughter Lidia than she had been during Tina's adolescent years. Tina and her mother have talked many times about mutual regrets and are more at peace with each other.

What Can Help Ease Parental Regrets

In many ways, the years of parent-child conflict when both have ADHD are a situation of "complex trauma" for both parents and children. (Complex trauma is a relatively new concept to describe the effects of frequent smaller daily traumas, in contrast to the trauma caused by a single traumatic event.) Complex trauma is very common among family members with untreated ADHD because both parents and children feel stressed, frustrated, and overwhelmed—a situation likely to result in frequent conflicts, verbal abuse, even physical altercations, and, to varying degrees, family dysfunction.

Family therapy, even on a time-limited basis, can be a very healing experience both for older parents and their adult children. The goal of the therapy is to foster understanding, forgiveness, and better communication. Many middle-aged adults with ADHD, now raising their own child with ADHD, tell me that they have a much clearer perspective on the conflicts they experienced with their own parents. *"I was so resentful and angry in my twenties,"* one woman shared, *"but now that I am raising a daughter with ADHD, I can understand how hard it was for my own parents as they raised me."*

Parenting Patterns That Contribute to Prolonged Dependence

As the song says, "Growing up is hard to do." Many older parents with ADHD find themselves worrying about and emotionally and/ or financially supporting adult children with ADHD. The part of our brain—its prefrontal lobes—that helps us behave in a "mature" way is slower to fully develop in those with ADHD. I often tell parents that they are likely to see a big improvement in self-sufficiency as their adult child approaches age thirty. It's critical, however, for parents to keep setting limits and expectations so that their slower-to-mature child continues on the path toward self-sufficiency. Let's look at some parenting patterns that can inhibit maturation and growth.

Snowplow Parenting

"Snowplow" parenting is a recently coined term for parents who try to "plow" all the obstacles out of the way of their child so that they have a smooth path to follow. Many parents fall into a long-standing pattern of being their child's problem-solver. Parents love their children and want them to succeed, so they "run interference" for their child, with the best of intentions—meeting with their child's teacher every year to ask for accommodations, stepping in when their child is overwhelmed with homework, doing their child's laundry far past the age when they are quite capable of doing it for themselves. And this pattern, quite naturally, can continue into young adulthood and beyond. It's a habit that can be hard for parents to break, as well as one that an adult child takes for granted because it's all they've ever known.

Alan, a man in his early sixties, talked with resignation and frustration about his son Alex's seemingly endless path toward college graduation. Alan's ADHD had certainly caused difficulties for him in adult life as he drifted from one job to another with no particular plan. But he had been a good student and had earned a graduate degree. Whereas Alan had been passive and fairly compliant, Alex was the opposite: he was highly verbal, highly social, and argued with his teachers about why he had to do homework during high school. His mother, Beth, was a snowplow parent. She made excuses for Alex and fought his battles for him, including being the behind-the-scenes author of his college essays. Once he was in college, she constantly called the dean, his professors, and disability support providers, asking for exceptions to be made on his behalf. Despite all her efforts, he was put on academic probation and, when his grades continued to fall, he was sent home. A semester later, after much lobbying on the part of his mother, he returned to college. At last count, he was in his sixth year of undergraduate school. I'm not sure what else he learned in college, but he certainly learned that the rules don't apply to him.

Alex is not prepared for adulthood. Almost certainly, he will return to live at home and wait for his parents to find him a job that is to his liking.

Ostrich Parenting—If I Ignore It, Maybe It Will Go Away

Some parents operate without a plan, just hoping that their adult child will eventually grow up and figure out how to take care of themselves. But when parents continue to provide all the goods and services as when their adult child was a teen, there is no clear message that the latter needs to develop the skills to live as an independent adult. The phrase I tell many parents is, "Your job isn't to take care of your children, but to teach them how to take care of themselves." In some adolescents, this process is natural. They look forward to getting their driver's license and their first job. They are eager to leave home after high school, either for work or for college. These young adults may have more executive functioning abilities and more self-confidence. For most young adults with ADHD, however, maturation is much slower—several years slower. And they may need very explicit help in developing the "adulting" skills that other teens seem to acquire naturally.

In the story that follows, Claire, an older woman with ADHD, expressed her utter discouragement regarding Gina, an adult daughter who had done well academically but had never moved away from home or looked for employment. Everything had been handed to Gina, and at twenty-eight years of age, she demonstrated the immaturity of a much younger person. Gina is a college and law school graduate, but despite her academic abilities, she is deeply immature; she has remained at home after law school, not looking for work in the field of law and feeling completely stuck. Gina says, with anger, that she never wanted to study law in the first place and that her father "made her do it."

Gina has not worked since law school and is dating someone who also lives with his parents. Any job that Gina has ever had has been given to her by a family friend. She went straight from college to law school because, in her mother's estimation, she didn't want to be confronted by the challenges of work. During law school she lived at home. "My husband copes by staying removed from both me and Gina," Claire shared. "It's going to be entirely up to me to insist that she leave. My husband won't help. These days, I just find activities to get away from my daughter."

Claire, her husband, and Gina were stuck and badly needed the help of a therapist to move forward. One of the long-standing family issues in this family is that Claire and her husband have never developed a plan or worked as a team to place reasonable demands to help their daughter along the path toward independence. This family needs to work with a family therapist to help the parents communicate and make long-overdue decisions regarding Gina, to help her gradually make the transition to independence. But how do you break out of a long-established codependent relationship that slows or even blocks your adult child from becoming self-reliant and self-sufficient?

Inability to Set Boundaries with an Adult Child

In some cases, an adult child has long since left home but continues to have unreasonable expectations of parental support, often because the parents have not learned to set boundaries. Launching children with ADHD into successful adulthood is no guarantee that they will not come back for emotional and financial support when they hit the inevitable bumps in the road.

Setting Emotional Boundaries

Quite a few older parents find themselves feeling exhausted and overwhelmed as the crises in the lives of their adult children impact them. Emotional boundaries involve establishing how much and how often parents feel it's appropriate for adult children to call them when they are in an emotional crisis. Parents need to encourage their adult children, to help them develop confidence in their own ability to solve problems and to build a social support network for themselves rather than always calling home. This is the normal course of growing emotional maturity. As we mature, we rely upon our parents less and less for emotional support and build a network of friends, roommates, partners, and spouses to whom we turn for advice or simply a listening ear.

> Phyllis was an older woman with ADHD, retired from a very successful professional life. She'd been one of those many women who could focus very well at work, while her executive functioning skills at home were less in evidence. At home, things were managed well as her children were growing up because she had a full-time housekeeper and a husband who handled the paperwork and finances. After retirement, instead of enjoying the calm, relaxed lifestyle she had dreamed of, Phyllis found herself in a state of anxiety and overwhelm due to her daughter Annie's very difficult divorce. Annie fell apart when she learned that her husband had had an affair. Her husband moved out and suddenly Annie had to look for work instead of being the stay-at-home mother of two young children. She turned to Phyllis endlessly for support, weeping daily and telling her mother she just couldn't handle everything that she was suddenly responsible for. Phyllis

was called upon for babysitting, long phone calls for daily moral support, and financial assistance as well. Phyllis's blood pressure began to rise, her sleep was impacted, and her stress level went through the roof.

Phyllis needed to establish clear boundaries. She felt that Annie assumed that her retired mother had all the time in the world to help her with her problems. The fix wasn't immediate, but Phyllis's therapy helped her set clear limits on how much babysitting she could provide and insisted that Annie get into therapy herself rather than relying so much on her mother. A year later, Annie had found a job, had found good daycare for her two preschoolers, and no longer looked to her parents to solve all her problems.

Setting Financial Boundaries

Many parents, with the best of intentions, become the "bank of Mom and Dad" to a still-dependent twenty-something. It's quite often the case that young adults with ADHD are not prepared to be fully financially independent in their early to mid-twenties and parents fall into a habit of bailing their young adult children out. While this may be necessary, it's critically important to set "financial boundaries" with your young adult, letting them know how much you are willing to contribute and how long you are willing to contribute to their monthly expenses before you expect them to make choices that will allow them to be entirely independent.

Rob had never finished college and had returned home at age twenty. He continued to live in his parents' home for years while he worked at minimum-wage jobs intermittently; he was either fired or quit the job because he "didn't like his boss." His father was retired and his mother was nearing retirement when, in desperation, the parents rented a small cottage in a remote wooded area a few miles away. Rob considered himself an amateur environmentalist and imagined conducting a second "Walden Pond" experience while living in the cottage. After a couple of years, his mother became increasingly desperate. At that point, already in her seventies, she was only working to be able to financially support her son and was very eager to retire. Meanwhile the son, now in his midthirties, remained unemployed and was less and less functional. These parents ultimately needed very active support to find some sort of supervised living situation for their son as it had become increasingly clear that his ADHD and autism, combined with many years of not working, had rendered him incapable of full independence. Rob's parents would have helped themselves and their son much more had they sought assistance many years earlier. Their well-intended financial support during his twenties and thirties had only made the situation far worse. Setting financial boundaries ("We can't afford to support you indefinitely") and engaging social services set this family on a better course.

Leo had both ADHD and learning disabilities. Leo's mother, an older divorced woman close to retirement, didn't seem to have the will and determination to push her son out of the nest. Whenever she became frustrated and suggested he move out, he countered by saying he would kill himself if she evicted him. This emotional blackmail was quite effective. Even after he eventually earned his BA, a dozen years in the making, he continued to live at home, to work only intermittently while entertaining himself by refurbishing cars. His mother died when Leo was thirty-nine. He had never lived on his own or supported himself. Leo squandered his small inheritance in the course of a couple of years by spending it on a very expensive automobile and on dating women for whom he bought expensive clothing, jewelry, and vacations. Needless to *say, his life in middle age was very difficult. He rented out rooms in the townhouse he had inherited to be able to cover the mortgage and led a very hand-to-mouth existence.*

Belated Financial Boundaries

Whereas Leo never left home, Janice, also diagnosed with ADHD, had left home at a young age but was still depending upon her parents for most things.

> *Janice had impulsively dropped out of college to marry her boyfriend, who also had ADHD. The combination of this young couple's immaturity and ADHD led to a disastrous string of decisions. Her parents were bombarded with phone calls after every crisis. Janice had lost her job; her husband had lost his job; their car had broken down and needed costly repairs. The problems were endless and, for at least a decade, her parents were endlessly sending money and emotional support, bailing out the leaky boat that their daughter and her husband had sailed off on. Finally, as the parents neared retirement, they talked to a counselor at their church who strengthened their resolve to stop repeatedly rescuing Janice and her husband. They sent money to help with the latest disaster, accompanied by a message that this would be the last financial bailout.*

This sort of decision can be painful and difficult to make. Typically, the hovering, problem-solving relationship between parents and their child with ADHD has developed since early school years and the patterns and expectations are hard to break. Some parents have had to resort to asking their highly dysfunctional adult child with ADHD to stop calling them until that child has made the decision to get help to manage their own problems.

Family-Focused Therapy to Help Adult Children Move Toward Independence

A Treatment Program to Promote Independence in Adult Children

"Failure to launch" has become a catchphrase to describe young people in their twenties who drop out of school, barely work or don't work at all, and live with their parents, being largely or entirely supported by them. "Adulting" is hard, but it is especially difficult when you have all the executive functioning challenges of ADHD. Let's look at some parenting patterns that can result in a "failure to launch" adult child and solutions that can help.

One treatment program that has shown positive benefit was developed by Eli Lebowitz, PhD, at Yale.[1] Instead of working directly with young adults, his treatment approach is to work exclusively with the parents. He encourages the parents to better understand the dilemma that parents and their still-dependent adult children face and understand everyone's role in maintaining the dysfunctional codependence. Rather than judging the parents as overindulgent and the young adults as spoiled and lazy, the therapist needs to have a deep and sympathetic understanding of how well-intentioned parents fall into and remain in a codependency trap. Dr. Lebowitz's program also focuses on the very real suffering of the young adult. Although it can be so easy to judge them as spoiled and immature, Lebowitz writes that "young people struggling to function independently and overwhelmed by the demands of adulthood frequently suffer shame and alienation, as same-aged peers accumulate accomplishments while they accrue increasing disability."

A destructive cycle often develops between parent and adult child. The adult child relies on parents for help to avoid anxiety-producing challenges that feel insurmountable, while the accommodations made by the parents only serve to reinforce the adult child's patterns of avoidance and lack of efficacy. Many parents fear that continuing to accommodate their adult child will only reinforce dependency and are also driven by resentment about the constraints that their adult child's needs have imposed on them. The parents react from both fear and resentment, making occasional attempts to decrease their support, both emotional and financial, only to be met by feelings of anger and betrayal on the part of their adult child. Angry outbursts, sometimes physically violent outbursts, send the parents in "full retreat."

In Dr. Lebowitz's program, parents are supported and encouraged to see the very real anxiety and feelings of overwhelm that their dependent adult child experiences. The problems are viewed from a family systems perspective. While the parents begin to expect more from their adult child, they are also encouraged to sympathize with their child, rather than fall into blaming and shaming them for their inability to function in a more adult capacity.

Together the family talks about the process as something that is critical to help move the adult child toward feeling confident and competent as they take baby steps to learn self-sufficiency. When changes are made gradually, with sympathetic support from the parents and with the input and participation of the adult child, the dynamic can change from anger and confrontation to a growth orientation that helps both the parents and their adult child feel that positive change is occurring.

Tough Love with a Soft Landing

Even mental health professionals who don't have real expertise in treating young adults with ADHD can fall into a pattern of judging and blaming the young adult and encouraging the parents to take a "tough love" stance. Sometimes parents, long frustrated and feeling trapped, follow the tough love advice only to create a destructive crisis. Some young adults, in a state of shock, feeling "kicked to the curb," with no preparation, can become suicidal. Alternatively, they can become dangerously aggressive toward their parents because they feel unfairly and suddenly abandoned. In other cases, these young adults with no real independent-living skills are prone to leap into an inappropriate romantic relationship—taking an "any port in a storm" approach.

Withdrawing housing and financial support does not mean that the young adult with ADHD can suddenly figure things out and make a life for themselves. The following story is a tough love approach with a soft landing.

> One woman came to me almost desperate to move her extremely unmotivated son out of her house. Lucas had dropped out of college and had been living at home for nearly a year, not working, sleeping long hours, video gaming, and watching TV. He provocatively stated that he expected to end up as a street person if his mother didn't take care of him. Despite constant prodding, he did not look for work. His widowed mother was ready for retirement and eager to build a life for herself that didn't consist of dealing with her son every day.
>
> She found a room for rent in the basement of a home near the local community college and set her son up there. He felt safer and more comfortable living in a family home rather than in an apartment completely by himself. His mother offered to pay the rent and provide a very modest income for food and necessities for six months. After six months, she would continue to support him in this modest fashion only if he enrolled in courses at the community college and passed his courses. If he wanted money for a car, for entertainment, or other nonnecessities, he would have to find part-time employment. And, if he didn't enroll in school, after six months his mother would only pay half the rent. This gave Lucas a six-month "runway" to find work to pay the very modest rent. Meanwhile, she put her family home on the market with the

intention to move into an apartment in an active adult community nearby, giving Lucas the very concrete message that he could not come home again.

Lucas began to move ever so slowly toward independence. The wife in the family home where he rented a room showed an interest in him and hired him to do odd jobs around her house. This was a very safe environment in which to learn to work and manage a modest income. With his mother's guidance, he visited the nearby community college and decided to enroll in a year-long certificate course that gave him the skills to provide low-level tech support online. Lucas had always been interested in computers and loved the job he found after graduation. He could do it from home and avoid the stress of a commute and the expense of a car. A year after Lucas moved out of his mother's home, he was clearly on his way to greater independence. And his mother could breathe a sigh of relief that her life was no longer consumed by daily struggles with Lucas.

Utilizing Family Circumstances

I have worked with several families that were able to provide a "soft landing" for their adult child because they were small business owners able to bring their child into the family business. One couple that ran a small printing company hired their daughter with ADHD to work in the shop, answering the phone, taking orders, and gradually learning more about her parents' business. Another family that I worked with was able to provide their son with on-the-job training because his father did small-scale home renovations. The father was able to gradually show his son how to accomplish a broad range of handyman tasks over the course of several years. This son lived at home after high school and eventually moved into an apartment with an older brother a few years later—another soft landing.

How Do You Know If Your Child Is Unable to Launch?

It's important to distinguish between "failure" to launch and inability to launch. Sometimes an adult child has severe ADHD, possibly accompanied by autism spectrum disorder, bipolar disorder, severe social anxiety, and/or severe learning disorders. Such an adult child may be truly unable to maintain a job that pays a living wage, and may find it terrifying and overwhelming to be "on their own" without support and supervision.

For parents who are not sure whether their child is able to launch, I strongly recommend that they seek an assessment by a qualified mental health professional. Following the assessment, parents need to work closely with a professional who can provide guidance about what their adult child's needs are and how they can be met. Adult children that are severely impaired may qualify for Social Security Disability Insurance payments to help support them in their adult lives. They may also be eligible for job training through the Rehabilitative Services Administration (RSA). Often, older parents need assistance in understanding the maze of disability law and understanding how to apply for disability benefits, supervised housing, and other supports for their adult child.

In some families, the adult child unable to fully take care of themselves simply continues to live at home. This causes increasing concern as parents age: they know that they won't be around forever, taking care of their adult child. Such parents need to engage in a great deal of exploration to find a safe landing spot for their adult child after they can no longer care for their adult child at home.

Help a Child with ADHD along a Path to Success

There is no question that raising a child with ADHD is challenging, but there are wonderful success stories. While many factors can make

ADHD more challenging, many others can help move a child with ADHD along a path to success. Children who have the benefit of good treatment, strong family support, and fewer comorbidities can become highly successful adults. Young adults who make constructive choices—to stay in school; not to have children or get married before they are prepared; to engage in healthy daily habits, such as exercise, adequate sleep, and a healthy diet; and to make friends that will support them in becoming their best selves—can follow a path toward a successful, independent adulthood.

There are many reasons that adult children fail to launch. Helping them to successfully launch is every parent's goal, but it can't be achieved overnight. Here are some issues that are important to consider:

- **What could be a small positive step in the right direction?** Demanding a large and sudden increase in responsibility is likely to throw your young adult into a tailspin that can make matters worse. Instead, problem-solve with your adult child to determine a first step that isn't paralyzing or overwhelming.

- **Is college right for your child right now?** Many parents fear that if their child drops out of college, they will never go back. Instead, talk to your young adult about other options for now, with the idea that they can go back to school when they have a sense of direction and really feel ready. ADHD brains take longer to mature. A young adult with ADHD may fail at school in their early twenties and be ready to excel in school in their mid- to late twenties.

- **Is your adult child hiding from life because they fear failure?** Young adults with ADHD often feel overwhelmed, especially if they have failed in college and are back home with little sense of hope and direction. Instead of angry encounters, try sympathizing with your young adult and supporting them as they look for a job. They may need support and hand-holding initially. Going online to job sites with your young adult, searching for interesting entry-level jobs, and then helping them make an application is likely to bear more fruit than simply feeling angry because they stay home and never look for a job by themselves.

- **Are there alternatives to college, such as certificate programs?** For students with ADHD who have never liked school, college can seem meaningless, just "more of the same" as they try to grind their way through two years of general education requirements. Go online with them to see what types of certificates are offered at the local community college. Often, these courses are very hands-on and skill-focused and last only a year or so.

- **Could they attend college from home?** Many young adults with ADHD are simply not prepared to go away from home and family and manage to keep themselves on track, studying and going to class in a campus environment where there are countless distractions. I have helped many students who "crashed and burned" their freshman year when trying to go away to college, who were able to study and succeed when they were back in their home environment and attending college locally.

- **Are there ways for them to learn life skills before attempting college?** I often counsel parents that there are too many skills to learn at the same time once a young adult is out of high school. While staying home and working, a young adult can learn to get to bed on time, get up on time, get to work on time, earn money and then manage it, pay bills and budget for them, do their own laundry, maintain their car and remember to put gas in the tank, and so on. It can be helpful for them to work in a job that teaches them accountability and responsibility to help them learn to navigate the adult world of work. Once they have built these life-management skills, success at college may be much more manageable.

Growing up is a long process. Young adults with ADHD who impulsively leave home due to family conflicts or because parents think they should "be on their own" at age eighteen fall into self-defeating patterns and self-defeating relationships. The more your adult child can develop self-sufficiency while still under your roof, the more likely they will be to succeed once they leave home.

- **Encourage your child to enter a job that has opportunity for growth and advancement.** So many young adults work in jobs that offer no possibility for advancement. The longer they remain in these jobs, the more demoralized they may feel. Although some of these jobs are good ways to earn money while going to school part-time, they are not future-building jobs for the many younger adults with ADHD who are not suited for college. Young adults can greatly benefit from the guidance of parents or others to identify jobs in which they can grow and develop.

- **Set clear guidelines at home that help your young adult build self-sufficiency skills:**

  - A requirement to either work or take classes.

  - A requirement to do their part around the house—with clearly defined expectations.

  - A requirement to do their own laundry and keep their room somewhat organized.

  - A requirement, if they are working, to hand over 50 percent of their earnings to cover room and board. Parents can set this money aside to help their adult child with the cost of setting themselves up later to live independently—costs such as first and last month's rent, security deposits, automobile insurance, and so on. Many young adults, when they are paying little or nothing for room and board, think of their salary as a big allowance to spend recreationally on weekends. The cost of truly paying their own living expenses comes as a shock if they have had a "free ride" at home, not to mention that "free rides" help foster ongoing dependence.

- **Parents need to be patient but persistent**, always supporting their young adult child emotionally while supporting them step by step toward adult life management skills.

Of course, some young adults will never gain full self-sufficiency due to accidents, injuries, or health issues. Professional guidance can help parents to distinguish between true disabling conditions and a young adult who has been enabled in their avoidance of adulthood.

KEY TAKEAWAYS FROM THIS CHAPTER

✔ Parenting is especially challenging when both the parent and the child have ADHD.

✔ Having ADHD in childhood typically results in maturity delayed by several years.

✔ Today's older parents with ADHD typically didn't have the help and understanding regarding ADHD that are more available in today's generation of parents.

✔ "Failure to launch" patterns are typically due to a combination of lack of executive functioning skills on the part of the young adult and parenting patterns that have also contributed to delayed maturation.

✔ Counseling can be very useful to help older adults come to terms with parental regret that they may feel and to build healthy bonds with their adult child with ADHD.

✔ Parents may need help to change patterns:

- ○ Snowplow parents who try to move all their child's problems out of the way

- ○ Ostrich parents who try to ignore the problems, hoping that they will go away

- ○ Boundaryless parents who don't set financial or emotional limits with their adult child

✔ Some adult children with ADHD may never be able to become fully independent, due to severity of symptoms, significant comorbid conditions, or due to brain injury related to ADHD—professional help may be needed to plan a secure future for these adult children.

✔ There are many success stories—stories of parents who had no diagnosis or treatment for their own ADHD, who have made sure that their children, now adults, got the help that they needed during their growing-up years.

Making Ends Meet

Reducing financial stress for older adults with ADHD

Being financially prepared for retirement can be challenging when you have ADHD. This is true for a couple of reasons. First, those with ADHD are less likely to earn a consistent, comfortable income during their working years. And second, saving is more difficult when you have ADHD because saving requires long-term planning and long-term self-restraint in addition to earning enough income to be able to set money aside each month for retirement.

With the demise of most company retirement plans and the limited support offered by Social Security, we need to reframe our notion of "retirement." Many adults with ADHD will need to work as long as they can or find other ways to create income in retirement. In this chapter, I will share ADHD-friendly ways to learn better money management as well as stories of older adults with ADHD who have found creative solutions to reducing expenses and finding sources of postretirement income.

In Their Own Words: Older ADHD Adults and Finances

ADHD and careful financial management are rarely found together. For those with ADHD, the allure of an immediate reward holds much greater sway over them than the long-term rewards of an adequate retirement income. Some people characterize those with ADHD as having a very immediate sense of time, with time being divided into "now" and "not now."[1] And, of course, retirement is "not now" until it becomes "now."

Here are a few comments in response to my standard interview question, "Are you financially prepared for retirement, or will you need to work in retirement?"

"Who is? I'll either need to work or win the lottery."

"Lost my last job two years ago. Scraping by on my pension and doing some freelance work. Don't have enough to really retire."

"Are you financially prepared for retirement? No, no, and no! Will you need to work in retirement? Yes, yes, and yes."

"Currently working as a handyman while collecting Social Security."

"I have no savings and live on Social Security and the small amount that I earn; my finances are living proof of my inability to manage money."

"Financially, it's been horrible. I was forced out of my last job. Retired three years ago. I worked doing caregiving for the elderly, but it was too emotionally difficult. Then cleaned houses, but I can't now because of back problems. I'm not good with finances, never have been. I have no equity in my house—had to borrow against my house to pay bills."

ADHD-Friendly Money Management

Seventy percent of all Americans[2] live paycheck to paycheck during their working years[3] and can't imagine putting aside something for retirement. When you add attention deficit disorder to the mix, financial management becomes even more challenging. In this section, I will share money-management approaches that I have taught to many adults with ADHD who were struggling with impulsive spending and other poor money management approaches.

Money management systems recommended by financial managers or accountants typically involve lots of record-keeping, a highly ADHD-unfriendly activity. If money management systems are going to work for older adults with ADHD, they need to take ADHD patterns into account:

- **Forgetfulness**—"I thought I paid that bill last month; I thought I had canceled my HBO subscription; why in the world is my credit card bill so high?"

- **Inattention to detail**—"I didn't notice that the subscription renews automatically."

- **Dislike of paperwork**—"I just pile up the papers and never get around to dealing with them."

- **Disorganization**—"I know I saw that somewhere!"

- **Impulsive spending patterns**—"I've never had a budget; I just spend money."

- **Short-term thinking**—"I'm just happy if I can pay my bills at the end of the month."

Most plans for gaining control of your spending start with "keep an accurate record of every expense for the next month. Save your receipts, then write everything down in categories." The people who suggest these plans clearly don't understand much about ADHD. Should an older adult with ADHD keep such a record, they would then simply have a record of expenditures, planned and unplanned, which will only give a picture of how badly they are doing without a road map to reach the land of managed finances.

Here is a more ADHD-friendly approach:

- **Make a list of all of your fixed monthly expenses** (housing, car payments, gas, insurance payments, utilities, internet and phone, average monthly food costs, monthly condo fees, medical bills, etc.) and create a total.
- **Subtract your total fixed expenses from your total monthly post-tax income.** What you have left is what is available to spend on *anything else,* including the following:
  - Clothing
  - Entertainment
  - Household maintenance
  - Gifts
  - Travel
  - Eating out

That's right, all the fun stuff! If you are like many older adults with ADHD, there is precious little left over after your fixed expenses are deducted. But whatever is left is your discretionary income.

- **If there is no money left over, then big decisions need to be made to reduce monthly expenses.** You may need to speak to a financial counselor to figure out how to reduce expenses for housing, transportation, food, and so on.
- **Managing discretionary spending.** If there is money left over after calculating your monthly living expenses, what remains is your budget for discretionary spending. Divide your discretionary income by 4.5 (to make up for months with more than four weeks) and that becomes your weekly allowance for *all* discretionary spending.

- **Set up a separate checking account for discretionary spending from which you spend using a debit card.** You can easily arrange for your bank to transfer your "discretionary spending" to this spending account each week. Use a debit card for this account—and use it whether you are spending online or in person. Using a debit card will prevent you from overspending, unlike using a credit card. Check your remaining weekly balance each time you consider a purchase, whether for a cup of coffee or a pair of shoes. If there is not enough money in your weekly budget, then you "can't afford it" and will need to wait until the following week. This way you only need to wait a few days before you can make the purchase.

- **Use credit cards only for emergencies.**

- **Now, create an emergency slush fund**—that is, a fund of money that is only spent on urgent, important, and unexpected expenses—this might be a car repair, a house repair, a medical or dental bill, new eyeglasses, a new computer or smartphone. This isn't easy to do, but as was true for the following woman, most of us "leak" money—small amounts here and there every day that if we put into an emergency slush fund can add up over time to create an emergency slush fund and prevent us from borrowing money on our credit cards whenever there is an urgent and unexpected expense.

I once worked with a woman who was a single parent without a large income. She barely made ends meet from month to month. I suggested that she make a game of creating her slush fund—each time she wanted to purchase a magazine, a carry-out lunch, a cup of coffee from Starbucks, and so on, she should forgo the purchase and set that amount of money aside in her slush fund. She realized that she easily spent $15 a day on nonessential items. Because this was not a "forever plan" of forgoing all of life's little pleasures,

*she became excited about saving money for the first time. Each
evening, she went online and transferred money from her checking
account into a savings account that she had created at the same
bank. She loved seeing her savings account grow. In ways, she got
her "dopamine burst" from transferring the money every evening
just as effectively as she might have enjoyed a dopamine burst
through a small purchase. In a couple of months, she had over
$1,000 in her emergency slush fund, and at that point she began
looking for even more ways to save. And the more she saved, the
less stressed she felt. She was no longer at the mercy of unexpected
disasters, feeling forced to put charges on her credit card when
unplanned expenses arrived. She could cover them and continue
her savings pattern to build her slush fund back to its previous
level. All through making small changes in her daily spending
habits.*

- **Build "healthy" spending habits.** Building healthy spending
  habits is a lot like building healthy eating habits. If you go on a
  diet, all the studies show that it won't last long. Healthy eating
  habits develop by changing undesirable eating habits slowly, so
  that the new, healthy eating patterns become natural. If you go
  on a strict weight-loss program, you'll only feel deprived, and
  the diet won't last.

In a similar fashion, don't put yourself on such a strict spending
budget that all you think about is what you wish you were buying.
If it's all deprivation, your new spending approach won't last long.
Instead, try to change your overspending habits slowly, substituting
"healthy" spending habits. Here are some examples:

- Use your local library rather than purchasing books.
- Socialize through exercise—such as walking with a friend—
  rather than meeting a friend for a restaurant meal.

- Make coffee at home rather than buying it cup by cup every day (same goes for lunch or other meals).

- Look for new, interesting activities for seniors that are low cost or no cost.

- **Eliminate expensive gifts for friends and family.** Look for creative ways to celebrate birthdays and holidays so that they don't involve big expenses. Organize a special outing to celebrate a grandchild's birthday rather than purchasing an expensive gift that will likely be forgotten days or weeks later.

- **Reduce alcohol and/or cigarettes if they are part of your monthly expenses.** Alcohol and cigarettes aren't healthy for your body or your wallet. Cutting down on these habits will be good for your health and also be a significant money saver over the course of each month.

- **Identify ways that you "leak" money.** Many older retirees tell themselves that they don't have expensive spending habits because they are not taking expensive vacations or buying expensive retirement homes. But if you are on a limited budget, it's important to identify ways that you "leak" money—$5 here, $10 there. It adds up quickly if you are making minor, unnecessary purchases on a daily basis.

- **Don't trick yourself into unaffordable spending by telling yourself, "I'm worth it" or "At my age, I deserve it."** While you may feel you "deserve" something, that feeling is really based on expectations that have nothing to do with your budget. And that way of thinking only makes you feel deprived instead of allowing you to feel proud of managing your money well. If you are considering a purchase, take a step back to really consider whether it's something you need and whether your discretionary income can cover it (see the following steps for more on this).

- **Don't shop for entertainment—online or anywhere else.** It may only be a book here or a pair of shoes there, but these "little" expenses add up over the course of the month. If there are things that you need or want, write them down, just as if you were making a grocery list, along with the cost of the item. This moves you away from impulse purchases toward planned, thoughtful spending. Once you see your list, you may well decide that you strongly prefer some items on your list over other items and can make selective choices that still fall within your budget. Remember, *all* online purchases need to be deducted from your monthly cash "allowance." Otherwise, you are slowly going into debt.

- **Create a "Me Fund."** Once you have created your emergency slush fund, you can turn your attention toward "wants." Instead of "leaking" money for small things, put money aside for things you really want. You won't feel deprived, and you'll be rewarded in ways you'll remember. The woman who learned to "think small" also started a savings account using the money she didn't spend on snacks, coffee, and random purchases. She built up savings for things that meant more to her—a plane ticket to visit a family member or a special event with a friend.

- **Distinguish "needs" from "wants."** All of us see things we want—whether it's a new jacket, a dinner out at a nice restaurant, or a fancy car. With or without ADHD, it's easy to tell ourselves that we "need" that new car or new winter coat, when what is really the case is that our car or our winter coat can last longer, albeit with some repairs. Unfortunately, we live in a "throwaway society" where perfectly good clothing, books, furniture, and other household items are given away at the slightest sign of wear and tear. For older adults with ADHD, their attraction to the "new and shiny" can make it hard to have the self-discipline to tell themselves no. It's easy to rationalize purchases that we really can't afford. "Wants" can turn into "needs" in the mind of some adults with ADHD when the purchase allows them to feel less burdened by the tasks of the day—for example, ordering carry-out or having a restaurant meal because you feel too tired to cook, or just don't feel like it.

Linda was a woman with ADHD who had been married to a man who earned a high income. Following their late-in-life divorce, she struggled to come to terms with her radically reduced discretionary income. While she would be "okay," she could no longer afford to buy expensive clothing, drive a high-end car, go out to restaurants or the theater on weekends, and travel several times a year. At first, she spent more than she could afford, putting her future self at financial risk.

Gradually, Linda became more realistic. She moved to more affordable housing, started driving a more modest car, and interestingly, became increasingly content as she let go of the symbols of her former affluent life. Once she shifted her focus from what she had lost to what's next, she began to develop her considerable artistic talent and became an active member of the local arts community. She had learned to distinguish needs from wants and ended up building a life that was more satisfying than she expected.

Some ADHD-friendly strategies for avoiding impulsive spending:

- **Develop a 7-day rule.** "If I still think I need it a week later, then I'll consider buying it." The 7-day rule stops the immediate, impulsive spending that is so easy to do online.

- **Keep some "emergency meals" in the freezer.** There are now many affordable, healthy frozen dinners available in grocery stores (or even better, routinely cook extra servings of meals and freeze them to reheat on nights when you don't feel like cooking). Having a few on hand can help you avoid the costly impulse to order carry-out or go out to a restaurant when you don't feel like cooking.

- **Break your "Starbucks habit"** by upgrading your home coffee-maker. One woman told me that she now uses a coffeemaker at home that dispenses very good-quality coffee and also heats milk. While this coffeemaker is more expensive than a standard one, each cup of coffee costs her a tiny fraction of what she'd spend on coffee at a coffee shop.

- **Pack your lunch if you work outside the home.** It's healthier and costs a fraction of any meal you can buy.

Creative Ideas to Generate Income or Save Money after Retirement

One of the positive aspects of ADHD is that many who have it are gifted problem-solvers when the problem is an immediate one. Years in the future, retirement planning is not an immediate problem and receives little attention, but once retirement approaches or arrives, creative ideas may arrive along with it. Here are some stories from older adults with ADHD about creative ways to respond to a reduced income.

Part-Time Employment

Many retirees find part-time work to be a welcome addition to their daily life. Not only does it provide extra income, it also adds structure and stimulation to their days. It's a buffer against the social isolation that is a common risk for retirees. Other benefits include employee discounts and, with some companies, health insurance for part-time workers.

An increasing number of employers provide health insurance for part-time workers and reasonable hourly pay. Trader Joe's, Home Depot, Lowe's, Costco, and Starbucks, to name a few, are realizing the advantages of hiring mature, reliable adults to work part-time.

(More companies that offer health insurance plans to part-time workers can be found online.) Not everyone is in good health and can manage to work in retirement, but for those who can, it's an increasingly popular option. Many seniors whom I interviewed talked of enjoying the sense of purpose and social stimulation of part-time work.

> *Sarah, a woman with ADHD who had supported herself and her son as a single parent, had little money set aside for retirement. Her major asset was her townhouse in the Washington, DC, suburbs. She had grown up in North Carolina and decided to return to live near family in a more affordable house. Once there, she found she missed the daily interactions with people she had enjoyed at work and also missed the higher income she had been accustomed to. Soon, she found herself wandering over to the large resort hotel and golf course near her retirement community, a hub of activity in this largely rural area. A few days later, she inquired about employment. Sarah's intelligence and outgoing personality appealed to the hotel manager and she was offered a part-time job in the hotel gift shop. She excitedly talked about the golf celebrities that came through buying trinkets. While this job was not high-paying, it offered her far more than some extra spending money. It gave her a place to go, a time to be there, and a task to accomplish when she got there. It offered her human interaction several days a week and unexpectedly became one of the highlights of her new ADHD-friendly retirement lifestyle.*

Self-Employment

Self-employment is another route to increasing your retirement income. And self-employment can be very appealing because you have more control over when and how much you work.

The Happy Handyman

Ron, an older man with ADHD, supported himself in retirement by becoming the handyman to many elderly widows in his condo complex. They trusted him because he developed a personal relationship with each of them and worked hard to be available whenever there was a minor emergency. They referred their friends, and within a year of retirement he had a handyman business that kept him as busy as he needed to be. Not only did he generate income, but he also felt that he served a good purpose in his Florida retirement community.

RV Rental

Sean, a creative ADHDer, rapidly realized the high return on investment when he began renting his RV. He had bought it thinking that he might live in it and tour the country, but health issues intervened, and he was using it much less than he had anticipated. His RV rental brought in a surprising income.

Don't Toss It Out—Sell It!

Jenn and Mark both had ADHD. Mark grew up in a family where no one threw anything away. "You never know when you might need it" was the watchword in his family. After marriage, Mark continued the family tradition of hanging on to everything that came into his possession. While this can look like hoarding, in many cases it's driven by an ADHD-related difficulty with making decisions. After the kids grew up and moved out, Jenn and Mark were surrounded by an enormous accumulation of belongings, most of which were of no use to them. After both were diagnosed with ADHD in late middle age (prompted by their adult *son's diagnosis), Jenn began reading prodigiously about how to cope with ADHD. A natural researcher, she was an intelligent woman with a curious mind, and soon she was an authority on all sorts of supports and treatments for ADHD. At her initiation, she and her husband hired a professional organizer to help them start to off-load unnecessary belongings. Jenn had an "aha!" moment—instead of giving away all those countless items, she began to advertise them for sale on eBay, Craigslist, and Amazon and quickly had a thriving business. The basement storeroom of the house became her warehouse of items for sale, allowing the rest of the house to be gradually cleared out and organized. Soon she was making a profit of between $1,000 and $1,500 each month. By the time she and Mark entered retirement earlier than planned (Mark had lost his job when his company was sold), Jenn was an experienced reseller and enjoyed the game of finding goods for sale in bulk that she could resell at a tidy profit. She'd found a retirement activity that she could conduct from anywhere and could work as much or as little as she chose depending upon what else was going on in her life.*

As a self-employed senior, it's important to get information on what you'll need to set aside for taxes. Remember, you'll owe close to one-third of your income to your state and the federal government unless you live in a state without state income tax. Don't let yourself think of your income as "yours" and make the mistake of spending the money you owe in taxes. Taking your estimated taxes "off the top" and putting that money in a separate account from which you'll pay quarterly taxes is the best approach.

Consider Cohousing

I write more about cohousing in Chapter 14 where I discuss building an ADHD-friendly retirement. Cohousing, sharing housing with others, is becoming increasingly popular, as it can both cut down on your retirement expenses and also provide companionship so important to us in our later years. There is a rapidly growing number of options for seniors who want to explore shared housing.[4]

An older widowed woman with ADHD, Elaine continued to live alone in the house she had shared with her husband before his death. She knew that her housing costs were too high, yet she hesitated to leave. Elaine, who enjoyed having company around, created a comfortable space for herself in the basement, with her own bathroom, kitchenette, and outside entrance. Through a friend still working in the local school system, she was able to advertise her upper level bedrooms for rent to young, single teachers. Soon, she had three and then four very responsible young women, grateful for having an affordable place to live. The young women enjoyed one another's company and bonded. A year later, when one of them became engaged and moved out, she made sure that her room was rented to another single schoolteacher. Elaine and her young schoolteachers shared the common areas on the ground floor, and soon she was serving as informal house mother and enjoying the lively company of these young women. Meanwhile, with her mortgage paid off, she had increased her monthly income by nearly $2,500. Not bad for someone who had been lonely and barely scraping by before.

Rent Space to Increase Monthly Income

If you own a home, consider renting out part of it, as either a long-term rental, such as a basement apartment, or for short-term rentals, for example, listing it with Airbnb.

Lise had children and grandchildren who traveled to see her a couple of times a year and she wanted to make sure she had room for them to stay with her when they came. Her house had a large basement, so she blocked it off—with doors at the top and bottom of the basement stairs. This space for her children and grandchildren could double as an Airbnb that she could rent for a sizable nightly fee. She wasn't sure whether she'd like being a landlord, so she decided to try this as an experiment. Lise found that she actually enjoyed the role, welcoming people to her comfortable basement apartment, giving them tips on places to eat, and adding special touches, such as a welcome note and a bouquet of fresh flowers. She received top reviews from her tenants. Lise didn't know if she would do this long-term, but for now, she had solved her financial crunch while finding a way to stay in her home a few years longer.

Consider Moving to a "Tiny House"

If you are a homeowner, most likely your biggest source of financial security is the equity in your home. Many older adult homeowners have been able to pay off their mortgage by the time they retire. For others, even if a mortgage remains on their house, they have significant equity in their home that can become liquid cash should they decide to sell it. A very recent but rapidly growing phenomenon is the "tiny house" movement,[5] and a great many of these tiny houses are being purchased by retirees. A tiny house can be purchased for as little as $100,000 or less. Although not all states allow "tiny houses" because they do not meet local building codes, a growing number of states do.

A tiny house differs from a mobile home. It is often a two-story structure with a footprint of as little as 400 to 500 square feet. Some architects have designed very attractive tiny homes with large windows to create a sense of spaciousness and with porches or decks outside to expand the living space of this very affordable type of housing. Tiny house communities are being designed and built in many parts of the country. To learn more about the tiny house movement, just do an internet search for "tiny house." Two websites to consider are https://tinylivinglife.com and https://tinyhouse hugeideas.com.

Move to a Tax-Friendly State

Alaska, Florida, Nevada, South Dakota, Texas, Washington, and Wyoming are states that don't tax personal income, while thirty-six other states allow retirees to exclude all or part of their retirement income from their taxable income. Of course, it's difficult to move as a single person to an unfamiliar state, but Alice, a divorced older woman with ADHD, had a creative idea.

> Alice was active in sports near her home not far from Philadelphia. As she began to think of reducing costs, she considered moving to Florida, but she didn't want to move alone. She began doing research and found several sports-oriented communities in Florida for "active adults" where the housing was a fraction of the cost of her current house. Alice talked a friend into going with her to explore these "over 55" active communities and they liked what they saw. The more they talked of moving to the same community in Florida among their friends, the more others became interested. Alice and her friend both purchased condos in the same complex, spending "six months and a day" there to establish residency in Florida. When she returned from her winter in Florida to put her New Jersey house on the market, other members of her social group were interested. Over the course of two or three years, a lively group of longtime friends, all single, and several with ADHD, made the transition to the same Florida community, where there were no state taxes, the cost of living was much lower, and the weather much better.

Move to a Less Expensive Country

Not everyone can afford to move to a less costly country, and many others don't want to move that far away from family. But for those who have the means to fly home regularly, or can invite family to visit regularly, a growing number have elected to move to Mexico, Costa Rica, and Panama, to name a few, to enjoy the better climate and lower cost of living. You'll need to look into "global" or "international" health insurance plans. Even if you live abroad, you can still use Medicare when you return to the US, but while in another country, your global health insurance will be used.

> *Louise, a widowed woman with ADHD, was living in Arizona when I interviewed her. She told me that she had worked for the Peace Corps as a young adult and spoke fluent Spanish. After her youngest child graduated from college in a year or two, she planned to purchase a property in an ex-pat community in Latin America. "I could scrape by here in Arizona," she told me, "but in Latin America, I can live comfortably." She was looking forward to the adventure and to creating a completely different life for herself.*

KEY TAKEAWAYS FROM THIS CHAPTER

- ✔ ADHD tendencies can complicate saving for retirement.
- ✔ Even if you have not managed your money well in preparation for retirement, there are still many options available to you to improve your financial situation, including the following:
  - ○ Shared housing
  - ○ Less expensive housing

- Lowering taxes
- Finding ways to have an income stream in retirement

✔ It's never too late to build better financial habits and make good financial decisions.

✔ With your ADHD creativity, there are multiple ways to supplement your income in retirement.

Creating an ADHD-Friendly Retirement

Finding structure, support, stimulation, social connections

You probably have many years ahead of you, years in which you can enjoy a much better quality of life as you learn to implement the approaches that I've introduced in this book. This final chapter outlines ways to create an "ADHD-friendly environment" for yourself in your later years so that these years are satisfying and fulfilling.

What Is an ADHD-Friendly Environment for an Older Adult?

You may not be able to achieve all of these, but the following list outlines goals to aim for as you build an ADHD-friendly living environment:

- **Self-acceptance and understanding**—You can gain greater self-acceptance through learning about ADHD, through counseling, and through interacting with other older adults with ADHD online or in person.

- **Acceptance and understanding of your ADHD in those close to you**—Ideally, the people you live with or are closest to come to understand how you are impacted by ADHD and interact with you in a supportive and solution-focused way instead of simply criticizing or judging you.

- **A connection to your "tribe" of fellow ADHDers**—Connecting in either a virtual or in-person ADHD community—"your tribe"— can help support you on your ongoing journey to live well as an older adult with ADHD. Fellow ADHD "elders" can provide you with acceptance, understanding, camaraderie, and support. I have observed that finding fellow ADHDers is a very healing and supportive experience.

- **A more streamlined, decluttered home environment**—You don't have to do the decluttering alone, but the more that you can maintain a living environment that does not feel overwhelming, discouraging, or distracting, the better you can focus on what matters and brings you pleasure.

- **A reduced level of stress**—Sometimes we just fall into a rut, continuing to live in ways that are highly stressful. It may help to talk to others who can help you identify sources of chronic stress and then problem-solve to find ways to reduce or eliminate stressors in your life.

- **A daily practice of brain-healthy habits** can help you feel and function well. These habits can be built up slowly over time and don't require "perfection" to be able to be very helpful in improving your cognitive and overall functioning.

- **Daily routines** to take care of yourself, your home, and your needs—again, developing new habits takes time as well as structure and support from others.

Structure and support should become your mantra as you work to create an ADHD-friendly environment. Just as teenagers leaving home in young adulthood lose the structure and support that helped them function when living at home, older adults transitioning into retirement may experience similar challenges. In both instances, most of the structure and support that has helped them function is suddenly gone, often to ill effect. Just as young adults with ADHD are often unprepared for managing their daily lives away from home, older adults with ADHD are often unprepared for life in retirement, a life that may be unstructured and often socially isolated. Bernie's story is one example:

"I remember feeling lost years ago when I left home for college. I did pretty well at home, in spite of my undiagnosed ADHD. My parents reminded me of things and bailed me out a few times when I had done something dumb. And I had sports after school and friends. Then, I left for college and things fell apart. I sometimes didn't go to class, and often stayed up really late at night. I came close to flunking out before I realized I needed help to learn how to live on my own. It feels a bit like that now that I've retired. There's no road map for retirement. One day, I had routines, a place to go, a time I had to be there, and tasks I needed to do at work. Now, there is all this time and I just don't know what to do with it. Some days, I don't even get dressed and I'm watching TV or going on the internet way too much. It's not nearly as much fun as I thought it would be."

Bernie's experience of feeling lost in retirement is not unique. Mary's story of her sudden plunge into dysfunction vividly illustrates the risks of losing structure and support in your life.

Mary raised two daughters as a single parent while holding down a full-time job. It wasn't easy, but she managed. She had been a much-loved person at the local high school where she had taught art for more than twenty-five years. After retiring, Mary decided to move to be near her older daughter, Deborah. Several months after Mary's move, Deborah contacted me, reporting that her mother had never fully unpacked following her move. Boxes were stacked high against the walls of her new apartment. Mary's nights and days had turned upside down so that she was staying up most of the night and then sleeping well into the day. She had stopped eating nutritious meals and was basically living on snacks. Mary had lost the familiar routines and social contacts she had enjoyed in the community where she had lived for so many years and needed to find a way to find structure and support in her new environment. For her, the solution was found when she moved into a senior assisted-living complex that provided meals, activities, and social contacts.

Structure and Support Can Help You Maintain Brain-Healthy Daily Habits

Remember MENDSS habits (meditation, exercise, nature, diet, sleep, and social connections)? These are the brain-healthy daily habits I wrote about in Chapter 9. You are much more likely to exercise, social-ize, or get out into the natural environment if there is structure in your life to make these activities happen. Structure and support can be provided in a senior living facility or can be created more infor-mally by having a walking buddy or joining senior exercise groups. Meditation or other stress-reducing tools can be built into your life by joining an in-person or online group in which seniors practice med-itation or yoga. A healthy diet can be supported by the many meal services that now exist, if cooking feels too burdensome.

Decluttering and Simplifying to Focus on What Matters

So many adults find themselves overwhelmed by a lifetime of accu-mulation. On top of that, several of the older adults I worked with found that they had a double burden because their parents had passed away without downsizing, which meant that a new flood of unnecessary belongings entered their living space, requiring lots of decisions. It's all too easy to just feel overwhelmed and do nothing, especially if you have ADHD. Here are some things that you can do to make decluttering easier.

Hire a Professional Organizer

If you feel overwhelmed and have the means to do so, it may be an excellent investment to hire a professional organizer. Some of them specialize in helping older adults downsize. Just having the company of someone who is there with you, asking the right questions and helping you stay focused on the task, can make a world of difference. Many of these organizers also provide a service to haul unwanted items away from your home, donating them and recycling as much as possible before taking the remainder to the dump.

Downsize by Moving into a Retirement Community

Some active adult communities provide the services of a person who can use the floor plan of the unit you plan to rent or purchase (two-bedroom, one-bedroom with den, etc.) to carefully measure and help you decide what will fit into your new space, even where the furniture should be placed for maximum utility.

> Claire felt so overwhelmed by her belongings (she and her husband had both been pack rats and collectors) that I recommended that she use such a service. They helped her pack her clothing and personal belongings; helped her pack up the few dishes, plates, glasses, pots, and pans she could use in the small kitchen of her new apartment; and tagged the furniture to be moved. Claire left, following the moving van, to take the relatively brief trip to her new apartment

in a spacious and welcoming "over 55" community. Once she unpacked—which was easy to do because she hadn't brought much with her—she could turn her attention back to the large older home she had lived in for so many years. Her real estate agent who was contracted to handle the sale of the property "staged" the house using some of the furniture that remained and added a few pieces that she kept in storage for the purpose of staging homes. The agent arranged for everything else to be picked up by a service that donates and recycles unwanted items and, voilà, Claire had side-stepped the onerous task of sorting through a lifetime of belongings—one that would have overwhelmed her and would have taken more than a year.

Declutter and Off-Load with the Help of Family or Friends

Many of us don't have the means to hire a professional organizer or move into a retirement community that offers these services. If this is your situation, look to family members or friends who may be able to help.

I once facilitated a support group of older women with ADHD. Out-of-control clutter was one of their biggest challenges. As they quickly got to know and trust one another, they came into the group reporting, with laughs and smiles, that they had started helping one another to do major "dig-outs" of their homes. Many people with ADHD report that it's much easier to dig out and off-load someone else's belongings than to deal with their own.

Not everyone is so fortunate as to have an adult child who is available and willing to help with the dig-out of a lifetime.

One woman I worked with invited her three children to come and take whatever belongings they wanted, other than the few things she planned to keep when she moved into her small retirement apartment. She told them that she could no longer be the repository of childhood belongings or family heirlooms and would give away whatever they didn't take. Her son responded that he had no time to come and participate, and that he had no need for any of her household items. Her two daughters came for a long weekend and packed up a number of family mementos, leaving the lion's share of the decluttering and off-loading to their mother. She hired a local hauling company that advertised that it donated and recycled as much as possible. This was an inexpensive service and it took only a few hours to off-load all her household belongings aside from the items she planned to take with her—clothing, kitchen items, and furniture for her bedroom and living room in her small retirement rental apartment. After the sentimental items had been retrieved by her daughters, she found that the rest of the downsizing was much easier. She simply moved from room to room with a member of the hauling company, pointing out what she wanted him to remove. The pressure to make immediate decisions while the hauling company employees were in her house made the process much easier. Once done, her son offered to rent a truck and move her remaining belongings to her new retirement home.

ADHD-Friendly Transition from Work to Retirement

Moving into retirement can be challenging for everyone and those challenges are magnified if you are an adult with ADHD. Our working years give us structure, a built-in social life, and a sense of purpose. Once these are gone, retirement brings a void that, for many, is difficult to fill. Older adults with ADHD typically thrive on structure and stimulation but find it hard to create those things for themselves. Many tend to fall back on default stimulation—overeating, drinking too much alcohol, shopping online, overusing social media, and watching too much television. When the transition from working years to retirement isn't an all-or-nothing affair, it's easier to begin to more slowly create structure, find healthy sources of stimulation, and build other activities that can provide you with a sense of purpose in retirement. Here are some more gradual approaches to retirement used by some of the ADHD seniors I've spoken with.

Some of us are able to gradually reduce our work hours, or to change how we work as we approach retirement. Those who work for themselves have more control over the process of gradual retirement.

Hank had worked in his family's business for nearly thirty years. The business was sold with the agreement that Hank would remain on hand as needed to guide and train the new owners and to introduce them to long-standing clients of the company. At first, Hank was frustrated by this condition, but after several months, he realized that it was a win-win agreement. He had time to plan exciting trips, including a long-distance bike ride he'd always dreamed of, and he felt good about his new role in the old company. He retained his identity as an expert while dipping his toe into retirement.

Alice had a very demanding job as an editor and project manager for an underfunded nonprofit organization. They were always trying to do more with less and this impacted all the employees, but especially Alice. Her ADHD therapist encouraged her to advocate for herself at work, proposing that she move into retirement through working at home half-time for a year before ending her employment altogether. This was a win-win for Alice and her employer. She remained on board for twelve months, providing training and support for her replacement, while also having time to gradually shift her focus from work to retirement years. As an editor, she had always wanted to write a book. The ideas had swirled around in her head for years, but the demands of her job meant that she never had time or energy for her own writing.

During this transition year, she gradually started writing and was in full-gear writing mode by the time her full retirement rolled around a year later.

Chase chose the gradual retirement option as well. He had worked all his life for his family's company started by his father, a very successful chain of high-end hardware stores. He and his brother had inherited the business from their father and now the next generation was poised to take over. Chase was a high-energy ADHDer, on the more hyperactive end of the continuum. As he expressed it, "Being on the golf course a few days a week isn't going to do it for me." His brother, however, was in poor health and eager for full-time retirement. Chase made a gradual transition. Roles were clarified and managing authority was shifted to his middle-aged son and niece, while Chase took the tasks of marketing, introducing new product lines, and creating special events to bring customers into their stores. He loved the variety and the lower stress of his new role and anticipated working many more years in this capacity.

Work Part-Time

In Chapter 13, I wrote about ADHD seniors with a financial need to bring in extra income during retirement, but there are other reasons that part-time work might be a great option—stimulation, a sense of purpose, and social connections.

Martha, after retiring from her career as a schoolteacher, moved south to a community near to her family, close to where she had grown up. She was able to purchase a modest two-bedroom ranch house. Her longtime friends came to visit occasionally, but it was a five-hour drive from the Washington, DC, area where she had lived and worked during her career. Her friends' visits dwindled in frequency over a couple of years and she began to feel lonely and isolated. At the suggestion of a friend, she applied for a part-time job in a small town nearby that attracted tourists. She was trained as a historical tour guide and worked a few hours each week. Working twenty hours a week gave her added income, provided structure to her days, and gave her a social outlet as she enjoyed interacting with people on her tours.

Continue to Work—in a Second Career or on a Long-Postponed Passion

In Jo Ann Jenkins's recent best-selling book, *Disrupt Aging*,[1] she writes about the critical importance of society starting to view aging (and retirement) through a more up-to-date lens. We moved from the Beatles' image of knitting sweaters by the fireside to moving to the Sun Belt and playing golf, and now even that seems dated. Ms. Jenkins, the CEO of AARP, the huge advocacy organization for people over age fifty, writes, "we must change the way we view ourselves and our inner lives *from aging as decline* to *aging as continuous growth*."

Early retirement has been, for many, a status symbol, demonstrating to the world that you have "made it." You have enough money so that you don't need to continue to work. But earning money is only one reason to work. There are many others, including social contact, the satisfaction of making a contribution to your community, intellectual stimulation, and a sense of purpose. In addition, for those with ADHD, work provides much-needed structure to what otherwise can become formless, unproductive days.

Many of us, especially those with ADHD, may not have found great satisfaction in our work. Quite a few older adults with ADHD that I interviewed told me of jobs that had become so highly stressful that it was endangering their mental and physical health. I am not suggesting that these individuals should not have left their job. What I *am* suggesting is that we stop thinking in such a black-and-white way about work vs retirement. What if we began thinking of retirement as our opportunity to do a different kind of work that perhaps we'd always wanted to do? Rather than a means to a paycheck, work can become an activity that brings meaning, purpose, autonomy, and satisfaction to our lives. This can be a second career or the serious pursuit of a long-postponed dream. In a second career, we can be less concerned about maximizing our earning power and can focus instead on our own satisfaction.

ADHD-Friendly Housing Options

Move to More ADHD-Friendly Housing

Many older adults with ADHD do well in active adult communities. These typically offer a range of meetings, clubs, and activities. There is nothing to plan or organize; all you need to do is show up. This is perfect for an aging person with ADHD who has a lot of interests but who struggles to organize activities or finds it difficult to find like-minded individuals. It's like summer camp for older people.

On the other hand, if you are like many seniors, you might prefer to "age in place," remaining in the home in which you have lived for many years. It's important to understand that there are several reasons that aging in place may not be a very ADHD-friendly option:

- Living in a single-family home involves ongoing maintenance and repairs, calling on executive functioning skills that are often in short supply among older adults.
- Living in a single-family home often leads to increasing social isolation as old friends and neighbors move away or pass away.

- Also, living alone or as an aging couple in a single-family home provides none of the structure and support that exists in communities designed for the over-55 crowd.

The idea of moving, especially when you have ADHD, can feel overwhelming. You may feel dread at having to deal with all of the belongings you have accumulated. Plus, moving requires lots of decisions: Where can I afford to move? Should I stay here or move closer to one of my kids? Should I move into a multilevel care facility? Should I move to an active older-adult community? Should I move in with one of my kids? Should I move to Florida? The decision-making alone can often completely stall decisions until a sudden downturn in health requires an immediate and ill-planned decision.

As you think about where and how you will live, keep in mind that an ADHD-friendly living environment is one that automatically provides or supports the daily habits that you want to develop and maintain: healthy meals, stimulating activities, exercise opportunities, and social connections are, in general, a more ADHD-friendly choice than living alone in relative isolation where everything depends upon you. Lower-cost choices include subsidized senior housing or cohousing, a growing movement here in the US where older adults, more often women, seek out other seniors to share housing and meals with. Amie Clark writes more about this in her article "Elder Cohousing: The Future of Eldercare."[2] More common (and typically more costly) choices include active over-55 adult communities and multilevel assisted-living communities.

Finding Connections and Purpose after Retirement

Community connections and a sense of purpose are important for many people in retirement, especially for those whose sense of purpose and community prior to retirement were connected with the career they have left behind. As one man I interviewed told me, "It's hard to still feel relevant now that I'm retired."

Become Active in a Spiritual or Religious Community

A number of older adults I talked with said that their spiritual community has become the center of their social lives. For some, that means weekly service attendance and perhaps a midweek group. Those with higher energy levels and greater need for stimulation become involved in multiple group activities.

The key is to take ADHD into account when you decide what to volunteer for. Roles that call for planning and organization skills may not be a good match. Those that call for diving in and helping with an already established activity usually work best. For example, a woman I interviewed, Mary, loves gardening and has volunteered to help maintain the landscaping around her church. But she knows her limits. While she does weeding, mulching, and flower planting, she's not involved in setting the facilities management budget for the church.

Engage in Volunteer Work

It can be difficult to find meaningful volunteer activities. So many adults told me that their volunteer work served mainly as a way to have interaction with other volunteers. The volunteer work itself held no special appeal because it involved performing mundane tasks, such as checking people in at a voting site or helping set up for an event.

If you have had a professional career, it's likely that you will crave some degree of responsibility and stimulation in your volunteer activities. Instead of perusing a list of volunteer opportunities for seniors, a different approach is to identify an organization whose mission you support and contact it to explore whether you could bring value to that organization. Depending upon your background, you might make a great board member of a struggling nonprofit; if you have a finance or accounting background, you could offer those services to a nonprofit, serving as its treasurer.

Betty had played a role in creating an internal newsletter for the organization she worked for prior to her retirement. She contacted the local senior center in her suburban town outside Boston to learn about the various activities they offered. In her discussion with its staff, they told her of their monthly newsletter. Her ears perked up: "Here's something I'm good at that I could help with." She mentioned her prior experience with a newsletter, sharing that she knew how to do editing and layout, and even wrote articles for the employee newsletter where she had worked. The senior center staff, always overworked and underfunded, were immediately interested in what Betty might contribute. Within a year, she was in charge of the newsletter and greatly enjoying canvassing her community for human-interest stories related to the senior population. Not only that, she visited local establishments in her role as editor of the newsletter and was able to negotiate discounts for seniors from local businesses that advertised in the newsletter. Her volunteer activity helped her integrate into her community in ways she had never had time for during her working years. She was doing something that she was good at and loved doing. She had meaning in her life and more social connections than ever.

Another woman with ADHD I interviewed, Ellen, a retired English teacher, volunteered at the local juvenile detention center, where she started a book group that has become popular. She reports that the young detainees are among the most enthusiastic and dedicated students she has ever had. She enjoys having more freedom and flexibility, but also told me that her two hours each week at the detention center are one of the highlights of her week. She can continue to teach young adults and share her interest in literature and understands that her contribution to the lives of these young detainees is much greater than if she were working as a substitute teacher for one of the local high schools.

Take Courses Designed for Seniors

You may fantasize about learning Italian or writing a memoir, but the key to such projects is structure, structure, structure. There are courses designed specifically for seniors in many communities. Numerous studies done in the past decade demonstrate that overall well-being and quality of life among seniors is enhanced by participation in lifelong learning.[3] Many older adults want to develop stronger computer skills. Organized classes can provide the structure needed to keep a senior with ADHD on track. There are many resources. Here are a few to get you started:

OLLI (Osher Lifelong Learning Institutes) offers noncredit courses with no homework or grades at member colleges and universities across the US. At last count, there are 120 educational institutions that participate and they are growing increasingly popular. Courses may be taught by faculty members of the college or university, but are often taught by older adults who participate in OLLI and have a particular area of expertise that they want to share. Courses are typically six to eight weeks long and also provide a great way to meet other older adults with similar interests.

Community college courses—Check with your local community college. Almost all community colleges now offer free courses to seniors who are aged sixty-plus. Some allow seniors to audit classes at no charge, for no credit, whereas others offer free courses for college credit, a wonderful opportunity for seniors who have always wanted to continue their college education.

Senior Planet AARP has two places where you can sign up for free online classes and workshops:

- ○ **Senior Planet's upcoming events**—https://seniorplanet .org/classes/

- ○ **AARP's Virtual Community Center** offers free online classes to seniors—https://local.aarp.org/virtual-commu nity-center/.

The Importance of a Social Support Network When Preparing for Retirement

Finding people who know us, care for us, and accept us is never easy, but it can be especially challenging when you have ADHD. People in retirement tend to look for communities based on common interests or needs, such as an organized retirement community, an arts community, or a golf community.

Older adults with ADHD often find more difficulty than other adults in finding a place where they fit in, resulting in troubling loneliness and isolation. Finding or creating an older adult ADHD support group can be an excellent place to start. Fortunately, Meetup groups are very easy to create online. All you need is a topic—"Older with ADHD"—plus a time and a place to meet. One man I interviewed moved away after his wife of thirty years asked for a divorce. He settled in western North Carolina, where he liked the weather and hoped he could find friends in the community. He created three different Meetup groups—one for older adults with ADHD and two others to discuss topics of interest to him. Within a few months of his arrival, he had made several friends by taking the initiative to form these groups.

If you are shy, feel socially awkward, or have difficulty initiating social gatherings, often the best way to have social connections is to find a retirement community that offers a broad range of meetings and activities. That way there is nothing to initiate. All you need to do is show up.

It's critically important to stay socially connected. For some, seeing people once a week is enough; for others, daily interactions are a must. But for all of us, social connectedness is critical to good health and good brain functioning. Loneliness is becoming an increasing problem in our modern society where people move away from family and may continue to move due to career opportunities. As recent studies have demonstrated, loneliness is especially acute among older people and can be directly linked to depression, high levels of stress hormones, fragmented sleep, declining health, and shorter life span.[4] Shared housing, a viable, affordable option chosen by an increasing number of older adults, predominantly women, can be a powerful antidote to social isolation.

Learning to Manage ADHD Is Always a Work in Progress

We are impacted by ADHD in so many different ways, and we can't necessarily change all the factors that make our life with ADHD more stressful. But you can develop a positive problem-solving approach to the stressors in your life.

Step 1

List the changes you want to make. Do you have someone to brainstorm with as you make this list? It can help to have the perspective of someone who knows you well but isn't caught up in the feelings of overwhelm you might be feeling. If you are confused and not sure where to start, talk through your list with someone who can provide helpful feedback.

As an example, your list might look something like this:

I need to:

• Dig out of my house, but it feels impossible and overwhelming.

• Get my finances in order—should I earn some extra income, or reduce my monthly expenses?

• Learn more about ADHD and talk to other older adults who are on this same journey.

• Ask for support from my partner/family to learn more about ADHD and support me in making changes.

• Build a reasonable, healthy daily routine.

• Think about my health problems and whether I will need more care and support soon.

• Put more people and activities in my life.

Step 2

Prioritize what you are going to change in your efforts to create an ADHD-friendly retirement. Remember, "E.A.S.T. (Everything at the Same Time)" is least successful. Pick just one and get it done!

You can prioritize your list by talking with a friend, a family member, or a coach. Choose someone who knows you well and can help you plan and prioritize.

What is missing in your life that makes your environment not ADHD-friendly? Ask yourself, "What would help me feel that I am moving in the right direction?"

Step 3

Find the structure and support you need to begin to make necessary changes. This could be something like the following:

- A walking buddy to support your need for regular exercise

- A mutual dig-out buddy to begin to declutter your home

- A friend or family member to help you problem-solve

- An online ADHD support group for older adults that can provide understanding, support, and suggestions to help you work toward creating a more ADHD-friendly retirement

KEY TAKEAWAYS FROM THIS CHAPTER

In creating an ADHD-friendly environment as an older adult, keep in mind these things:

✔ **There are many ways to find structure and support.** If hiring a professional coach, organizer, or therapist isn't in your budget, look for support from friends, family members, and members of the ADHD community.

✔ **Look for senior housing options that can provide structure, support, social connections, and stimulation.**

✔ **Creating an ADHD-friendly life is always a work in progress.** Don't get discouraged if everything isn't "fixed" in short order.

✔ **Be kind to yourself!** Encourage yourself, set small goals, be forgiving when you fall short, and then get back at it.

✔ **Catch those automatic negative thoughts you've lived with for so long and rephrase them.** Instead of, "There I go again! I always screw things up," tell yourself, "Yes, I fell back into old patterns, but I'm moving in the right direction."

My Message to You

I hope that this book has helped you understand how ADHD impacts older adults and what approaches are helpful. Most important, if you are an older adult with ADHD, or believe that you may have ADHD, I hope that through reading this book you have come to better understand your needs and will find ways to create an ADHD-friendly environment that suits you.

This is the first book written for or about older adults with ADHD. I don't pretend to have all the answers, but I have laid out, to the best of my ability, what I have learned as I have seen older adults with ADHD in therapy, as well as spoken to and observed many older adults with ADHD.

My message is simple. "Treating" ADHD is much more than taking medication or working with a coach. Both of those are often very helpful. But just as important are brain-friendly daily habits, along with creating or finding an environment that will meet your needs for social connection, structure, and support. Older adults living in isolation, especially those with ADHD, are at risk for depression, loneliness, and poor health.

If you need assistance, look for it. If you are living in a state of disorganized overwhelm, get regular help to maintain some reasonable level of order in your home. If you are taking poor care of yourself physically, look for ways to get regular sleep, get regular exercise, and eat a healthy diet—through joining an ADHD support group, working with an ADHD coach, belonging to a community that provides these things, and/or participating in a senior center in your community. If you find yourself sinking into social isolation, into poor self-care, into a sense of purposelessness, don't blame yourself; instead, work to change your circumstances.

Those with ADHD thrive when they have daily structure in their lives through work, friendships, volunteer work, and/or through living in an active adult community with multiple activities available. There are many things that you can do to lead a more satisfying life as an older adult with ADHD.

ADHD in Older Adults Self-Report Questionnaire

Kathleen Nadeau, PhD

This questionnaire is copyrighted and is available only for personal use without the written permission of the author.

Instructions: Please respond to each item, rating it from 0 to 5, with 0 indicating "not at all" and 5 indicating "very much." The items that you rate as a 4 or 5 in your current life are the issues to focus on with your therapist, coach, or psychiatrist.

This questionnaire cannot be used to make a diagnosis. Instead, it should be used as part of a structured interview to share with the professionals who are treating you.

Midlife	Now	Symptom
		Overall stress level
		Absentmindedness
		Forgetting things I've been told
		Impulse to do "one more thing" when I don't have enough time

Midlife	Now	Symptom
		Tendency to run late
		Difficulty managing finances
		Difficulty paying bills on time
		Difficulty filing tax returns on time
		Difficulty handling paperwork
		Impulse purchases
		Messiness
		Tendency to interrupt others in conversation
		Difficulty completing projects
		Difficulty putting things back where they belong
		Losing track of time
		Difficulty planning my day
		Difficulty sticking to my plan for the day
		Difficulty with meal planning
		Difficulty with meal preparation
		Difficulty with keeping in touch with friends
		Conflicts or misunderstandings with friends
		Taking on too many projects
		Conflicts in marriage or primary relationship
		Impatience
		Night owl tendencies
		Keeping an irregular schedule
		Spending too much time on digital devices
		Difficulty getting regular exercise
		Frequent family conflicts
		Feeling overwhelmed
		Overeating and/or night eating
		Difficulty maintaining a healthy weight
		Depression/despondency
		Anxiety/worries

Midlife	Now	Symptom
		Boredom/restlessness
		Alcohol consumption
		Cigarettes/tobacco
		Overall life satisfaction

ADHD in Older Adults Self-Report Questionnaire

ADHD Medication Benefits and Side Effects Tracking Form

Keeping a chart like this and sharing it with your physician will help both you and your physician to carefully track the benefits and negative side effects of medication, allowing your prescriber to more accurately determine your need for a different dose, delivery system, or type of medication.

Use a new chart each week and don't compare your answers from previous charts you've completed until after you've rated your responses for the current week. This will prevent your earlier answers from influencing your current answers.

Please rate each benefit and negative side effect from 1 to 5, where 1 indicates a very small effect (either positive or negative) and 5 indicates a large effect.

Date: from _____ to _____

Medication(s) Dose/Time & Frequency Time Medication Wears Off

1) _____

2) _____

3) _____

4) _____

Side Effects	Sunday	Monday	Tuesday	Wednesday	Thursday	Friday	Saturday
Headache							
Loss of appetite							
Jitteriness							
Insomnia							

Benefits	Sunday	Monday	Tuesday	Wednesday	Thursday	Friday	Saturday
More focused							
Calm							
More able to complete tasks							
Fewer misplaced belongings							
Less forgetful							
Less emotionally reactive							

ADHD Medication Benefits and Side Effects Tracking Form

APPENDIX B

Benefits	Sunday	Monday	Tuesday	Wednesday	Thursday	Friday	Saturday
More aware of time/more on time							
Less Impulsive							
More motivation							
Fewer conflicts with others							

ADHD Resources

Organizations

CHADD is a long-established advocacy organization for those with ADHD across the life span. It lists professionals who specialize in ADHD as well as organizations that treat ADHD. https://chadd .org/organization-directory/

ADDA is a long-established ADHD nonprofit organization that provides a host of helpful online support groups, work groups, seminars, and educational materials for adults with ADHD. This is one of the best places to find fellow ADHDers and to meet with them regularly in groups focused on a large variety of ADHD topics. https://add.org

CHADD and ADDA now hold an annual meeting together where you can meet and interact with fellow adults with ADHD and hear lectures by many of the top experts in the field.

Online Resources

Help for sleep problems: Read "20 of the Best Guided Meditations for Sleep and Insomnia." https://www.lifehack.org/844530/best -guided-meditation-for-sleep

Focusmate is a well-organized, highly affordable way to provide yourself with company and accountability as you work to complete tasks that you find difficult to get started on. "Focusmate changes the way you work by connecting you to other professionals who have committed to being accountable for finishing their most important work. You choose a time to work, and Focusmate pairs you with an accountability partner for a live, virtual coworking session that will keep you on task." https://www.focusmate.com

ADHD reWired is a large, active online coaching community of adults with ADHD that offers podcasts, coaching groups, and accountability groups. Following six months of participation in a coaching group (at a fee of approximately $380 per month), "alumni" of these groups can continue to participate in accountability groups and access podcasts for a nominal monthly fee. Alumni of their coaching groups form an ongoing supportive community for adults with ADHD. https://www.adhdrewired.com

YouTube

How to ADHD: Created by actress Jessica McCabe, this You-Tube channel has over a million subscribers and comes highly recommended by older adults with ADHD with whom I've spoken. It's lively, informative, and accurate. https://www.youtube.com/c/How toADHD/about

Magazines

ATTENTION! Magazine is published by CHADD and is available free to all members of CHADD. It contains information for people with ADHD of all ages. https://chadd.org/attention-magazine

ADDitude Magazine is a nationally distributed ADHD-focused magazine that provides evidence-based information for professionals who specialize in treating ADHD, as well as information for those with

ADHD. *ADDitude*'s articles are, in many cases, written by leaders in the field and all articles are reviewed and approved by the magazine's professional advisory board. https://www.additudemag.com

Books

Fogg, BJ. *Tiny Habits: The Small Changes That Change Everything.* New York: Harvest, 2021.

Kolberg, Judith, and Kathleen G. Nadeau. *ADD-Friendly Ways to Organize Your Life.* New York: Routledge, 2002.

Ratey, John J. *Spark: The Revolutionary New Science of Exercise and the Brain.* New York: Little, Brown, 2008. A highly readable book about the importance of aerobic exercise and how it changes our brain chemistry, reducing ADHD symptoms and improving memory and learning.

Tuckman, Ari. *More Attention, Less Deficit: Success Strategies for Adults with ADHD.* Plantation, FL: Specialty Press, 2009. By a well-known ADHD specialist and psychotherapist.

Zylowska, Lidia. *The Mindfulness Prescription for Adult ADHD: An 8-Step Program for Strengthening Attention, Managing Emotions, and Achieving Your Goals.* New York: Trumpeter, 2012. This is a proven, evidence-based program for managing your ADHD.

Finding Affordable Treatment

To advocate for insurance coverage of stimulant medications, readers can visit the following section of Dr. David Goodman's website to learn more: https://addadult.com/cant-get-adhd-medication-approved-insurance/.

CHADD has an article on finding affordable services, which can be found at https://chadd.org/attention-article/19-tips-for-finding-low-cost-adhd-treatment/.

Prescription Assistance Programs

The following organizations may be able to assist you if you need help paying for the medications that you need.

- **The Partnership for Prescription Assistance**—For more information, call 1-888-477-2669 or go to https://screening.mhanational.org/content/partnership-prescription-assistance/.
- **Rx Hope** offers an assistance program directory along with information about assistance programs for specific medications. https://www.rxhope.com/

- **Mental Health America (local and/or state)**—This is a resource for information about prescription assistance programs. https://mhanational.org/
- **Medicare Rights Center** offers information about state and national prescription assistance programs, drug discount cards, and mail order and internet pharmacies. https://www.medicare rights.org/

In addition, many pharmaceutical companies offer medication discounts to qualified individuals. Here is a list of some of those programs:

Medication	Program Details
Concerta	Concerta savings program, https://www.concerta.net/savings.html. Eligible patients using commercial or private insurance can save on out-of-pocket costs.
Daytrana	Savings on Daytrana program, https://www.daytrana.com. Eligible patients pay as little as $20 on up to 12 prescriptions.
Evekeo	Evekeo co-pay savings program, https://www.evekeo.com. If your co-pay exceeds $30 for insured patients or $75 for uninsured patients, show your savings card info to the pharmacist for a discount.
Focalin XR	Focalin XR co-pay card, https://www.focalinxr.com/savings. Eligible patients pay only $10 for a 30-tablet prescription.
Intuniv	Takeda, https://www.takeda.com/en-us/what-we-do/patient-services/helpathand/, available by application, provides assistance for people who have no insurance or who do not have enough insurance and need help getting their Takeda medicines.
Journay PM	Jornay PM savings offer, https://www.jornaypm.com/savings. Pay $0 for your first prescription. Then, pay $25 per prescription if Jornay PM is covered by your insurance, or $75 per prescription if Jornay PM is not covered by your insurance. Restrictions apply.

APPENDIX D

Medication	Program Details
Mydayis	Mydayis co-pay program, https://www.mydayis.com /prescription-support/copay-program. Eligible patients pay as little as $30 for a prescription fill until the end of the program.
Strattera	Lilly Cares Foundation patient assistance program, https://www.lillycares.com, helps eligible patients receive Lilly medications at no cost. *Does not apply to generic versions of Strattera*
Vyvanse	Vyvanse savings card, https://www.vyvanse.com. Eligible patients may pay as little as $30 per prescription for a maximum savings of $60 each time a prescription is filled.
Wellbutrin XL	Wellbutrin XL co-pay savings program, https://www .wellbutrinxl.com. Eligible patients pay as little as $5 per 30-day supply.

NOTES

INTRODUCTION

1. Y. Ginsberg et al., "Underdiagnosis of Attention-Deficit/Hyperactivity Disorder in Adult Patients: A Review of the Literature," *The Primary Care Companion for CNS Disorders* 16, no. 3 (2014): PCC.13r01600, https://doi.org/10.4088/PCC.13r01600; J. J. S. Kooij et al., "Distinguishing Comorbidity and Successful Management of Adult ADHD," *Journal of Attention Disorders* 16, no. 5 suppl. (2016): 3S–19S, https://doi.org:10.1177/1087054711435361.

CHAPTER 1 ADHD IN OLDER ADULTS: WHY IT MATTERS

1. Kathleen G. Nadeau and Patricia O. Quinn, *Understanding Women with ADHD* (Chevy Chase, MD: Advantage Books, 1999).
2. William E. Gibson, "Age 65+ Adults Are Projected to Outnumber Children by 2030," AARP, https://www.aarp.org/home-family/friends-family/info-2018/census-baby-boomers-fd.html.
3. K. Henkens et al., "What We Need to Know about Retirement: Pressing Issues for the Coming Decade," *Gerontologist* 58, no. 5 (2018): 805–812.
4. National Council on Aging, "Get the Facts on Economic Security for Seniors," 2021, https://www.ncoa.org/article/get-the-facts-on-economic-security-for-seniors.
5. J. Tanskanen and T. Anttila, "A Prospective Study of Social Isolation, Loneliness, and Mortality in Finland," *American Journal of Public Health* 106, no. 11 (2016): 2042–2048.

CHAPTER 2 THE CHALLENGES OF GETTING OLDER

1. S. H. Chapman, M. P. LaPlante, and G. Wilensky, "Life Expectancy and Health Status of the Aged," *Social Security Bulletin* 49, no. 10 (1986): 24–48.
2. V. L. Bengtson and F. J. Whittington, "From Ageism to the Longevity Revolution: Robert Butler, Pioneer," *Gerontologist* 54, no. 6 (2014): 1064–1069.

3. R. de la Sablonnière, "Toward a Psychology of Social Change: A Typology of Social Change," *Frontiers in Psychology* 8 (2017).

4. Patrick Nolan and Gerhard Lenski, *Human Societies: An Introduction to Macrosociology*, 11th ed. (Boulder, CO: Paradigm, 2011).

5. Louise C. Hawkley and John T. Cacioppo, "Loneliness Matters: A Theoretical and Empirical Review of Consequences and Mechanisms," *Annals of Behavioral Medicine: A Publication of the Society of Behavioral Medicine* 40, no. 2 (2010): 218–227.

6. Hawkley and Cacioppo, "Loneliness Matters."

7. Hawkley and Cacioppo, "Loneliness Matters."

8. Greg Miller, "Social Neuroscience: Why Loneliness Is Hazardous to Your Health," *Science* 331 (2011): 138–140.

9. Miller, "Social Neuroscience."

10. National Institute on Retirement Security New Report, "40% of Older Americans Rely Solely on Social Security for Retirement Income," 2020, https://www.nirsonline.org/2020/01/new-report-40-of-older-americans-rely-solely-on-social-security-for-retirement-income/.

11. N. Roy et al., "Choosing Between Staying at Home or Moving: A Systematic Review of Factors Influencing Housing Decisions among Frail Older Adults," *PLoS ONE* 13, no. 1 (2018).

12. *Business Insider*, "The Fastest Growing Metro Area in the US Is a Republican-Leaning Retirement Community in Florida," 2021, https://www.businessinsider.com/the-villages-florida-msa-metro-area-republican-exurban-census-2021-8.

13. L. Hantrais, J. Brannen, and F. Bennett, "Family Change, Intergenerational Relations and Policy Implications," *Contemporary Social Science* 15, no. 3 (2020): 275–290.

14. A. N. McKee and J. E. Morley, "Obesity in the Elderly" (updated 2021), in K. R. et al., eds., Endotext (South Dartmouth, MA: MDText.com, Inc.; 2021).

15. E. Commisso et al., "Identifying and Understanding the Health and Social Care Needs of Older Adults with Multiple Chronic Conditions and Their Caregivers: A Scoping Review," *BMC Geriatrics* 18, no. 231 (2018).

16. Dale E. Bredesen, *The End of Alzheimer's: The First Program to Prevent and Reverse Cognitive Decline* (New York: Avery, 2017).

17. K. E. Assmann et al., "Unsaturated Fatty Acid Intakes During Midlife Are Positively Associated with Later Cognitive Function in Older Adults with Modulating Effects of Antioxidant Supplementation," *Journal of Nutrition* 148, no. 12 (2018): 1938–1945.

CHAPTER 3 IT'S HARD TO UNDERSTAND IT IF YOU HAVEN'T LIVED IT

1. M. S. Jellinek, "Don't Let ADHD Crush Children's Self-Esteem," *Clinical Psychiatry News* (May 2010): 12.
2. S. P. Hinshaw, "Preadolescent Girls with Attention-Deficit/Hyperactivity Disorder: Background Characteristics, Comorbidity, Cognitive and Social Functioning, and Parenting Practices," *Journal of Consulting and Clinical Psychology* 70, no. 5 (2002).
3. G. D. de Boo and P. J. M. Prins, "Social Incompetence in Children with ADHD: Possible Moderators and Mediators in Social-Skills Training," *Clinical Psychology Review* 27 (2007): 78–97; C. L. Huang-Pollock et al., "Can Executive Functions Explain Relation Between ADHD and Social Adjustment?," *Journal of Abnormal Child Psychology* 37 (2009): 679–691.
4. C. L. Bagwell et al., "Attention-Deficit Hyperactivity Disorder and Problems in Peer Relations: Predictions from Childhood to Adolescence," *Journal of the American Academy of Child and Adolescent Psychiatry* 40 (2001): 1285–1292; M. J. Kofler et al., "Developmental Trajectories of Aggression, Prosocial Behavior, and Social–Cognitive Problem Solving in Emerging Adolescents with Clinically Elevated Attention-Deficit/Hyperactivity Disorder Symptoms," *Journal of Abnormal Psychology* 124, no. 4 (2015): 1027–1042.
5. S. R. Friedman et al., "Aspects of Social and Emotional Competence in Adult Attention Deficit/Hyperactivity Disorder," *Neuropsychology* 17 (2003): 50–58.
6. William Dodson, quoted in Devon Frye, "Children with ADHD Avoid Failure and Punishment More Than Others, Study Says," *ADDitude*, 2016, https://www.additudemag.com/children-with-adhd-avoid-failure-punishment/; G. Weiss et al., "Psychiatric Status of Hyperactive as Adults: A Controlled Prospective 15-Year Follow-Up of 63 Hyperactive Children," *Journal of the American Academy of Child Psychiatry* 24, no. 2 (1985): 211–220.
7. Margaret Weiss, Lily Trokenberg Hechtman, and Gabrielle Weiss, *ADHD in Adulthood: A Guide to Current Theory, Diagnosis and Treatment* (Baltimore: Johns Hopkins University Press, 1999).
8. J. Mahadevan, A. Kandasamy, and V. Benegal, "Situating Adult Attention-Deficit/Hyperactivity Disorder in the Externalizing Spectrum: Etiological, Diagnostic, and Treatment Considerations," *Indian Journal of Psychiatry* 61, no. 1 (2019): 3–12.
9. V. A. Harpin, "The Effect of ADHD on the Life of an Individual, Their Family, and Community from Preschool to Adult Life," *Archives of Disease in Childhood* 90 (2005): 2–7.

10. Social Security Administration, "Policy Basics: Top Ten Facts about Social Security," https://www.cbpp.org/research/social-security/top-ten-facts -about-social-security.

11. S. Gnanavel et al., "Attention Deficit Hyperactivity Disorder and Comorbidity: A Review of Literature," *World Journal of Clinical Cases* 7, no. 17 (2019): 2420–2426.

CHAPTER 4 HOW DO YOU KNOW YOU HAVE ADHD?

1. B. L. Fischer et al., "The Identification and Assessment of Late-Life ADHD in Memory Clinics," *Journal of Attention Disorders* 16, no. 4 (2012): 333–338, https://doi.org/10.1177/1087054711398886.

2. L. Zhang et al., "Attention Deficit/Hyperactivity Disorder and Alzheimer's Disease and Any Dementia: A Multi-generation Cohort Study in Sweden," *Alzheimer's & Dementia* 1, no. 9 (2021).

3. A. Golimstok et al., "Previous Adult Attention-Deficit and Hyperactivity Disorder Symptoms and Risk of Dementia with Lewy Bodies: A Case-Control Study," *European Journal of Neurology* 18, no. 11 (2011): 78.

4. D. E. Bredesen, "Reversal of Cognitive Decline: A Novel Therapeutic Program," *Aging* (Albany, NY) 6, no. 9, (2014): 707–717.

5. A. Palmini, "Professionally Successful Adults with Attention-Deficit/ Hyperactivity Disorder (ADHD): Compensation Strategies and Subjective Effects of Pharmacological Treatment," *Dementia & Neuropsychologia* 2, no. 1 (2008): 63–70.

6. American Psychiatric Association, *Diagnostic and Statistical Manual of Mental Disorders*, 5th ed. (DSM-5), (Washington, DC: American Psychiatric Publishing, 2013).

7. J. D. McLennan, "Understanding Attention Deficit Hyperactivity Disorder as a Continuum," *Le Médecin de famille canadien* 62, no. 12 (2016): 979–982.

8. L. Cumyn, L. French, and L. Hechtman, "Comorbidity in Adults with Attention-Deficit Hyperactivity Disorder," *Canadian Journal of Psychiatry* 54, no. 10 (2009): 673–683.

9. M. H. Sibley et al., "Variable Patterns of Remission from ADHD in the Multimodal Treatment Study of ADHD," *American Journal of Psychiatry*, ePub, August 13, 2021, https://doi.org/10.1176/appi.ajp.2021.21010032.

10. Thomas E. Brown, *Outside the Box: Rethinking ADD/ADHD in Children and Adults: A Practical Guide* (Arlington, VA: American Psychiatric Association Publishing, 2017).

11. B. K. Ashinoff and A. Abu-Akel, "Hyperfocus: The Forgotten Frontier of Attention," *Psychological Research* 85, no. 1 (2021): 1–19.

12. C. M. Koen, A. J. Carmichael, and K. E. Koen, "Attention Deficit Disorder and the Americans with Disabilities Act: Is Anyone Paying Attention?" *Health Care Manager* (Frederick) 36, no. 2 (April–June 2017): 116–122.

13. J. A. Sedgwick, A. Merwood, and P. Asherson, "The Positive Aspects of Attention Deficit Hyperactivity Disorder: A Qualitative Investigation of Successful Adults with ADHD," *ADHD Attention Deficit Hyperactivity Disorder* 11 (2019): 241–253.

14. J. W. Lee, K. Seo, and G. H. Bahn, "The Positive Aspects of Attention-Deficit/Hyperactivity Disorder among Famous People," *Psychiatry Investigation* 17, no. 5 (2020): 424–431.

15. C. G. Palmer et al., "Wildland Firefighters and Attention Deficit Hyperactivity Disorder (ADHD)," Proceedings of the Second Conference on the Human Dimensions of Wildland Fire, 2011.

16. Thom Hartmann, *ADHD: A Hunter in a Farmer's World* (New York: Healing Arts Press, 2019).

17. Y. Ginsberg et al., "Underdiagnosis of Attention-Deficit/Hyperactivity Disorder in Adult Patients: A Review of the Literature," *Primary Care Companion for CNS Disorders* 16, no. 3 (2014), PCC.13r01600.

18. Cumyn, French, and Hechtman, "Comorbidity in Adults with Attention-Deficit Hyperactivity Disorder."

19. Ginsberg et al., "Underdiagnosis of Attention-Deficit/Hyperactivity Disorder in Adult Patients."

20. American Psychiatric Association, *Diagnostic and Statistical Manual of Mental Disorders* (DSM-5).

21. J. N. Epstein and R. E. Loren, "Changes in the Definition of ADHD in DSM-5: Subtle but Important," *Neuropsychiatry* 3, no. 5 (2013): 455–458.

22. E. M. Mahone and M. B. Denckla, "Attention Deficit/Hyperactivity Disorder: A Historical Neuropsychological Perspective," *Journal of the International Neuropsychological Society: JINS* 23, nos. 9–10 (2017): 916–929.

23. Palmini, "Professionally Successful Adults with Attention-Deficit/Hyperactivity Disorder (ADHD)."

24. S. Young et al., "Females with ADHD: An Expert Consensus Statement Taking a Lifespan Approach Providing Guidance for the Identification and Treatment of Attention-Deficit/Hyperactivity Disorder in Girls and Women," *BMC Psychiatry* 20, no. 1 (2020): 404.

25. M. Combs et al., "Perceived Stress and ADHD Symptoms in Adults," *Journal of Attention Disorders* 19, no. 5 (2015): 425–434.

26. J. Kooij et al., "Internal and External Validity of Attention-Deficit Hyperactivity Disorder in a Population-Based Sample of Adults," *Psychological Medicine* 35, no. 6 (2005): 817–827.

27. R. A. Barkley and M. Fischer, "Hyperactive Child Syndrome and Estimated Life Expectancy at Young Adult Follow-Up: The Role of ADHD Persistence and Other Potential Predictors," *Journal of Attention Disorders* 23, no. 9 (2019): 907–923.

28. D. W. Goodman et al., "Assessment of Physician Practices in Adult Attention-Deficit/Hyperactivity Disorder," *Primary Care Companion for CNS Disorders* 14, no. 4 (2012): PCC.11m01312.

29. Alzheimer's Association, "2020 Alzheimer's Disease Facts and Figures. Alzheimer's and Dementia," *Journal of the Alzheimer's Association* 16, no. 3 (2020): 391–460.

30. Alzheimer's Association, "2020 Alzheimer's Disease Facts and Figures."

31. R. S. Wright et al., "Diet Quality and Cognitive Function in an Urban Sample: Findings from the Healthy Aging in Neighborhoods of Diversity Across the Life Span (HANDLS) Study," *Public Health Nutrition* 20, no. 1 (2017): 92–101.

32. K. R. Murphy and L. A. Adler, "Assessing Attention-Deficit/Hyperactivity Disorder in Adults: Focus on Rating Scales," *Journal of Clinical Psychiatry* 65, suppl. 3 (2004): 12–17.

33. C. J. Miller, J. H. Newcorn, and J. M. Halperin, "Fading Memories: Retrospective Recall Inaccuracies in ADHD," *Journal of Attention Disorders* 14, no. 1 (2010): 7–14.

34. R. C. Kessler et al., "Validity of the World Health Organization Adult ADHD Self-Report Scale (ASRS) Screener in a Representative Sample of Health Plan Members," *International Journal of Methods in Psychiatric Research* 16, no. 2 (2007): 52–65.

CHAPTER 5 STIMULANT MEDICATION FOR OLDER ADULTS WITH ADHD

1. D. Kolar et al., "Treatment of Adults with Attention-Deficit/Hyperactivity Disorder," *Neuropsychiatric Disease and Treatment* 4, no. 2 (2008): 389–403.

2. L. Matheson et al., "Adult ADHD Patient Experiences of Impairment, Service Provision and Clinical Management in England: A Qualitative Study," *BMC Health Services Research* 13, no. 184 (2013).

3. T. E. Brown et al., "The Patient Perspective: Unmet Treatment Needs in Adults with Attention-Deficit/Hyperactivity Disorder," *Primary Care Companion for CNS Disorders* 21, no. 3 (2019): 25767.

4. Matheson et al., "Adult ADHD Patient Experiences of Impairment, Service Provision and Clinical Management in England."

5. S. Cortese et al., "Comparative Efficacy and Tolerability of Medications for Attention-Deficit Hyperactivity Disorder in Children, Adolescents

and Adults: A Systematic Review and Network Meta-analysis," *Lancet Psychiatry* 5, no. 9 (2018): 727–738.

6. T. Torgersen et al., "Optimal Management of ADHD in Older Adults," *Neuropsychiatric Disease and Treatment* 12 (2016): 79–87.

7. T. Spencer et al., "A Large, Double-Blind, Randomized Clinical Trial of Methylphenidate in the Treatment of Adults with Attention-Deficit /Hyperactivity Disorder," *Biological Psychiatry* 57, no. 5 (2005): 456–463.

8. L. A. Habel et al., "ADHD Medications and Risk of Serious Cardiovascular Events in Young and Middle-Aged Adults," *Journal of the American Medical Association* 306, no. 24 (2011): 2673–2683.

9. Email communication from William Dodson, MD, February 12, 2021.

10. Email communication from William Dodson, MD.

11. Kolar et al., "Treatment of Adults with Attention-Deficit/Hyperactivity Disorder."

12. L. Cumyn, L. French, and L. Hechtman, "Comorbidity in Adults with Attention-Deficit Hyperactivity Disorder," *Canadian Journal of Psychiatry* 54, no. 10 (2009): 673–683.

13. T. A. Rowland and S. Marwaha, "Epidemiology and Risk Factors for Bipolar Disorder," *Therapeutic Advances in Psychopharmacology* 8, no. 9 (2018): 251–269.

14. Cumyn, French, and Hechtman, "Comorbidity in Adults with Attention-Deficit Hyperactivity Disorder."

15. J. Geffen and K. Forster, "Treatment of Adult ADHD: A Clinical Perspective," *Therapeutic Advances in Psychopharmacology* 8, no. 1 (2018): 25–32.

16. Geffen and Forster, "Treatment of Adult ADHD."

17. D. W. Goodman et al., "Assessment of Physician Practices in Adult Attention-Deficit/Hyperactivity Disorder," *Primary Care Companion for CNS Disorders* 14, no. 4 (2012): PCC.11m01312.

18. K. L. M. Sassi et al., "Amphetamine Use in the Elderly: A Systematic Review of the Literature," *Current Neuropharmacology* 18, no. 2 (2020): 126–135.

19. J. D. Franzen et al., "Psychostimulants for Older Adults: Certain Agents May Improve Apathy, ADHD, Depression, and Other Conditions," *Current Psychiatry* 11, no. 1 (2012): 23–32.

20. Sassi et al., "Amphetamine Use in the Elderly."

21. T. E. Brown et al., "The Patient Perspective: Unmet Treatment Needs in Adults with Attention-Deficit/Hyperactivity Disorder," *Primary Care Companion of CNS Disorders* 21, no. 3 (2019): 25767.

22. Matheson et al., "Adult ADHD Patient Experiences of Impairment, Service Provision and Clinical Management in England."

23. K. Budur et al., "Non-Stimulant Treatment for Attention Deficit Hyperactivity Disorder," *Psychiatry* (Edgmont, PA) 2, no. 7 (2005): 44–48.

24. A. Arnett and M. Stein, "Refining Treatment Choices for ADHD," *Lancet Psychiatry* 5, no. 9 (2018): 691–692.

CHAPTER 6 LEARN TO UNDERSTAND, ACCEPT, AND THRIVE WITH ADHD

1. B. Franke et al., "Live Fast, Die Young? A Review on the Developmental Trajectories of ADHD Across the Lifespan," *European Neuropsychopharmacology* 28, no. 10 (2018): 1059–1088.
2. The Psychology Interjurisdictional Compact (PSYPACT), https://psypact .site-ym.com/.
3. J. Geffen and K. Forster, "Treatment of Adult ADHD: A Clinical Perspective," *Therapeutic Advances in Psychopharmacology* 8, no. 1 (2018): 25–32.
4. J. T. Nigg et al., "Evaluating Chronic Emotional Dysregulation and Irritability in Relation to ADHD and Depression: Genetic Risk in Children with ADHD," *Journal of Child Psychology and Psychiatry, and Allied Disciplines* 61, no. 2 (2020): 205–214.
5. C. López-Pinar et al., "Long-Term Efficacy of Psychosocial Treatments for Adults with Attention-Deficit/Hyperactivity Disorder: A Meta-analytic Review," *Frontiers in Psychology* 4, no. 9 (2018): 638.
6. Franke et al., "Live Fast, Die Young?"
7. J. T. Nigg et al., "Toward a Revised Nosology for Attention-Deficit/Hyperactivity Disorder Heterogeneity," *Biological Psychiatry: Cognitive Neuroscience and Neuroimaging* 5, no. 8 (2020): 726–737.

CHAPTER 7 WAYS TO HELP YOURSELF

1. Judith Kohlberg and Kathleen G. Nadeau, *ADD-Friendly Ways to Organize Your Life* (New York: Routledge, 2002).
2. BJ Fogg, *Tiny Habits: The Small Changes That Change Everything* (New York: Harvest, 2021).
3. Russell A. Barkley with Christine M. Benton, *Taking Charge of Adult ADHD*, 2nd ed. (New York: Guilford Press, 2021).
4. Lidia Zylowska and John T. Mitchell, *Mindfulness for Adult ADHD: A Clinician's Guide* (New York: Guilford Press, 2021).

CHAPTER 8 WORKING WITH AN ADHD COACH

1. S. J. C. Schrevel, C. Dedding, and J. E. W. Broerse, "Why Do Adults with ADHD Choose Strength-Based Coaching over Public Mental Health Care? A Qualitative Case Study from the Netherlands," *SAGE Open* (July 2016), https://doi.org/10.1177/2158244016662498.
2. M. V. Solanto et al., "Efficacy of Meta-cognitive Therapy for Adult ADHD," *American Journal of Psychiatry* 167, no. 8 (2010): 958–968.

3. I. Bloemen, W. Verbeeck, and S. Tuinier, "The Effect of Group Coaching in Adult ADHD," *European Psychiatry* 22, S1 (2007): S205; E. Ahmann et al., "A Descriptive Review of ADHD Coaching Research: Implications for College Students," *Journal of Postsecondary Education and Disability* 31, no. 1 (2009): 17–39.

4. E. Ahmann, M. Saviet, and L. J. Tuttle, "Interventions for ADHD in Children and Teens: A Focus on ADHD Coaching," *Pediatric Nursing* 43, no. 3 (2017): 121–131; S. B. Goudreau and M. Knight, "Executive Function Coaching: Assisting with Transitioning from Secondary to Postsecondary Education," *Journal of Attention Disorders* 22, no. 4 (2018): 379–387; T. L. Maitland et al., "The Impact of Coaching on Academic Success: A Focus on University Students with Learning Disabilities and Attention Deficit/Hyperactivity Disorder," paper presented at the conference of AHEAD: Association on Higher Education and Disability, Denver, CO, 2010; Dianne R. Stober and Anthony M. Grant, eds., *Evidence Based Coaching Handbook* (Hoboken, NJ: Wiley & Sons, 2006), 1–14.

5. L. E. Knouse et al., "Recent Developments in the Psychosocial Treatment of Adult ADHD," *Expert Review in Neurotherapy* 8 (2008): 1537–1548; J. A. Kubik, "Efficacy of ADHD Coaching for Adults with ADHD," *Journal of Attention Disorders* 13 (2010): 442–453; Frances Prevatt and Abigail L. Levrini, *ADHD Coaching: A Guide for Mental Health Professionals* (Washington, DC: American Psychological Association, 2015).

6. Patrick Williams and Deborah C. Davis, *Therapist as Life Coach: An Introduction for Counselors and Other Helping Professionals,* rev. and expanded ed. (New York: W. W. Norton, 2007); J. Geffen and K. Forster, "Treatment of Adult ADHD: A Clinical Perspective," *Therapeutic Advances in Psychopharmacology* 8, no. 1 (2018): 25–32.

7. S. McMains and S. Kastner, "Interactions of Top-Down and Bottom-Up Mechanisms in Human Visual Cortex," *Journal of Neuroscience* 31, no. 2 (2011): 587–597.

8. D. F. Tolin and A. Villavicencio, "Inattention, but Not OCD, Predicts the Core Features of Hoarding Disorder," *Behaviour Research and Therapy* 49, no. 2 (2011): 120–125, https://doi.org/10.1016/j.brat.2010.12.002.

9. Judith Kolberg and Kathleen G. Nadeau, *ADD-Friendly Ways to Organize Your Life* (New York: Routledge, 2016).

10. L. R. Vartanian and A. M. Porter, "Weight Stigma and Eating Behavior: A Review of the Literature," *Appetite* 102 (2016): 3–14.

11. Kolberg and Nadeau, *ADD-Friendly Ways to Organize Your Life.*

12. James Clear, *Atomic Habits: An Easy and Proven Way to Build Good Habits and Break Bad Ones* (London: Penguin Random House UK, 2018).

13. BJ Fogg, *Tiny Habits: The Small Changes That Change Everything* (New York: Harvest, 2021).

CHAPTER 9 BRAIN-HEALTHY DAILY HABITS

1. S. V. Faraone and H. Larsson, "Genetics of Attention Deficit Hyperactivity Disorder," *Molecular Psychiatry* 24, no. 4 (2019): 562–575.

2. S. H. Kollins et al., "Increased Subjective and Reinforcing Effects of Initial Nicotine Exposure in Young Adults with Attention Deficit Hyperactivity Disorder (ADHD) Compared to Matched Peers: Results from an Experimental Model of First-Time Tobacco Use," *Neuropsychopharmacology* 45 (2020): 851–856.

3. E. Shareghfarid et al., "Empirically Derived Dietary Patterns and Food Groups Intake in Relation with Attention Deficit/Hyperactivity Disorder (ADD): A Systematic Review and Meta-analysis," *Clinical Nutrition ESPEN* 36 (2019): 28–35.

4. J. Biederman et al., "Does Attention-Deficit Hyperactivity Disorder Impact the Developmental Course of Drug and Alcohol Abuse and Dependence?," *Biological Psychiatry* 4, no. 4 (1998): 269–273.

5. A. Björk et al., "Health, Lifestyle Habits and Physical Fitness among Adults with ADHD Compared with a Random Sample of a Swedish General Population," *Society, Health & Vulnerability* 9, no. 1 (2018).

6. C. Fadeuilhe et al., "Insomnia Disorder in Adult Attention-Deficit/ Hyperactivity Disorder Patients: Clinical, Comorbidity, and Treatment Correlates," *Frontiers in Psychiatry* 12 (2021).

7. V. Harpin, "The Effect of ADHD on the Life of an Individual, Their Family, and Community from Preschool to Adult Life," *Archives of Disease in Childhood* 90 (2004).

8. S. Cortese et al., "Association Between ADHD and Obesity: A Systematic Review and Meta-Analysis," *American Journal of Psychiatry* 173, no. 1 (2016): 34–43.

9. Q. Chen et al., "Common Psychiatric and Metabolic Comorbidity of Adult Attention-Deficit/Hyperactivity Disorder: A Population-Based Cross-Sectional Study," *PLoS ONE* 13, no. 9 (2018).

10. M. A. Katzman et al., "Adult ADHD and Comorbid Disorders: Clinical Implications of a Dimensional Approach," *BMC Psychiatry* 17, no. 1 (2017): 12888-017.

11. W. Sroykham and Y. Wongsawat, "Effects of Brain Activity, Morning Salivary Cortisol, and Emotion Regulation on Cognitive Impairment in Elderly People," *Medicine* (Baltimore) 98, no. 26 (2019): e16114.

12. R. A. Barkley and M. Fischer, "Hyperactive Child Syndrome and Esti-mated Life Expectancy at Young Adult Follow-Up: The Role of ADHD Persistence and Other Potential Predictors," *Journal of Attention Disorders* 23, no. 9 (2019): 907–923.

13. L. Dahlberg et al., "Predictors of Loneliness among Older Women and Men in Sweden: A National Longitudinal Study," *Aging and Mental Health* 19, no. 5 (2015): 409–417.

14. D. Bredesen, "Reversal of Cognitive Decline: A Novel Therapeutic Program," *Aging* 6, no. 9 (2014): 707–717; C. Gustafson, "Dale E. Bredesen, MD: Reversing Cognitive Decline," *Integrative Medicine* (Encinitas, CA) 14, no. 5 (2015): 26–29; Dale E. Bredesen, *The End of Alzheimer's: The First Program to Prevent and Reverse Cognitive Decline* (New York: Avery, 2017).

15. Reversal of Cognitive Decline (ReCODE) Study (RECODE), https://clinicaltrials.gov/ct2/show/NCT03883633.

16. A. I. Guerdjikova et al., "Novel Pharmacologic Treatment in Acute Binge Eating Disorder—Role of Lisdexamfetamine," *Neuropsychiatric Disease and Treatment* 1 (2016): 833–841.

17. E. Sobanski et al., "Sleep in Adults with Attention Deficit Hyperactiv-ity Disorder (ADHD) Before and During Treatment with Methylphe-nidate: A Controlled Polysomnographic Study," *Sleep* 31, no. 3 (2008): 375–381.

18. Lidia Zylowska, *The Mindfulness Prescription for Adult ADHD: An 8-Step Program for Strengthening Attention, Managing Emotions, and Achieving Your Goals* (New York: Trumpeter, 2012).

19. Zylowska, *The Mindfulness Prescription for Adult ADHD*, ix–xi.

20. C. Thompson, E. Quigley, and A. Taylor, "The Influence of a Short-Term Mindfulness Meditation Intervention on Emotion and Visual Atten-tion," *Journal of Cognitive Enhancers* 5 (2021): 73–82.

21. John J. Ratey, *Spark: The Revolutionary New Science of Exercise and the Brain* (New York: Little, Brown, 2008).

22. M. R. Islam et al., "Exercise Hormone Irisin Is a Critical Regulator of Cognitive Function," *Nature Metabolism* 3 (2021): 1058–1070.

23. Y. Netz, "Is There a Preferred Mode of Exercise for Cognition Enhance-ment in Older Age?" *A Narrative Review* 6, no. 57 (2019).

24. A. Sheppard and M. C. Broughton, "Promoting Wellbeing and Health Through Active Participation in Music and Dance: A Systematic Review," *International Journal of Qualitative Studies on Health and Well-Being* 15, no. 1 (2020).

25. Y. Wu et al., "The Effects of Tai Chi Exercise on Cognitive Function in Older Adults: A Meta-Analysis," *Journal of Sport and Health Science* 2, no. 4 (2013): 193–203.

26. R. Abbott and H. Lavretsky, "Tai Chi and Qigong for the Treatment and Prevention of Mental Disorders," *Psychiatric Clinics of North America* 36, no. 1 (2013): 109.

27. F. Herold et al., "Functional and/or Structural Brain Changes in Response to Resistance Exercises and Resistance Training Lead to Cognitive Improvements—A Systematic Review," *European Review of Aging and Physical Activity: Official Journal of the European Group for Research into Elderly and Physical Activity* 16, no. 10 (2019).

28. H. White and P. Shah, "Attention in Urban and Natural Environments," *Yale Journal of Biology and Medicine* 92, no. 1 (2019): 115–120.

29. S. Kaplan, "The Restorative Benefits of Nature—Toward an Integrative Framework," *Journal of Environmental Psychology* 15 (1995): 169–182.

30. B. Jiang, R. Schmillen, and W. C. Sullivan, "How to Waste a Break: Using Portable Electronic Devices Substantially Counteracts Attention Enhancement Effects of Green Spaces," *Environment and Behavior* 51, nos. 9–10 (2019): 1133–1160.

31. P. J. Allen et al., "Rationale and Consequences of Reclassifying Obesity as an Addictive Disorder: Neurobiology, Food Environment and Social Policy Perspectives," *Physiology & Behavior* 107, no. 1 (2012): 126–137; N. P. Avena, P. Rada, and B. G. Hoebel, "Evidence for Sugar Addiction: Behavioral and Neurochemical Effects of Intermittent, Excessive Sugar Intake," *Neuroscience & Biobehavioral Reviews* 32, no. 1 (2008): 20–39.

32. A. F. A. Schellekens et al., "Often Overlooked and Ignored, but Do Not Underestimate Its Relevance: ADHD in Addiction—Addiction in ADHD," *European Addiction Research* 26 (2020): 169–172.

33. Schellekens et al., "Often Overlooked and Ignored."

34. F. Lenoir et al., "Intense Sweetness Surpasses Cocaine Reward," *PLoS ONE* 2, no. 8 (2007): e698.

35. A. Poulton et al., "Stimulants for the Control of Hedonic Appetite," *Frontiers in Pharmacology* 7 (2016): 105–110.

36. Avena, Rada, and Hoebel, "Evidence for Sugar Addiction."

37. J. J. Rucklidge et al., "Vitamin-Mineral Treatment of Attention-Deficit Hyperactivity Disorder in Adults: Double-Blind Randomised Placebo-Controlled Trial," *British Journal of Psychiatry* 204, no. 4 (2014): 306–315.

38. K. F. Holton and J. T. Nigg, "The Association of Lifestyle Factors and ADHD in Children," *Journal of Attention Disorders* 24, no. 11 (2020): 1511–1520.

39. M. Warthon-Medina et al., "Zinc Intake, Status and Indices of Cognitive Function in Adults and Children: A Systematic Review and Meta-Analysis," *European Journal of Clinical Nutrition* 69 (2015): 649–661.

40. C. Portugal-Nunes et al., "Iron Status Is Associated with Mood, Cognition, and Functional Ability in Older Adults: A Cross-Sectional Study," *Nutrients* 12, no. 11 (2020).

41. E. Derbyshire, "Brain Health Across the Lifespan: A Systematic Review on the Role of Omega-3 Fatty Acid Supplements," *Nutrients* 10, no. 8 (2018).

42. N. C. Peeri et al., "Association of Magnesium Intake and Vitamin D Status with Cognitive Function in Older Adults: An Analysis of US National Health and Nutrition Examination Survey (NHANES) 2011 to 2014," *European Journal of Nutrition* 60, no. 1 (2021): 465–474.

43. L. M. Hablitz et al., "Circadian Control of Brain Glymphatic and Lymphatic Fluid Flow," *Nature Communications* 11, no. 4411 (2020).

44. A. M. V. Wennberg et al., "Sleep Disturbance, Cognitive Decline, and Dementia: A Review," *Seminars in Neurology* 37, no. 4 (2017): 395–406.

45. W. Dodson and Y. Zhang, "Sleep Disturbances Associated with Adult ADHD," new research program and abstracts of the 152nd annual meeting of the American Psychiatric Association, May 1999; J. J. Kooij, L. P. Aeckerlin, and J. K. Buitelaar, "Functioning, Comorbidity and Treatment of 141 Adults with ADHD at a Psychiatric Outpatients' Department," *Nederlands Tijdschrift voor Geneeskunde* 145 (2001): 1498–1501; M. Schredl, B. Alm, and E. Sobanski, "Sleep Quality in Adult Patients with Attention Deficit Hyperactivity Disorder (ADHD)," *European Archives of Psychiatry and Clinical Neuroscience* 257 (2007): 164–168.

46. Fadeuilhe et al., "Insomnia Disorder in Adult Attention-Deficit/Hyperactivity Disorder Patients."

47. Mayo Clinic, "Melatonin," https://www.mayoclinic.org/drugs-supplements -melatonin/art-20363071.

48. S. Kasper, M. Gastpar, W. E. Müller et al., "Silexan, an orally administered Lavandula oil preparation, is effective in the treatment of 'subsyndromal' anxiety disorder: a randomized, double-blind, placebo controlled trial," *International Clinical Psychopharmacology* 25, no. 5 (2010): 277–287.

49. G. Cannard, "Complementary Therapies: On the Scent of a Good Night's Sleep," *Nursing Standard* 9 (1995).

50. S. Shannon et al., "Cannabidiol in Anxiety and Sleep: A Large Case Series," *Permanente Journal* 23 (2019): 18-041.

51. J. Martino, J. Pegg, and E. P. Frates, "The Connection Prescription: Using the Power of Social Interactions and the Deep Desire for Connectedness

to Empower Health and Wellness," *American Journal of Lifestyle Medicine* 11, no. 6 (2015): 466–475.

52. S. J. Scott, *Habit Stacking: 127 Small Changes to Improve Your Health, Wealth, and Happiness (Most Are Five Minutes or Less)* (Pasadena, CA; Old Town Publishing, 2017).

CHAPTER 10 GETTING CONNECTED, STAYING CONNECTED

1. H. M. O'Rourke, L. Collins, and S. Sidani, "Interventions to Address Social Connectedness and Loneliness for Older Adults: A Scoping Review," *BMC Geriatrics* 18, no. 1 (2018): 1–13.

2. S. Hinshaw, "Preadolescent Girls with Attention-Deficit/Hyperactivity Disorder: I. Background Characteristics, Comorbidity, Cognitive and Social Functioning, and Parenting Practices," *Journal of Consulting and Clinical Psychology* 70, no. 5 (2002): 1086–1098.

3. S. Young, "The Adolescent Outcome of Hyperactive Girls: Self-Report of Psychosocial Status," *Journal of Child Psychology and Psychiatry* 46, no. 3 (2005): 255–262.

4. J. S. Owens et al., "A Critical Review of Self-Perceptions and the Positive Illusory Bias in Children with ADHD," *Clinical Child and Family Psychology Review* 10, no. 4 (2007): 335–351.

5. C. L. Bagwell, "Attention-Deficit Hyperactivity Disorder and Problems in Peer Relations: Predictions from Childhood to Adolescence," *Journal of the American Academy of Child and Adolescent Psychiatry* 20 (2001): 1285–1292; M. Flicek, "Social Status of Boys with Academic Problems and Attention-Deficit Hyperactivity Disorder," *Journal of Abnormal Child Psychology* 20 (1992): 353–366; T. Heiman, "An Examination of Peer Relationships of Children With and Without Attention Deficit Hyperactivity Disorder," *School Psychology International* 26 (2005): 330–339; B. Hoza et al., "What Aspects of Peer Relationships Are Impaired in Children with Attention-Deficit/Hyperactivity Disorder?," *Journal of Consulting and Clinical Psychology* 73, no. 3 (2005): 411.

6. Y. Holst and L. B. Thorell, "Functional Impairments among Adults with ADHD: A Comparison with Adults with Other Psychiatric Disorders and Links to Executive Deficits," *Applied Neuropsychology: Adult* 27, no. 3 (2020): 243–255.

7. Holst and Thorell, "Functional Impairments among Adults with ADHD."

CHAPTER 11 MARRIAGE AND ADHD IN OLDER COUPLES

1. Melissa Orlov, *The ADHD Effect on Marriage: Understand and Rebuild Your Relationship in Six Steps* (Plantation, FL: A.D.D. Warehouse, 2010).
2. Orlov, *The ADHD Effect on Marriage*; Russell A. Barkley, *When an Adult You Love Has ADHD: Professional Advice for Parents, Partners, and Siblings* (Washington, DC: APA Life Tools, 2017); Gina Pera, *Is It You, Me, or Adult A.D.D.?: Stopping the Roller Coaster When Someone You Love Has Attention Deficit Disorder* (Chicago: Alarm Press, 2008); Pera and Arthur L. Robin, eds., *Adult ADHD-Focused Couple Therapy: Clinical Interventions* (Abingdon, Oxfordshire, UK: Routledge, 2016).

CHAPTER 12 THE LONG AND WINDING ROAD

1. E. R. Lebowitz, "Family Impairment Associated with Childhood Obsessive-Compulsive Disorder," *Journal of the American Academy of Child and Adolescent Psychiatry* 56, no. 3 (2017): 187–188.

CHAPTER 13 MAKING ENDS MEET

1. R. A. Barkley, K. R. Murphy, and T. Bush, "Time Perception and Reproduction in Young Adults with Attention Deficit Hyperactivity Disorder," *Neuropsychology* 15, no. 3 (2001): 351–360.
2. Zack Friedman, "Shock Poll: 7 in 10 Americans Live Paycheck to Paycheck," *Forbes*, February 8, 2022, https://www.forbes.com/sites/zackfriedman/2022/02/08/shock-poll-7-in-10-americans-live-paycheck-to-paycheck/?sh=6a63d72955f6.
3. Board of Governors of the Federal Reserve, *System Report on the Economic Well-Being of US Households in 2015*, May 2016, 59–60.
4. Sally Abrahms, "House Sharing for Boomer Women Who Would Rather Not Live Alone: Having Roommates Saves Money and Provides Valuable Companionship," *AARP Bulletin*, https://www.aarp.org/home-family/your-home/info-05-2013/older-women-roommates-house-sharing.html.
5. Randy Rieland, "Tiny Retirement: Is It for You? 7 Things to Consider Before Buying a Tiny Home," AARP, March 29, 2018, https://www.aarp.org/home-family/your-home/info-2018/tiny-house-retirement-fd.html.

CHAPTER 14 CREATING AN ADHD-FRIENDLY RETIREMENT

1. Jo Ann Jenkins, *Disrupt Aging: A Bold New Path to Living Your Best Life at Every Age* (New York: PublicAffairs, 2016).
2. Amie Clark, "Elder Cohousing: The Future of Eldercare," March 23, 2022, The Senior List, https://www.theseniorlist.com/cohousing/; J. Carrere et al.,

"The Effects of Cohousing Model on People's Health and Wellbeing: A Scoping Review," *Public Health Reviews* 41 (2020): 22; Sally Abrahms, "House Sharing for Boomer Women Who Would Rather Not Live Alone: Having Roommates Saves Money and Provides Valuable Companionship," *AARP Bulletin,* https://www.aarp.org/home-family/your-home/info-05-2013/older-women-roommates-house-sharing.html.

3. C. A. Talmage et al., "Directions for 21st Century Lifelong Learning Institutes: Elucidating Questions from Osher Lifelong Learning Institute Studies," *Alberta Journal of Educational Research* 64 (2018): 109–125; M. Narushima, J. Liu, and N. Diestelkamp, "Lifelong Learning in Active Ageing Discourse: Its Conserving Effect on Wellbeing, Health and Vulnerability," *Ageing and Society* 3, no. 4 (2018): 651–675; J. Park, K. Lee, and H. Dabelko-Schoeny, "A Comprehensive Evaluation of a Lifelong Learning Program: Program 60," *International Journal of Aging and Human Development* 84, no. 1 (December 2016): 88–106.

4. J. Yanguas, S., Pinazo-Henandis, and F. J. Tarazona-Santabalbina, "The Complexity of Loneliness," *Acta Bio-Medica: Atenei Parmensis* 89, no. 2 (2018): 302–314.

ACKNOWLEDGMENTS

I am deeply grateful to the many people who have generously given me their time and their wisdom in helping me bring this book to completion, including Dr. Veronica Chang, along with our psychology intern, Braha Eisenstat, who were tremendously helpful in the organization and compilation of information gathered from all the older adults with ADHD whom I interviewed. My thanks also to Alex West, who provided enormous support with organizing references. I want to thank William Dodson, MD, and Venkadesh Handratta, MD, for their efforts in reviewing the medication chapter and guiding me on issues related to ADHD medication in older adults. I send warm wishes and many thanks to the participants of the "Wise Agers" group, an online support group of older adults with ADHD that was offered by my clinic, the Chesapeake Center, at the commencement of the COVID-19 pandemic and which is self-led and ongoing today. They provided me with support and many insights into the issues faced by older adults. I also want to thank Dr. Susan Van Ost, who cofacilitated the Wise Agers group with me and whose wisdom and humor were much appreciated. I very much appreciate the information on the greater need for physician training on the diagnosis and treatment of ADHD in older adults provided by David Goodman, MD, as well as his support in referring older patients with ADHD to me to interview as part of this project. Many thanks to Kim Livingston, who sent me a draft of her wonderful memoir about growing up

ACKNOWLEDGMENTS

as a female with ADHD and then agreed to allow me to interview her for this book. Thanks to James Ochoa, LPC, in Austin, Texas, for his generous support in sending his patients my way to be interviewed for this book. And finally, many thanks to all of the older adults who generously gave of their time to complete my questionnaire and be interviewed by me as I gathered information for this book.

INDEX

"normal" age-related cognitive changes and, 64–65
questionnaires to assist in diagnosis, 67–69
reasons for late diagnosis, 57–61
reasons to have proper diagnosis, 48–49
reasons to seek diagnosis, 55–56
reasons why mental health professionals fail to consider ADHD as diagnosis, 61–63
regrets over late diagnosis, 56–57
report of life management problems and, 44
report of relationship/interpersonal problems and, 44–45
report of school-related problems and, 44
report of work-related problems and, 44
therapeutic effect of correct, 115
variations of ADHD, 49–50
waxing and waning symptoms and, 51
Diagnostic and Statistical Manual, 5th edition (DSM-5), 50–51
dialectical behavior therapy (DBT), 121
diet, 178–185
addiction tendencies and, 180–182
ADHD tendencies that make healthy eating more challenging, 179
brain-healthy, 138
micronutrients, 184–185
dietary changes, prevention of cognitive decline and, 23
dimensional disorder, ADHD as, 33
dinner group, monthly, 197–198
disability
ADHD classified as, 3–4, 53
defined, 3–4
discretionary income, 269
discretionary spending, 269–270
disorder, ADHD coach helping with, 153–156
disorganization
money management for adults with ADHD and, 268
older adults with ADHD and, 110
Disrupt Aging (Jenkins), 293
distractibility, difficulty making social connections and, 206
distractions cluttering time, 157–159

divorce, among older adults with ADHD, 36, 237–238
dopamine
ADHD and brain, 12
eating and, 181
stimulants' effect on, 80
downsizing, by moving into retirement community, 288–289
downsizing experts, 134
dyslexia, combined with ADHD, 1
dysregulated attentional system, ADHD and, 52–53

E.A.S.T. (everything at the same time) is least successful, 128, 167, 301
eating
clutter and unhealthy, 155
coaching adults with ADHD in healthy, 38
See also diet
eating disorders, ADHD and, 51, 182
e-communication, ADHD coach helping with, 150–151
education
about ADHD, 125–128
courses designed for seniors, 298–299
Education for All Handicapped Children Act (1975), 2
elder coaches, 147
"Elder Cohousing: The Future of Eldercare" (Clark), 295
"emergency meals," avoiding impulsive spending and keeping on hand, 274
emergency slush fund, 270–271
emotional boundaries, setting, 252–253
emotional concerns, older adults with ADHD and, 110
emotional dysregulation, 117
emotional reactivity, mindfulness meditation and, 170–171
emotional regulation skills, developing, 121
emotional sensitivity, low self-esteem contributing to, 121–122
emotional volatility, ADHD and, 113
emotions
ADHD-related struggle with, 39
impulsivity and, 122
problem resolutions in marriage and, 221
empathy, within marriage, 220, 242

gifted and talented programs, children with inattention testing for, 3
Ginsburg, Ruth Bader, 62
girls with ADHD, 3
 social skills and, 200
 social struggles of, 202
 underdiagnosis of, 60
GMAT examiners, lawsuits for failure to accommodate persons with ADHD, 4
goals
 problem-solving to reach, 130–133
 self-management strategies to achieve, 128–130
Goodman, David, 62, 95, 101, 102
green breaks, 138, 176–178
GRE examiners, lawsuits for failure to accommodate persons with ADHD, 4
group ADHD coaching, 141–142
guanfacine, 85, 87

habits
 ADHD coach and development of, 160–161
 ADHD coach helping with developing decluttering, 155–156
 aging and difficulty maintaining healthy, 24
 brain-healthy daily, 115, 123, 138, 287
 developing "healthy" spending, 271–275
 making daily habit of reaching out to someone, 214
 to streamline daily routine, 159–160
 See also daily habits
habit stacking, 194
Habit Stacking (Scott), 194
hands-on approach, during therapy sessions, 116
Hartmann, Thom, 54
health
 effects of loneliness on, 21
 self-care to support, 22–23, 25, 38
health insurance
 ADHD treatment coverage, 101–103, 107
 for part-time workers, 275–276
health/safety concerns about taking stimulant medications, 97–98, 107
help
 asking for, 304
 making peace with needing, 134

heritability of ADHD, 33, 67
high achievers, with ADHD, 50
Hinshaw, Stephen, 27, 200
hoarding
 ADHD coach helping with, 151–153
 defined, 151
homework, ADHD therapy and, 114
housing
 ADHD-friendly options, 294–295
 aging and possible need for change in, 21–22, 24
 cohousing, 278–279
 moving to less expensive country, 282
 moving to tax-friendly state, 281
 near other seniors, 198
 renting space to increase monthly income, 279–280
 senior-friendly living circumstances, 36–37
 shared, 300
 "tiny house," 280–281
hyperactive/impulsive ADHD, 58, 59, 165
hyperactivity, as symptom of ADHD, 2
hyperfocus, ADHD and, 52–53
hyperpalatable foods, 180, 182–184

"if-only's"
 ADHD diagnosis and, 56–57
 undiagnosed ADHD and, 13
impulsive spending
 money management for adults with ADHD and, 268
 strategies for avoiding, 274–275
impulsivity
 adults with ADHD and, 15
 emotions and, 122
 in marriages with ADHD partner(s), 218
 medication to reduce, 87
inattention, difficulty making social connections and, 206
inattentive ADHD, 58, 59, 165
income, ideas to generate after retirement, 275–282
information
 finding, about ADHD, 125–128
 visual presentation of, 9
insomnia
 ADHD and, 186–188
 as side effect of stimulants, 82–83
interest groups, joining, 213

INDEX